DECORATIONS FOR HOLIDAYS & CELEBRATIONS

American cornhusk doll, c. 1880. The costume is that of a Victorian lady. Index of American Design. *Courtesy of the National Gallery of Art, Washington.*

DECORATIONS FOR HOLIDAYS & CELEBRATIONS

Ideas, Inspiration, and Techniques for Making Festival Objects
from Natural Materials, Decorated Eggs, Kitchen Crafts,
Fabric, Wood, Paper, Metal, and Glass

by BARBARA B. STEPHAN

CROWN PUBLISHERS, INC., NEW YORK

To my parents, Gerard and Virginia Brooks, who have always
made holidays joyous occasions

Printed in the United States of America
Published simultaneously in Canada by
General Publishing Company Limited

Designed by Laurie Zuckerman

LIBRARY OF CONGRESS CATALOGING IN PUBLICATION DATA
Stephen, Barbara B.
Decorations for holidays and celebrations.
(Crown's arts and crafts series)
Bibliography: p.
Includes index.
1. Holiday decorations. I. Title.
TT900.H6S73   745.59'41   77-13228
ISBN: 0-517-515938 (cloth)
0-517-515946 (paper)

10 9 8 7 6 5

Contents

Acknowledgments

I am deeply indebted to the artists and craftsmen whose work appears in this book. All those who so generously supplied photos or allowed me to photograph their work have received credit in the captions accompanying their illustrations. Appreciation must also be expressed to the scores of anonymous craftsmen whose work is represented and who can be identified only by region or country.

Particular thanks should go to the following individuals and institutions: Matti S. Kosonen, President, Finn-Matkos; Henry J. Harlow, Curator, Old Sturbridge Village; Michael Daniel, Southern Highlands Handicraft Guild; Mona Helcermanas-Benge; The Upson Company; Gibson Greeting Cards, Inc.; Hallmark Cards, Inc.; Maid of Scandinavia; The Smithers Company; National Gallery of Art; Danish Information Office; Swedish Information Office; Swedish National Tourist Office; and the Swiss National Tourist Office.

I am grateful for the support and guidance of my editor, Brandt Aymar; without his encouragement when I broached the subject of my first book project to him, I might never have entered the field of writing.

Thanks also to my husband, John J. Stephan, who saw the living room turned into a photographic studio, the bathroom into a darkroom, and much of the rest of the house similarly transformed, yet managed to take it all with good humor and still offer advice and encouragement.

Finally, special appreciation goes to my parents, to whom this book is dedicated, for always adding that "certain something" that turns a holiday into a joyous occasion.

Barabara B. Stephan

Note: All photos and projects are by the author unless otherwise credited.

The "Klause" of Wollishofen in Switzerland wear elaborate head-dresses when they parade through the streets on December 6. Horn-blowing and bell-ringing characterize the noisy procession, which combines elements of ancient New Year's and Christmas observances. *Courtesy of the Swiss National Tourist Office.*

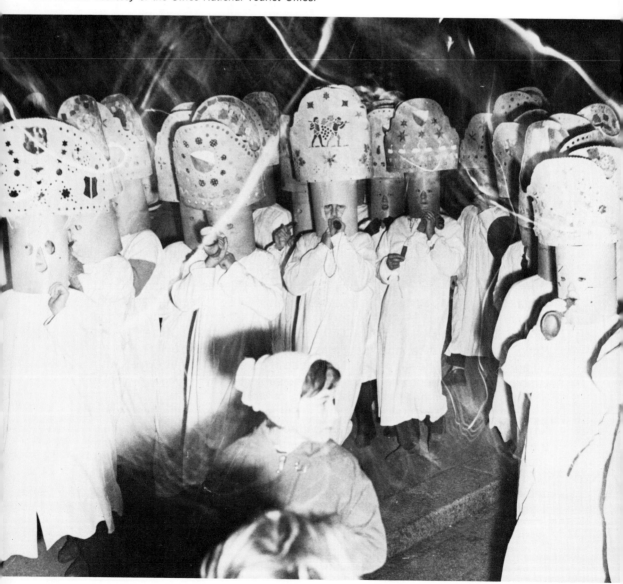

Introduction: The Meaning of Holidays

Holidays are joyous occasions, a time for giving rein to the creative spirit. The events we celebrate—Christmas, Passover, Easter, among others—have without a doubt become powerful sources of inspiration for artistic expression. Whole creative endeavors—egg decorating, for example, and the art of working with straw—have developed in association with holiday observances.

The celebrations of life—the births, marriages, and anniversaries, the national and secular as well as the religious holidays—can of course be observed without reference to the past. But the symbols chosen to express the joy of the occasion will undoubtedly be drawn from the rich and often ancient heritage that forms the fabric of our lives. The mistletoe, the Easter rabbit, the Paschal lamb, the heart-shaped greeting card, the rising sun, the Christmas tree—all can be seen not only as colorful images but also as meaningful expressions of a profound relationship between man and his environment. Knowingly or unknowingly, the artist or craftsman who uses such imagery is helping to perpetuate the sensibilities of the past and to give meaning and continuity to modern life.

Celebrations: A Look at the Past

From time immemorial, man has set aside certain days as times of ritual and celebration. Predominant among early celebrations were the rites aimed at ensuring the supply of food in a precarious world, expressed in animal cults in hunting societies, and in vegetation cults in gathering and early agricultural societies. With the growth of settled communities and the concurrent shift in

1

emphasis from food gathering to food production, such concerns as the fertility of the soil, the succession of the seasons, the amount of sunshine and rainfall, and the progress of sowing and reaping became the center of interest of ritual organization. As a result, the major festivals tended to occur with the change of the seasons—at the midwinter solstice or the vernal equinox—or at the time of harvest or bringing the flocks in from the fields.

Despite the fact that modern industrial society is far removed from its agrarian past, contemporary holidays reflect earlier traditions to a remarkable degree. Christmas, Passover, and Easter, though religious celebrations, have their roots in the festivals of midwinter and spring; the secular rites of New Year's, Halloween, Valentine's Day, and May Day are similarly traceable to seasonal observances. Practices such as the coloring of eggs at Easter, the lighting of bonfires at Halloween, and the decoration of homes with greenery at Christmas are far more closely associated with nature worship than with the events the customs are taken to represent. Far from detracting from the character of modern holidays, the persistence of ancient rituals and symbols has actually enriched and enhanced their observance.

New Year's (January 1)

New Year's was celebrated in most ancient societies, but the time of the festival varied greatly. In Egypt, the new year began when the Nile overflowed its banks in summer, bringing water to the parched lands; the Babylonians, Persians, and early Romans celebrated at the time of the spring equinox (March 21), when nature showed new life; the Celtic and Teutonic peoples of northern Europe marked the new year in November, a time that marked the return of the cattle to the barns in winter and the slaughter of the surplus herd. Common to many of the new year celebrations were masked processions, representing the return of dead souls; noise and revel, often associated with driving out evil spirits; and fire rites, symbolizing the extinguishing and rejuvenation of the sun.

It was by decree, rather than custom, that January 1 became the first day of the Julian calendar, adopted by Julius Caesar in the first century B.C. But it was not until the sixteenth century and the calendar reforms of Pope Gregory that Christian Europe began to accept this day as the start of the new year. Older dates for celebrating new year's rites are still reflected in Mardi Gras (Carnival in South America and parts of Europe), with its frenzied revels and masked processions, and Halloween (from the Druidic New Year), with its bonfires and costumed devils and ghosts.

Valentine's Day (February 14)

The customs of Valentine's Day can probably be traced to the Roman Lupercalia, originally a pastoral fertility festival celebrated in the month of February. During the festival, young men would draw girls' names from a box in order to find their partners for the coming year. Though the custom was frowned upon by the early Christians, it was easy enough for the Church to make use of the holiday by substituting a saint's feast day for the Lupercalian celebration, and exchanging the names drawn from those of young maidens to those of saints with virtues worthy of emulation. The fact that Saint Valentine's Day was chosen for the Christian holiday may have been coincidental, for there were at least three and perhaps as many as seven historical figures named Valentine whose feast days were observed on February 14.

Despite Church efforts, Saint Valentine's Day reverted to its original form during the Middle Ages, perhaps because of the conventional medieval belief that birds picked their mates starting on February 14. Valentine himself emerged as the patron saint of lovers, and love tokens and gifts were widely exchanged in his name. Today the holiday is reserved for the exchange of cards and gifts, and the religious associations of the celebration are almost completely forgotten.

Pennsylvania Dutch puzzle purse, handmade, 1797. The lover's token is embellished with hearts and birds, recalling the medieval belief that birds choose their mates on February 14. *Courtesy of Hallmark Cards, Inc.*

Passover and Easter

Passover, the feast commemorating the Angel of Death "passing over" the Jewish firstborn and the exodus of the Jews from Egypt, has been celebrated for over three thousand years and is said to be one of the oldest festivals in existence. It appears to be a composite celebration, representing the merging of two traditions, one pastoral (incorporating the sacrifice of the Paschal lamb, the firstborn of the flock) and the other agricultural (including the offering of the first sheaf from the barley harvest, and the feast of unleavened bread, or *matzah*). To the concepts of fertility and spring renewal are added the tradition of Exodus, with its emphasis on thanksgiving for redemption from slavery and joy in the rebirth of a free nation. Every year in Jewish households the story of deliverance is retold during the communal meal in the ceremony known as the *Seder.*

Since Christ was crucified during Passover, it was only natural that Christian commemoration of his resurrection should incorporate elements of the Jewish festival. Saint Paul referred to Christ as the Paschal lamb, and exhorted Christians to keep the feast of unleavened bread in which Christ had participated with his followers (The Last Supper). The themes of sacrifice and redemption which so colored the Passover festival were reiterated and reinforced in Christ's death and resurrection, along with the deliverance it implied for those of faith.

PAINTED EGGS. Anne Byrd Easley. The hare and the egg, both ancient fertility symbols, have long been associated with the celebration of Easter. *Photo by Mona Helcermanas-Benge.*

EASTER BUNNY. Jenny Choy. The hare is not found in North America, so the bringer of eggs became an Easter rabbit when transferred to the New World.

HE IS RISEN! Becky Patterson. Fabric appliqué with weathered wood. The cross has become the most powerful symbol of the Easter season. *Courtesy of the artist.*

Since the Christian Passover coincided with the spring holidays and rebirth rites celebrated by many of the peoples to whom Christianity spread, non-Hebrew elements were also incorporated in the feast. In this manner the tradition of the hare and the egg—the hare being a lunar symbol, and both hare and egg representing fertility—came to be merged in the Easter celebration. Sunrise services, and, in the Roman liturgy, the blessing of a newly kindled fire, are customs that hark back to the lighting of New Year's fires, a kind of sympathetic magic welcoming the sun. The English word for Easter may have been derived from the name of an Anglo-Saxon fertility goddess *(Eostre)* whose festival was celebrated at the vernal equinox, and who, according to legend, had opened the gates of Valhalla to the murdered Sun God.

Easter customs surrounding the hare and the egg were carried to the New World by the German-speaking immigrants known as the Pennsylvania Dutch, but the celebration was largely ignored by most other settlers, to whose stern religious beliefs Easter revels were repugnant. Not until the latter part of the nineteenth century, especially during the Civil War, did Easter begin to be celebrated as it had been in Europe. The fact that Easter was chosen as the day for memorial services for the war dead helped to return the festival to prominence, and gradually some of the folk customs associated with the holiday began to revive.

Thanksgiving

More than any other major holiday, Thanksgiving is a celebration that appears to link modern man with his agrarian past. Celebrated in the fall, at the time of harvest, it is reminiscent of many ancient festivals: the Jewish feast of Sukkot; the Feast of Demeter, in honor of the Greek goddess of grain; the Roman Cerelia, presided over by the cereal goddess Ceres; and the November Feast of Saint Martins, celebrated in much of northern and central Europe.

Despite this long and popular tradition, the American Thanksgiving is much less closely linked with early harvest festivals than it at first appears. Indeed the Puritans, who celebrated the first Thanksgiving in the autumn of 1621, would have been shocked to learn of the heathen precedents to their feast of gratitude. Hardly festival-oriented, they scorned even the Christian holidays of Easter and Christmas as tainted with idolatry, and considered their day of thanks to be purely of their own making.

Days of thanksgiving were commemorated only sporadically from the time of the Pilgrims until the nineteenth century, and had it not been for the vigorous efforts of Sarah J. B. Hale, the original holiday might never have assumed its present prominence. This remarkable woman, editor of the *Ladies' Magazine* and later *Godey's Lady's Book,* campaigned tirelessly for a nationwide observance. In 1863, her wish was at last achieved when President Lincoln issued the first national proclamation fixing the last Thursday in November "as a day of thanksgiving and praise to our beneficent Father." At first religious in character, the holiday has become greatly secularized, with family feasting and sport now the prime concerns of the day.

Cornhusk dolls. Czechoslovakia. The earliest cornhusk dolls were harvest figures fashioned by the Indians of the Americas.

Christmas

Since there was no reliable record of the date of Christ's birth, and since the early Church voiced considerable opposition to the pagan practice of commemorating anniversaries, Christmas was not widely observed for the first several hundred years of the Christian era. In the third century, efforts were made to ascertain the date of the Nativity, and in the fourth century the Bishop of Rome finally settled on December 25 as the time of Jesus' birth.

The choice of December 25—a very unlikely date historically—may have been made in an attempt to turn people away from competing influences. These included the Roman festival of Saturnalia (December 17–23) and the powerful Mithraic cult, which celebrated December 25 as *Natalis Solis Invicta,* the birthday of the Sun God. Though there was resistance within the Church to the selection of a pagan date, the observation of the Nativity at the time of the midwinter solstice had the inevitable effect of bringing the Christ legend into close association with the themes of light and dark, and the rebirth of the sun. Thus in the Christmas liturgy, Christ becomes the "Light Eternal," the "Sun of Justice," bringing enlightenment to those "who sit in darkness and the shadow of death."

Among the Teutonic and Celtic peoples of northern Europe the theme of new life emerging from darkness at the decline of the year coincided perfectly with the rites of the midwinter solstice and the feast of the new year, so that there was little difficulty in merging the Nativity with existing folk festivals. Indeed, many of the customs and traditions that were to become an intimate part of the Christmas celebration originated in this area: the decorations with greenery and fir trees, symbolic of eternal life; the hanging of the mistletoe, a plant sacred to the Druids; and the lighting of a Yule log and Yule candles, remnants of the fire rites of the new year.

In such a receptive climate, Christmas soon became the most popular festival of the year, and it remained so until the Reformation brought certain changes in religious observances. In England, the Puritans threatened to obliterate Christmas entirely, along with Easter, Whitsuntide, and the saints' days. The celebration revived in England with the Restoration, but the prejudice against Christmas was carried to the New World, and it was not until the wave of Irish and German immigration of the nineteenth century that the holiday was commonly celebrated and antagonism finally defused.

An example of the eclecticism of Christmas (and of most other holidays as well) can be seen in the traditions surrounding Santa Claus. The original Saint Nicholas, a fourth-century bishop in Asia Minor whose feast day was held on December 6, became legendary for his generosity and developed in the popular mind into a giver of gifts. Condemned as a pagan remnant during the Reformation, Saint Nicholas was replaced in some countries with the more secular Christmas Man (Father Christmas, Père Noël). The Dutch refused to relinquish their saint, however, and brought the observance of *Sinterklaas* Day (a form of *Sint Nikolaas*) to New Amsterdam in the New World. Here *Sinterklaas* gradually became anglicized into Santa Claus, the saint exchanged his title of bishop and his vestments of red and white for the familiar suit of Father Christmas, and the gift-giving night shifted to Christmas Eve.

Still another tradition was added when the Germans and German-speaking Swiss (known as the Pennsylvania Dutch) arrived with the legend of *Christkindl*—the Christ Child— bringing gifts on Christmas Eve. Soon anglicized and secularized to "Kriss Kringle," the Christ Child joined the pantheon of spirits—Saint Nicholas, *Sinterklaas,* Father Christmas—which were to make up the modern Santa Claus.

The feast day of Saint Lucia, Lady of Light, is celebrated on December 13 in Sweden. The custom harks back to the rites of the midwinter solstice, when fires were lit in sympathetic magic to entice the return of the sun. *Courtesy of the Swedish National Tourist Office.*

Greenery, a symbol of everlasting life, was used by the Romans in celebrating Saturnalia, and by the Celtic and Teutonic peoples of Europe in their midwinter festivities.

The legend of Christ's birth in a manger has become stylized in the hundreds of different crèches produced in various parts of the world. This example is from Peru.

"Merry Old Santa Claus" by Thomas Nast. From *Harper's Weekly*, January 1, 1881. Nast is largely responsible for the rotund and rosy-cheeked appearance of the modern Santa, a figure in whom the traditions of Saint Nicholas, Father Christmas, and Kriss Kringle are merged.

Large (15-inch diameter) wreath incorporating at least seventeen different kinds of pods, cones, and leaves collected in travels around the country. Patsy Gibson.

From the Wilds:
Pods, Cones,
and Greens

Nature's debris is the collector's bounty. Everywhere that plants thrive, treasure is produced—in the form of cones, seeds, dried flowers, leaves, and branches that litter the ground with the passing of each season. Though trips to the country may ensure the biggest bounty, there is wealth awaiting even the city dweller willing to explore the parks, vacant lots, and tree-lined streets of his neighborhood.

Despite a plentitude of natural materials, nature's abundance should not be abused. To ensure a responsible attitude toward collecting, always observe the following guidelines:

—Where private land is involved, consult the owners before removing any material.
—Collecting on state or federal lands may be prohibited or restricted to material that has fallen on the ground—consult park rangers or the proper administrative agencies.
—Try to take only plant material which is spent—cones and pots that have dropped their seeds, or leaves and branches that have fallen to the ground.
—Make a rule not to cause injury to any living plant. Many plants are in danger of extinction because overzealous collectors have pulled them from the ground, roots and all, when all they wanted were dried stalks or seed heads, which could have been cut with clippers.
—Become familiar with your area's conservation lists, and observe all local, state, and federal regulations pertaining to plant material.

Dried Materials: Cones, Pods, and Seeds

Pinecones

In general, collect cones when they are mature—after they have opened to release their seeds but before they are weathered by wind and rain. Wash dirty cones quickly, using a scrub brush (soaking will cause the scales to fold up), then place in a warm spot to dry. Anywhere from a day to two weeks will be required for the drying, depending on the size and maturity of the cones.

If the cones remain closed or are sticky with pitch, place in a shallow pan lined with aluminum foil and bake in a low (150° to 200°) oven for thirty minutes, or until the scales are open and the pitch melted. As well as speeding up the drying process, heat eliminates insect life. Many collectors make baking standard procedure for all the cones they gather.

Arrangements of dried materials are called "wood pretties" by the inhabitants of America's southern Appalachian Mountains. This particular wood pretty is composed of individually wired pods and cones joined into an attractive swag. *Photo by Michael Daniel. Courtesy of the Southern Highland Handicraft Guild.*

A tiny (5-inch diameter) but charming wreath by Esther L. Newell of Concord, New Hampshire. Eighty-year-old Mrs. Newell, who has made thousands of such wreaths, has the true collector's spirit. Of her materials she writes: "I use all kinds of small cones, rose hips, bitter sweet berries and berries from mountain laurel for color. More color can be added with dried tansy (yellow), dried chive blossoms (lavender), knot weed and any weed that will retain its color, straw flowers, and whatever you have. From the woods I get lichens, mosses, acorns, acorn caps, oak galls, beechnut burrs, and any interesting weed pod I see. From the garden there are poppy, columbine, lupin, Killarney bells, globe thistles, etc. I never go out to walk that I don't discover something new."

A partial listing of cones, pods, nuts, seeds, and pits useful for dried arrangements:

Cones	Pods	Nuts	Seeds	Pits
Casuarina (Ironwood)	Acacia	Acorn	Allspice	Apricot
Cedar	Beech:	Almond	Apple	Avocado
Cyprus	American	Black walnut	Bean	Cherry
Deodar cedar	European	Brazil nut	Cardomom	Peach
Douglas fir	Burdock	Butternut	Citrus	Plum
Hemlock:	Camphor	Chestnut	Cloves (bud)	Prune
Mountain	Castor bean	Filbert	Gourd	
Western	Catalpa	Hazelnut	Nutmeg	
Larch	Clematis	Hickory	Pumpkin	
Pine:	Cotton	Peanut	Squash	
Jeffrey	Eucalyptus	Pecan	Sunflower	
Lodgepole	Iris	Pistachio		
Pinyon	Jacaranda	Walnut		
Ponderosa	Lotus			
Scotch	Magnolia			
Sugar	Maple			
White	Milkweed			
Redwood	Mimosa			
Sequoia	Okra			
Spruce:	Poppy			
Black	Sweet gum			
Norway	Wisteria			
Sitka	Wood rose			
	Yucca			

Cut "flowers" from small pinecones with scissors. Choose cones that are fully opened, heating in a 200° oven if necessary. The cones are brittle and may shatter if cut just after they come out of the oven, so allow time to soften up.

A thick core makes large pinecones much harder to cut. Wear gloves and cut with hand-operated pruning snips or long-handled pruning shears. Pliers are good for pulling off individual petals. Note that the bottom of a cone makes a different kind of "flower" than does a cross section.

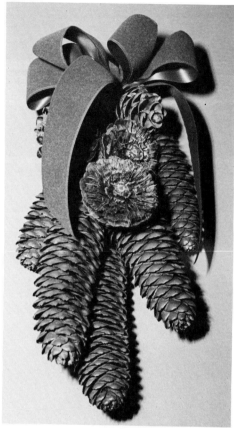

Pinecone sections glued to a wreath cut from cardboard. The bow is of glue-stiffened fabric (see Chapter 7).

A swag of cones and cone flowers, wired to a festive bow. *Photo by Michael Daniel. Courtesy of the Southern Highland Handicraft Guild.*

Pods and Nuts

As long as restraint is used in collecting scarce species, pods and nuts can be gathered at various stages of maturity for interesting color and shape variations. Green pods will often keep their color if dried on a screen in the dark, while mature pods may benefit from exposure to the sun. Some seed heads will turn to a beautiful golden tan if they are allowed to dry on the stalk, but don't postpone gathering too long, or wind and rain will take a toll.

Since insects can do extensive damage to a collection of dried pods and nuts, it is a good idea to follow the baking procedure described for cones. Use caution, however—a few segmented pods explode as they are heated. An alternative is to place the pods and nuts in a bag in the freezer for forty-eight hours, after which they should be insect-free.

Some clusters are fragile and may break apart as they dry. The problem can be minimized by harvesting seed-pods a little before maturity, when the stems are less brittle. Another solution is to dip the fully dried clusters in thinned white glue, shellac, varnish, or lacquer. Do not use white glue with pods that close when they become wet.

Seeds and Pits

Seeds and pits, including those from supermarket fruits and vegetables, make attractive additions to dried arrangements. Wash to remove any fleshy parts, then bake in a 150° to 200° oven for thirty minutes both to kill any insects or larvae and to prevent germination.

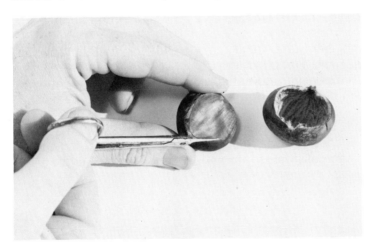

If you want to extract the meat of a chestnut in order to avoid insect infestation later on, cut away the back and pry out the inside.

To break walnuts evenly in two, give several sharp taps along the joint. Repeat on the other side and once on each end. Insert a knife point in the flat end and split. After the nutmeat is removed, reglue the halves, inserting a length of wire if desired.

Storage

All collected material should be fully dried and insect-free before being stored. Mildew must be avoided, since one damp item can ruin a whole container of specimens. Plastic bags are good for storage, since they allow you to see what is inside, and they also prevent reinfestation by insects (as long as there are no holes). Those seeds and nuts that attract rodents require stronger containers, such as cookie tins, glass jars, or even covered garbage cans for large quantities. Whatever the container, it is a good idea to add a quantity of moth crystals to continue to discourage insects, rodents, and mold.

Frameworks for Dried Arrangements

Wire

Wire wreaths can be purchased or made at home. The simplest wreath is made by shaping a metal coat hanger into a circle, leaving the hook in place for hanging. A two-wire wreath is much more practical, first because it can be made to any size, and second because materials wired to it cannot slip to the back the way they tend to do when fastened to a single-wire wreath. Stronger and more elaborate wire frames are available from florists and floral supply shops.

Chicken wire and hardware cloth are useful for certain flat and three-dimensional designs. For swags, crescents, or other flat forms, cut the wire mesh into the shape desired, cover the edges with masking tape, and wire the dried materials in place. Back with plywood or hardboard if the finished piece needs further support. For Christmas trees, topiaries, or other three-dimensional designs, bend wire mesh into shape, then "sew" the edges together using fine spool wire. Wear gloves when working with chicken wire and hardware cloth, and always use the proper wire snips for cutting.

Three wire wreaths. The simplest is a coat hanger, shaped into a circle. Next is a homemade wreath using two hoops of galvanized wire joined at several places around the frame. At lower right is a curved florist's wreath.

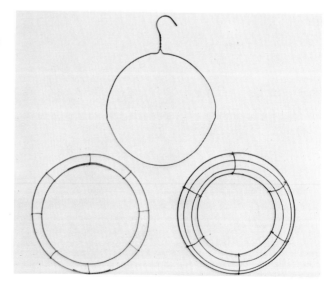

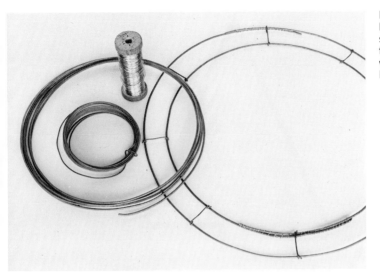

For a double-wire wreath, cut two lengths of heavy-duty wire, shape each into a circle (one slightly smaller than the other), and solder or bind the ends with spool wire. Cut lengths of medium-weight wire and use to join the two circles, keeping the spacing even all around.

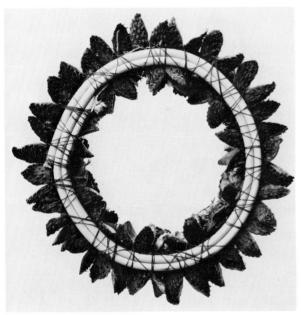

Lacking wire, a circular framework can still be made by bending reed, willow branches, or grape vines into a circle. In this Danish example, an inner and outer circle of beech burrs are wired to a double circle of reed; other materials are added and held in place with fine spool wire.

Front view of the small (5½-inch diameter) Danish wreath. Bits of moss help conceal the wire and fill out the circle.

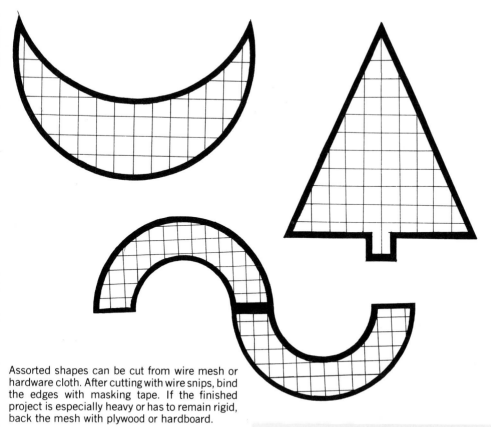

Assorted shapes can be cut from wire mesh or hardware cloth. After cutting with wire snips, bind the edges with masking tape. If the finished project is especially heavy or has to remain rigid, back the mesh with plywood or hardboard.

Cone wreath on wire mesh. Pat Polansky. One-quarter-inch mesh hardware cloth is cut into a wreath shape, and pods and cones wired on individually. The wreath is then backed with a piece of ¼-inch plywood.

Styrofoam

Styrofoam (expanded polystyrene produced by Dow Chemical Company) is a convenient material to work with because the tedious process of wiring can be eliminated—materials are simply glued or poked into place. A product of the petrochemical industry (which explains the rising prices), Styrofoam is lightweight but quite sturdy. It can be purchased in a number of shapes (wreaths, cones, balls), or can be cut by hand from sheets using a serrated kitchen knife, coping saw, or inexpensive battery-operated hot wire cutter (available in hobby shops). It is important to know that Styrofoam is flammable, and that is disintegrates if it comes in contact with certain solvent-based glues and some spray paints (check the label). Water-based glues and paints have no ill effect.

Although sometimes available dyed or flocked, Styrofoam is usually a stark white, which ought to be concealed before materials are attached. Color the Styrofoam with thinned poster or acrylic paints, shoe polish, or spray paint (if the label indicates the product is compatible with Styrofoam). Or wrap the Styrofoam with floral tape, raffia, strips of burlap, colored florist's foil, or other such material—just make sure that the covering used can be penetrated easily by stems, wooden picks, or floral pins. A third possibility—one that gives a naturalistic effect—is to coat the Styrofoam with white glue, then roll in powdered sphagnum moss.

Styrofoam shapes, especially those less than one inch thick, should be reinforced if they are to bear much weight. Corrugated cardboard, cut to size and glued to the Styrofoam, makes a good lightweight backing. For wreaths, a strong piece of wire wrapped around the outside perimeter and secured with floral tape will usually suffice.

Four Styrofoam wreath shapes. At back left is a heavy-duty florist's wreath, reinforced with wire and spray-painted green. At right is a flat wreath, 12 inches diameter, ⅝ inch thick. The wreaths in front have a curved surface, and are one and two inches thick. Also illustrated are candleholders with spiked tips and rubber-capped flower tubes, all of which can be inserted directly into Styrofoam.

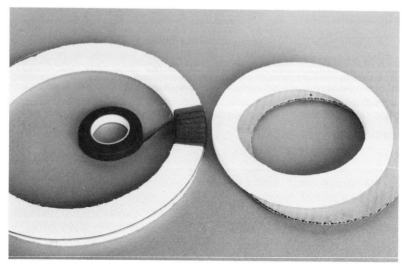

Styrofoam can be reinforced with wire and floral tape, as at left, or with corrugated cardboard *(right)*. Glue the cardboard in place or attach with tape.

One way to camouflage a Styrofoam wreath is to wrap it in long strips of burlap. Choose a color matching that of the materials to be attached.

Straw

Straw wreaths have some of the advantages of Styrofoam: they are lightweight, and materials can be inserted without wiring. In addition, the natural straw is quite attractive, and many prefer to leave some of it exposed when adding decorations.

Straw wreaths can either be purchased from floral supply or hobby shops, or they can be made by binding handfuls of barnyard straw, dried grasses, or long pine needles onto a circular wire framework. Use raffia or other natural material to hold the straw in place if part of the wreath foundation is to be left visible.

Corrugated Cardboard

Ordinary corrugated cardboard, the kind cut from supermarket boxes, is an inexpensive backing for small or lightweight projects. It can be cut with strong scissors, but a craft knife will make much faster work of the job. For added strength, glue two or more layers together with the corrugations at right angles, or, for wreaths, tape or sew a length of strong wire around the perimeter. Conceal the cardboard, if necessary, with floral tape, burlap, or fabric glued in place.

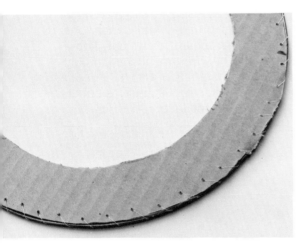

A reinforced cardboard wreath for lightweight projects. A length of heavy-gauge wire, sewn in place around the perimeter, adds strength and rigidity.

Use cardboard as a backing for leaves or other material that can be sewn in place. Choosing a large sturdy needle and heavy-duty thread, push the needle up through the cardboard and sew through the base of one leaf. Moving the needle about one inch away, stitch down through both layers to the back side. Continue to sew on leaves, placing each so as to conceal the previous stitch.

Wreath of sterculia leaves with coconut fiber bow. Helen Gibson. Magnolia, rhododendron, laurel, and other leaves could be handled in the same way.

Hardboard and Plywood

Hardboard and plywood provide sturdy backing for large projects as well as rigidity for smaller items that must not be bent. Be prepared for the addition of considerable extra weight, however, and make sure you have the appropriate hardware to support the project if it is to be hung.

Plywood is harder to cut than lumber of the equivalent thickness, but it resists warping and is better as a support. Sold in 4-by-8-foot (and sometimes 4-by-4-foot) panels, it is commonly available in thicknesses of one-eighth to three-quarters of an inch. For projects that will be subjected to considerable snow or rain, consider using one of the grades of exterior or marine plywood.

Hardboard is a material made of wood fibers pressed into panels one-eighth- and one-quarter-inch thick. Perforated hardboard, commonly known as pegboard, is handy for attaching wired items. The wires are pushed through the holes, then twisted together at the back. If materials are to be glued in place, turn the hardboard over to expose the back, since adhesives adhere better to this rough surface than to the smooth front face.

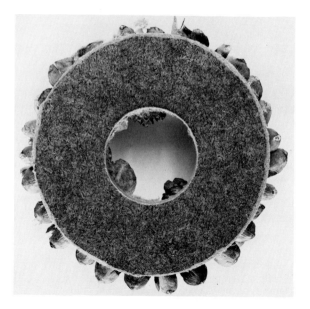

Hardboard backing for 5-inch-diameter wreath made by Esther L. Newell. Note that the smooth surface is turned to the back so that the pods and cones can be glued to the rough side.

Attaching Dried Materials to a Backing

Wire Frameworks

To attach items to hardware cloth, chicken wire, or wire armatures you will want to use flexible wire. Spool wire in gauges 28–38 and annealed or florist wire in gauges 18–26 are the most useful to have on hand. (The higher the number or gauge, the finer the wire.) Uncoated annealed wire is more flexible than painted florist wire, but florist wire is useful when a straight stem is needed.

For pinecones, wrap the wire completely around the lowest ring of scales, then twist the ends together at the base. Pods may have to be drilled at the base, one end of the wire inserted through the hole, and the ends twisted to secure. Treat flat scales and leaves like drilled pods, but make two holes at the base, side by side, so that the wired items hold firm. Dried material with stems need only to have the stems lengthened with wire attached with floral tape. When wiring any material, always leave enough extra wire to attach securely to the framework.

To wire a cone, wrap a length of wire around the lower ring of petals, bring the ends together at the base, and twist tightly. Use 18- or 20-gauge wire for large cones, 22- to 26-gauge for medium cones, and 28-gauge for small cones.

Wiring dried materials. 1). Drill pods at the base, pass a wire through the holes, and twist tightly. 2). Punch two holes in scales and leaves that have no stem. Thread wire in one hole and out the other; twist the ends together. 3). Attach wire with floral tape to leaves and pods with stems. Make a small crook in the top of the wire so that it can't pull out.

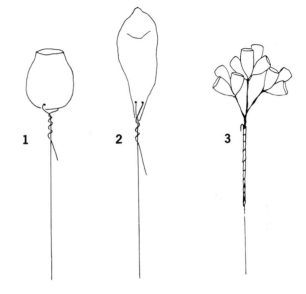

Attaching "stems" to pinecones and cone flowers. Drill a small hole in the base, then insert a length of cotton-covered wire or a toothpick that has first been dipped in glue. If cotton-covered wire is not available, use ordinary florist wire, but poke a little cotton in the hole to give the wire something to cling to.

To attach cones to a metal frame, wrap wires around both outer and inner circles, then twist the ends together. Wire larger cones on the outside and smaller cones toward the inside, then fill in the spaces in between. Skewered cones need only to be pushed into a Styrofoam base, but it is a good idea to first dip the wire or toothpick stems into white glue. To conceal the stark white Styrofoam, paint, cover with floral tape, or wrap with strips of burlap.

Styrofoam and Straw Frameworks

Short, straight stems are best for inserting into straw or Styrofoam framework. If the item to be attached has no stem, as in the case of nuts and pinecones, add one by drilling a hole in the bottom and inserting a toothpick or short length of #18 or #20 florist wire. Alternatively, the item can be attached with fine wire to wooden floral picks, which can then be pushed directly into the Styrofoam. Branches of greenery and some long-stemmed clusters are best held in place with sturdy wire florist pins.

To make sure that materials hold securely in a Styrofoam or straw framework, it is always a good idea to put a little thick white glue on the end of each wire, stem, or floral pick before inserting into the base.

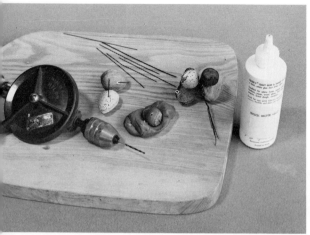

Secure nuts or other items to be drilled in a brace, or hold in place with a lump of plasticine or floral clay. Insert short lengths of wire if the items are to be poked into a straw or Styrofoam backing; use longer lengths of more flexible wire if they are to be wired to a metal or pegboard frame.

Metal florist pins can be used to hold long-stemmed items in place on a Styrofoam or straw backing. Wooden picks, available in both green and natural, are good for materials that have no stem.

An arrangement of magnolia leaves, pinecones, eucalyptus pods, and deodar cedar "roses" backed by a length of palm frond (stem end) spray-painted gold. Helen Gibson.

The basis for the arrangement is a block of Styrofoam concealed in gold foil. Leaves and cone clusters are wrapped with brown floral tape and held in place with metal florist pins; deodar cones are glued to a skewer and inserted directly through the palm frond into the Styrofoam backing.

Tree of pods and cones. Pat Polansky. The materials are all wired separately, then pushed into a 12-inch Styrofoam cone that is spray-painted brown.

Hawaiian wreath. Ray Wong. Eucalyptus leaves and seed pods, hairy lipstick plant pods, macadamia nut leaves, hau calyx, and harpulia pods are among the materials used in this elaborate wreath. The Styrofoam base is wrapped with banana fiber and the dried materials held in place with floral pins and wooden picks. A coat of spray glaze provides sheen and keeps some of the fragile materials from shattering.

Wreath of pods and cones collected in the southern Appalachian region. Gail DeBord. Note the symmetry of the arrangement and the focal points at top and bottom. *Photo by Michael Daniel. Courtesy of the Southern Highland Handicraft Guild.*

Attaching with Adhesives

Adhesives obviate the need for wiring, and often they are the most suitable choice for attaching dried materials to frameworks of Styrofoam, cardboard, wood, or hardboard. Among the adhesives that can be used are thick white glue, linoleum paste, ceramic tile cement, clear household cement, silicone glue, and melted glue from a hot-melt glue gun.

White glue, linoleum paste, and ceramic tile cement are water-based adhesives, meaning that cleanup is easy if tools are washed before the adhesive sets. White glue is the most easily available and probably the simplest to use. Do, however, choose the thicker "sticky" variety or the pastelike form in jars (both available in hobby stores) so that materials can be held in place without too much pinning or propping. Linoleum paste and ceramic tile cement are thicker than white glue (the first is of finger-paint consistency, the second more like butter), but usually require more time to dry. Note that the moisture in any of the water-based glues can cause small cones and seed pods to start to close; counteract this tendency by drying these items under a heat lamp or in some other warm place.

Clear household cement is a fast-drying adhesive good for gluing materials to wood or cardboard; it should not, however, be used on Styrofoam since the Styrofoam will melt. Household cement is inflammable and gives off irritating fumes, so always work in a well-ventilated area away from heat or flame.

MAKING A CONE TREE

To camouflage Styrofoam, coat with white glue and roll in milled sphagnum moss (or use unmilled sphagnum crumpled to a powder by rubbing between the hands).

Wind string in a spiral around the cone, holding in place with pins. Depending on the size of the cone and the variety of materials to be used, you may want to divide the base in halves or thirds, with a new spiral starting at each division. Arrange pods and cones in graduated sizes, saving the largest for the base and the smallest for the top. Glue in place with thick white glue, following the line of the string.

Fill a small vase with clay, and insert a dowel whose upper end is sharpened to a point. Pull the Styrofoam cone down over the dowel to hold in place.

Linoleum paste is an inexpensive, grayish-brown, water-based adhesive with the consistency of finger paint. Here it is spread thickly on the base of small hemlock cones to attach them to a circle of glue-stiffened burlap. Linoleum paste adheres items well, but requires at least several hours to dry. Since the moisture in the paste may make cones start to close, always dry in a warm place.

Above, right: Circle of hemlock cones, only two inches in diameter, makes a pretty Christmas ornament.

Ceramic tile cement, a white, water-based adhesive with the consistency of creamed butter, can be colored with acrylic or poster paints. Apply a thick coat to half the project to be decorated, then press the dried materials in place. Let dry thoroughly (the cones fall off if handled too soon), then repeat with the second half.

Pinecone kissing ball, using cross sections and tips of small spruce cones. The bow at the bottom is held in place with a long pin; the bow at the top is fastened to the support wire (see previous illustration).

Silicone cement, a translucent, rubbery adhesive squeezed from a tube, has the advantage of instant tack, and layers of material can be built up without waiting for the base layer to dry. It is not as strong as white glue, however, and probably should not be used on items that will receive a lot of handling.

MAKING A SPICE WREATH

A cardboard wreath, made from two circles of corrugated cardboard glued together with the corrugations at right angles, is covered with brown burlap.

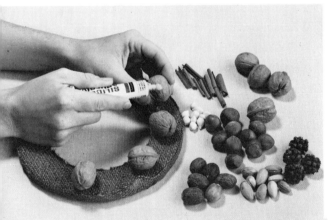

Silicone adhesive is tacky enough to hold materials in place even when freshly squeezed from the tube; thus multiple layers can be built up even before the bottom layer is dry. Materials to be used in the wreath include cinnamon, walnuts, cardamom, filberts, nutmeg, pistachio nuts, and miniature pommanders made by inserting cloves into a ball of bread-glue dough (see Chapter 6).

Below, left: Continue adding nuts and spices, using pins to hold the materials in place until the adhesive sets (about five minutes). Silicone cement remains flexible even when dry, and while it is excellent for fast work, it may not hold smooth-surfaced items securely, so it is a good idea to add a little white glue or clear household cement to reinforce crucial spots. Attach a wire loop hanger before completing the wreath.

The completed spice wreath, fragrant with the smell of cinnamon and cloves.

Glue guns work electrically to melt sticks of thermoplastic glue which harden to form an extremely strong, waterproof bond. Work goes very quickly—sometimes even too quickly, since the item to be joined must be attached to the framework immediately after the hot glue has been applied, or the glue will not stick. Although the newer glue guns are supposed to have flow controls that stop the adhesive from oozing out the moment pressure is released, they do not always perform up to expectations, so keep an aluminum pie plate or metal lid handy to catch drips when you put the tool down. Do not use this method on Styrofoam—the heat would melt the plastic.

An electric glue gun melts down and releases a strong, waterproof glue. The adhesive hardens almost immediately, so place the item in its proper position as soon as the glue is applied. Always keep an aluminum pie plate or tin can lid handy to catch drips after the gun is put down.

Right: Nut wreath on a ¼-inch plywood backing. Included are walnuts, almonds, Brazil nuts, filberts, hazelnuts, pecans, and pistachio nuts. A bow of brown velveteen complements the colors of the nuts.

Below: Pinecone bird from Denmark. The head is of papier-mâché, the eyes are beads, and the wings are of strong yellow paper.

Below, right: Tiny Italian Christmas crèche. Wooden figures are glued inside a walnut shell, which is attached to a wooden base decorated with lichens.

Pinecone doll from Denmark carries an armload of dried flowers and tiny cones.

Wrap a filbert or acorn head with a triangular scrap of cloth and glue onto a 2-inch pinecone from which the lower scales have been stripped. Add a skirt cut from a 5-inch-diameter circle of stiffened burlap adorned with a gathered apron. Glue berries, dried flowers, or pinecones in front to indicate hands.

Hawaiian crèche scene. Jean Judd. All materials—including the coconut stable, ironwood pod sheep, palm seed heads, and bamboo haloes—are native to Hawaii. The Christ child lies in a swaddling cloth on a log. Mary wears a necklace of shells; Joseph, behind her, carries a staff. The Wise Men, on the right, wear garments of three of Hawaii's ethnic groups (Hawaiian, Japanese, and Chinese), and a missionary family look on. A small angel graces the scene.

Finishes

Dried arrangements often benefit from a final spraying with clear lacquer or acrylic glaze. As well as adding sheen, the sprays serve to strengthen fragile materials and to discourage the accumulation of dust. Products vary slightly in body and run the gamut from high-gloss to almost-invisible matte finish, so choose the spray that produces the effect you prefer. Since Styrofoam is adversely affected by the solvents in some aerosols, make sure that the Styrofoam framework is well covered before applying clear sprays.

Dried Flowers and Leaves

A number of flowers, berries, and grasses will dry naturally, retaining their shape and color. Some of these can be harvested, fully dried, from the field; others benefit from being picked a little before maturity and suspended head down in a warm, dark place. (Darkness assures that maximum color will be preserved.) Remove most of the foliage from plants to be dried by hanging, then fasten in bunches with rubber bands or string and hang upside down in a garage, attic, or other dark, well-ventilated area. Drying will require several days to several weeks, depending on weather conditions and the particular plant involved.

Some flowers, such as globe amaranth and strawflowers, will have to have their stems replaced by wire before drying. Snip off the stems just below the flower head, and insert a length of floral wire up through the base of the flower and out the other side. Bend the top of the wire in a crook, then pull down so that the bent end becomes embedded in the flower head.

Leaves generally require only minimal treatment. Brush or rinse off any dirt, then place between sheets of newspaper and leave until dry. Do not weight the newspaper if you want the leaves to retain their natural curves.

Some leaves respond particularly well to glycerin treatment, retaining their color and remaining flexible indefinitely. One method involves cutting whole branches and placing the stems in a mixture of one part glycerin (from the druggists or a chemical-supply house) to two parts water. The absorption rate will vary with the foliage, and may require anywhere from several days to a month or more. Leaf color will generally intensify as the preservative is absorbed, but the dark greens and warm browns produced will be welcome in many arrangements.

Some foliage is delicate, and wilts before completing the glycerin treatment; other types may have heavy tough stems that inadequately absorb moisture. These kinds of plants should be completely immersed in the glycerin solution. When about two-thirds of each leaf is darkened and transparent looking, remove the leaves and place on newspaper, allowing to cure for several days.

Harvesting plants at different times of the year, using varying proportions of glycerin and water, and allowing the foliage to remain in the solution for varying lengths of time will all produce different effects and are worth experimentation.

Flowers, grasses, and berries which can be dried by hanging:

Flowers	Grasses
Artemisia	Bearded barley
Baby's breath	Fox tails
Bells of Ireland	Millet
Celosia	Oats
Chinese lantern	Pampas grass
Chives	Rye
Dock	Sea oats
Globe amaranth	Wheat
Goldenrod	**Berries**
Heather	
Honesty	Bayberry
Hydrangea	Bittersweet
Milkweed	Sumac
Mimosa	
Pearly everlasting	
Statice	
Strawflower	
Yarrow	

Foliage that preserves well in glycerin:

Bayberry	Laurel
Bells of Ireland	Leather fern
Beech	Lemon
Boxwood	Magnolia
Camelia	Maple
Clematis	Mountain ash
Dogwood	Myrtle
Eucalyptus	Peony
Forsythia	Periwinkle
Holly	Rhododendron
Hydrangea	Sweet gum
Ivy	

Attaching Dried Flowers and Leaves

Flowers and leaves that have been wired, or which have straight, stiff stems, can be inserted directly into frameworks of Styrofoam or straw; items with more fragile stems should be glued or held in place with florist pins or wooden picks. To attach loose bunches of dried flowers and foliage to a wire wreath, use a continuous length of spool wire. Wrap the wire round and round the metal frame, inserting a new bunch of material with every several revolutions. Leaves can be wired, glued, or (if a cardboard backing is used) sewn in place. When gluing, it is sometimes helpful to insert a bit of glue-covered moss or cotton between the leaf and the framework to provide a better grip.

There is a tendency for dried flowers to shatter (either due to eventual insect infestation or to the natural process of drying out and "going to seed"), so it is wise to protect dried arrangements with several coats of clear spray glaze.

Use a continuous length of spool wire to fasten dried flowers and foliage to a wire wreath frame. Wrap the wire around the frame, adding a new bunch of material every two or three revolutions. Each addition should be placed to conceal the wire holding the stems of the previous bunch.

Always spray arrangements of dried flowers with sealer or glaze to counteract the tendency of the materials to shatter. Use matte finish spray if you want the sealer to be invisible.

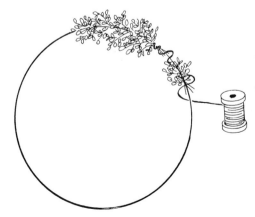

Statice wreath with flowers and a bow of dyed cornhusks. The statice is attached to a wire wreath using a continuous wiring method.

The same wreath has a totally different feeling if the accents are changed. Statice with deodar cedar "roses," brown bow.

Bunches of dried baby's breath are glued as accents between each pinecone flower.

Wreath of lavender, pink, and white statice with sprigs of baby's breath, fastened to a double-wire frame. Statice and baby's breath are among the "everlasting" flowers that dry naturally by the hanging method.

The base of each candle wreath is a pipe cleaner padded with bits of sphagnum moss. The tiny dried flowers are attached by the continuous wiring method.

Candle wreaths from Denmark.

Autumn wreath of strawflowers, statice, maple leaves, baby's breath, and assorted grasses. Flora-Dec Sales, Honolulu.

A sheaf of wheat, wrapped with a bow of glue-stiffened fabric (see Chapter 7). For a fuller arrangement, glue or wire the stalks around a core of cardboard tubing.

Compact wreath of dried flowers and seed heads, used to frame a mirror. Radha Chesick. *Photo courtesy of the artist.*

Working With Greens and Fresh Materials

Many hardy greens and flowers can be attached to wire, Styrofoam, or straw frameworks by most any of the methods previously discussed. But for foliage that wilts easily, and for wreaths and other arrangements meant to be displayed for a long period of time, it is important to provide some means of retaining moisture. One solution is to incorporate well-dampened sphagnum moss in the arrangement: sphagnum moss works like a sponge, soaking up and holding water, and it makes an excellent padding for wreaths and other Styrofoam or wire shapes. If wrapped with strips of green plastic or pieces of green florist's foil, the moss will stay damp for a long time.

Green florist's foam is another good choice for retaining moisture. Similar to but softer than ordinary Styrofoam, florist's foam should be fully saturated before fresh materials are inserted.

If neither moss nor foam is available, consider the old-fashioned method of using a vegetable or piece of fruit (apple, potato, orange, etc.) as the basis for an arrangement. Poke the stems of the foliage into the fruit (you may have to use a skewer to pierce the skin), and the greens will be able to draw on the fruit's natural moisture.

Greens suitable for arrangements:

Arborvitae	Holly	Redwood
Boxwood	Ivy	Rhododendron
Cedar	Juniper	Spruce
Fir	Laurel	White pine
Hemlock	Mistletoe	Yew

Keeping the greens moist is the secret for a long-lived wreath. Pack the curved back of a florist's wire wreath frame with dampened sphagnum moss, then begin winding with strips of plastic. (A green garbage bag cut into strips is used here.) The wrapping will create pockets into which clippings of evergreens are inserted.

Evergreen wreath with dried berries and cones. This is actually a double wreath—the berries and cones are attached to a single wire frame, which is wired in turn to the evergreen wreath. After the holiday season the wreath is taken apart and all the materials (except the greens) saved for reuse.

Miniature parcels wrapped in red and green dotted fabric enliven a Christmas wreath.

Glue fabric around a piece of Styrofoam cut to size with a serrated knife, coping saw, or hot-wire cutter. Tie the package with velvetlike nylon cord (sold at needlepoint shops) and fasten to a wooden pick.

Punchbowl wreath using nuts, lady apples, and kumquats. The fruit and nuts need only to be stacked in place. If kumquats are not available, "make" your own using clay made from bread and glue (see Chapter 6).

Advent wreath. It is important to keep greens fresh if they are to be used near candles, so prepare the wreath by packing the frame with sphagnum moss. Include in the packing four blocks of Styrofoam or green floral foam placed equidistant around the frame. Insert three or four lengths of wire in the base of each apple, leaving an inch or two extended, and force the wires through the greens into the blocks of foam. A lump of floral clay pushed into the hole made in each apple will keep the candles steady.

An alternative framework for an apple-candle wreath is moss-packed Styrofoam. Tuck the greens in pockets made by wrapping the Styrofoam with strips of green plastic.

Candle wreath using small lady apples.

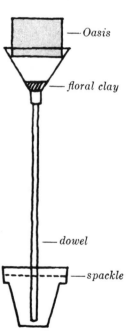

Mistletoe kissing ball. Place a saturated Oasis® flower holder on a circle of foil large enough to completely cover the Oasis®. Fold over and tie with decorative cord, making a long loop for hanging. Insert sprigs of mistletoe and Christmas greens, using a knife to puncture foil. Trim with stemmed Christmas ornaments and add a velvet bow at the top. Displacement of water occurs from stem insertion, so let the ball drain for half an hour before hanging. *Courtesy of Smithers-Oasis Division, The Smithers Company.*

Topiary tree. Place a firm dried branch or dowel stick in a 4-inch clay flower pot, anchoring the stick with spackle. The dowel stick may be painted or wrapped with ribbon. Fill the top of the pot with small pebbles. Secure a shallow funnel on top of the stick and seal with floral clay. Fit a saturated Oasis® flower holder in funnel. Insert short sprigs of boxwood or other foliage in a globe shape and add short-stemmed roses. *Courtesy of Smithers-Oasis Division, The Smithers Company.*

To make a garland of greens, start with a length of flexible rope (cotton washline, jute, hemp) and attach small bunches of evergreen trimmings using the continuous wiring method. If the garland is to be seen from behind, alternate clusters so that one goes on top, one under the rope.

Evergreen garland with calico bows. A long garland can be heavy, so make sure to provide adequate support when hanging.

A tree of lady apples.

A Styrofoam cone wrapped with floral tape is used as the foundation. The cone was a little squat, so an extra piece of Styrofoam was taped on the top. Use the larger apples at the bottom, smaller apples near the top.

A Note on Evergreens and Fire Safety

Keeping evergreens fresh and moist is the single most important step in preventing a fire hazard. If there is no way to introduce moisture, however (as in garlands of greens wired to long pieces of rope), consider treating the greens to reduce the chances of catching fire.

Various sprays sold to make plants wiltproof are available—they seal in moisture and thereby reduce the danger of fire. Or you can make a fire-retardant solution of ammonium sulfate (one pound chemical to one and one-half pints water), adding a little pine-oil emulsion if a Christmasy aroma is sought. After cutting the greens, stand them in this solution and leave in a cool spot until you are ready to make up the arrangement. For even greater protection, transfer some of the solution to a spray bottle and spray the finished arrangement.

Twelve-inch-diameter treetop star from Austria. Twelve- and 16-
point woven stars are hammered into a wooden framework. The
straw in the center is darkened by scorching with a hot iron.

From the Fields: Straw and Corn

When early man made the transition from hunter-gatherer to farmer, he placed his faith in the soil and in the crops that the soil would bring forth. Subject as his fortunes were to the change of the seasons, and to the ever-present threat of drought, pestilence, and plague, it is no wonder that he sought the help of the supernatural to ensure his livelihood. In most cases he prayed to a female deity, and celebrated her regenerative powers during planting and harvest festivals. In the Old World, where reliance was placed on grain (wheat, barley, rye, oats), the goddess was a Grain Mother, and straw images were made in her honor. In the New World, where corn and not grain was the focus of agricultural life, it was the Maize Mother whose magic was extolled, and it was from parts of the corn plant that images were constructed. The tradition of preserving the last sheaf of the harvest persisted in both the Old World and the New World, and became the basis for the decorative use of straw and corn, as harvest symbols or "corn dollies" ("corn" being British terminology for grain) in much of Europe, and as cornhusk figures in the Americas.

In recent years, there has been a revival of interest in work with straw and corn, partly because of a heightened sensitivity to the beauty of natural materials, and also because of a growing appreciation for the crafts of earlier generations. It is testimony to the growing popularity of both crafts that straw and cornhusks are now available commercially (in hobby shops or by mail order), and are likely to become even more easily available in coming years.

Straw

The grains most generally used for straw craft are wheat, rye, barley, and oats. Those living in a grain-growing region should have no difficulty finding a supply of one of these. Even if a farm is not available, suitable grains can often be found along the roadsides. In some areas, crops such as rye, oats, and barley are planted by subdivision developers or by highway crews to control erosion on slopes; in other areas, local wild grasses may provide a convenient substitute. It is even possible to grow grain at home. Seed is available from many mail-order seed companies, and can be planted in pots as well as in the open. The only special attention that might be required is staking (to protect the upright stalks in case of wind or heavy rain) and netting or screening (to keep birds from the ripening seed heads).

Commercial sources of straw are also available. Cleaned and prepared rye straw is sold in some hobby shops and by mail,* and florists usually stock wheat and oats. Although florist straw may seem expensive, the sheaves are long and generally in excellent condition, with the attractive seed heads intact. Loose straw can sometimes be found at the supermarket (as padding for melons and other fruits), in stables, or at feed stores where small quantities may be sold from broken bundles of hay. Although loose straw is likely to be broken and flattened, it is still suitable for making figures and certain types of straw stars.

Many straw techniques can also be worked in ordinary drinking straws, or in the long (17-inch) straws of white unsized paper which are now being marketed for craft purposes.*

Preparation

Ideally, field or garden straw should be gathered one to two weeks before reaching maturity so that the seed heads remain intact. Cut the stalks close to the ground, and spread on newspapers or an old cloth; place in a warm spot with good air circulation to dry. Drying will require a week to ten days depending on the weather, and can be hastened by moving the straw into the sun when the sky is clear.

To prepare harvested or purchased straw for working, cut with scissors just above each joint, and discard the leaf sheath which surrounds each segment of stalk. Sort the straws according to size.

Place the straw you intend to use in a pan of water, weighting if necessary to keep submerged, and allow to soak from 30 minutes to overnight. The length of time necessary depends greatly on the type and condition of the straw being used and must be learned by feel; in general, try not to soak longer than necessary. Wrap the softened straw in a damp cloth or newspaper, but do not wait too long before beginning work or the straw may mildew and discolor.

The dampened straw can be used whole and round, or it can be flattened by pressing with a hot iron. For some purposes it is desirable to split the straw before pressing. This is done by drawing a knife or fingernail down the length of the straw, then ironing until the straw is fully open and dry. The tougher

---

* See List of Suppliers.

straws will often have to be cut in two, but the more flexible varieties can often be opened out from a single slit, making one broad, flat strip. For darker color, continue to iron until the straw is scorched. The resulting light to medium brown shade provides an attractive contrast to the light golden color of unscorched straw.

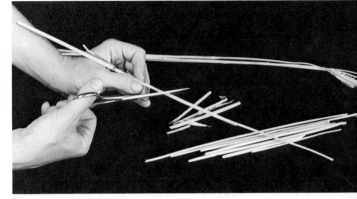

Preparing harvested and dried straw. Cut each segment just above the node, and slip off the leaf sheaths. The seed head may be left on the top segment if it is to be used decoratively. The straws can now be assorted according to size.

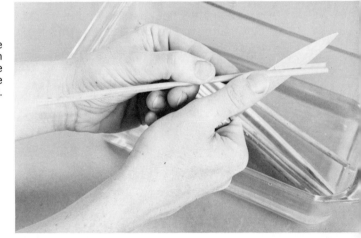

Straw must be soaked or tempered before being worked. Damp straw can be split with a knife or fingernail into two strips, or, if the straw is especially flexible, it can be opened out and flattened from a single slit.

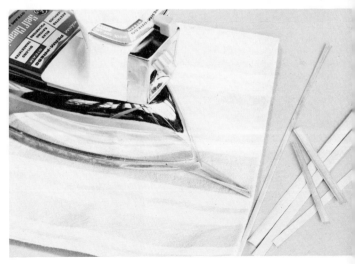

Flatten whole or split straws by ironing with a warm iron. Turn the iron up to hot to scorch the straw if a contrasting darker color is desired.

Woven Straw Stars

Woven straw stars can be made with round or flattened whole straw, or with widths of split and flattened straw. Four straws are used to produce the eight-point star which forms the basis for more complex shapes. Group the straws in pairs, placing the top two to form a cross, and the bottom two to form an X. Holding the center of the straws firmly between thumb and forefinger, weave a strong thread over the top straw, under the next, and over and under the succeeding straws until the circle is complete. Tie off the ends at the back of the star, leaving enough extra thread to form a loop for hanging. Tie firmly enough so that the star will not lose its shape, but not so tight as to crush the straws.

Double (sixteen-point) stars are formed by combining two simple stars. Join the pairs of straw in a cross, X, cross, X pattern, or simply form a cross with the top pair of straws and add the other straws in a spiral pattern underneath. Bind with thread in the over-and-under manner as for the simple star. If at first it feels awkward working with eight straws at once, simply bind two simple stars before joining them to make one double star.

More complex stars of thirty-two and sixty-four points can now be made by combining the double (sixteen-point) stars. For interesting variations, try using both flattened and unflattened straws, or straws that are long and narrow with those that are short and wide.

This simple 8-point star is the shape on which more complex woven stars are based. Place two straws to form a cross, and cover with two straws placed in an "X" pattern. Weave a thread over the top straw, and under and over the remaining straws, tying off at the beginning.

A simple 8-point star with smaller 8-point stars tied at the end of each point. Poland.

A double or 16-point star. The top 8-point star is of flattened whole straws; the bottom star is of ironed flattened strips. Make sure to hold the center of the straws firmly between thumb and forefinger while weaving the thread over and under the spokes.

A 12-point star. Note how the top three straws are arranged in a spiral, with the bottom three straws spaced between them.

Two 16-point stars with the flattened spokes cut in a decorative design. Poland.

Sixteen- and 24-point stars. The 24-point star is made by doubling the 12-point star.

A 32-point star. When working with this many straws, it is easiest to tie the two 16-point stars separately, then weave them together with a separate piece of thread.

A 32-point star formed as in the previous illustration, but with inner threads clipped and removed after the two stars are woven together.

MOBILE. Gisela Speidel. Eight- and 16-point stars are cut into various shapes and hung from silver wire.

Filigree Stars

The filigree star is an elaboration of the woven star, made by inserting strips of cut straw into the points of a woven star. The basic star must be made of whole, unflattened straw in order to accommodate the strips, which are cut in widths of 1/16 inch from straw that has been opened out and ironed flat. The strips can be left flat and straight, pinched together in the center to form a point, or drawn over a knife or scissor blade to form a rounded curve. Before inserting the strips into the spokes of the woven star, place a spot of glue on the ends so that the finished star will be sure to hold its shape.

Filigree stars. Thin strips cut from ironed straw are inserted in the spoke ends of woven stars.

A dab of glue will keep the strips secure in the straw spokes.

Bound and Tied Stars

In contrast to woven stars, which are fastened by over-and-under weaving, bound stars are made by fastening a bunch of soaked straws together in the center, and then forming a pattern by tying off the resulting spokes at various intervals. Alternately, the ends rather than the center are tied, and the bundles arranged in diamonds or triangles, which can then be combined in a variety of patterns. The thread used for binding these stars must be stronger than that used for woven stars (linen or buttonhole thread, or crochet cotton in white or a contrasting color is suitable), and the joints must be tied securely to ensure stability.

To make sure the shapes are symmetrical and the ties equidistant, it is helpful to work with the star pinned to a piece of polar graph paper (see Appendix).

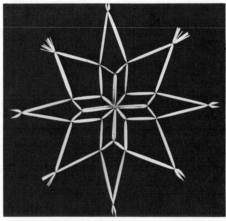

Large star. Bind 20 long, dampened straws tightly in the center, open out the spokes in groups of four, and tie each group at a point equidistant from the center. Separate the spokes into pairs, and tie each set to a pair from the neighboring spoke, making a star point.

Ten straws are bound in the center and at selected intervals out from the center. To help make the ties symmetrical, pin the center of a star to a piece of circular graph paper (see Appendix).

Fifteen straws are bound in the center and at one point out from the center, then separated and tied in long and short points.

Ten straws are bound in the center and at other points to produce a 5-point star.

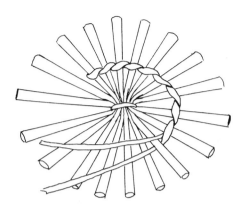

A woven star. Bind 30 or more straws in the center, then weave the ends of a doubled piece of dampened straw or raffia over and under the spokes, taking two at a time. Trim the star to shape.

Using a piece of raffia or damp straw folded in half, weave the ends alternately over and under the spokes of a bound star. When a full circle is reached, knot the ends of the raffia or straw around spoke number one and trim off any excess.

Star shaped by binding straws in bundles of four, then combining four such bundles in a decorative pattern. Heads of wheat are inserted in four of the points for a starburst effect.

Six-pointed star. Bind bundles of wet straw into equilateral triangles, then combine the triangles to form a 6-pointed star. Bind again wherever the triangles cross.

Braided, Plaited, and Woven Straw

Plaiting requires straw that has been dampened sufficiently and is flexible enough to bend without breaking. The simplest plait, sometimes called the catstep, is formed by folding two flattened straws back and forth across each other. The resulting chain can be shaped into a circle or small wreath, with bits of grain anchored at the joint for decoration. For a three- (or more) strand braid, it is helpful if the ends are secured in a clamp. Longer braids can be achieved if the small end of a new straw is inserted each time the end of a straw is reached; to conceal such joints, it is best if the lengths are staggered. Multistrand braids can be produced by hand, but it is also possible to purchase ready-made plait (such as that used by milliners) to shape into ornaments.

Instructions for a variety of plaits can be found not only in books on straw, but also in manuals dealing with basketry, palm frond weaving, and plaiting with leather and cord.

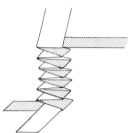

Catstep. Lay two well-dampened and flattened straws at right angles about an inch in from the ends, and fold back and forth across each other to build up a stack of accordionlike pleats.

Wreaths shaped from straws woven in the catstep pattern. Use two long straws, and start folding about an inch in from the ends. Continue folding to within an inch of the other end. Holding each end (a straight pin temporarily placed through the last fold helps), gently pull the ends apart, unwinding at the same time. Shape into a circle around a jar, overlap the ends, and tie. When dry the circle will keep its shape, and the ends can be trimmed or bits of grain added as decoration.

A wreath worked in paper straw. It is easier, since there is no chance of the straw splitting.

Three strands of straw are flattened and braided, and the resulting strip shaped into a heart.

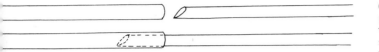

Often a new straw will have to be inserted when plaiting. Insert the small end of a new straw, trimmed to a point, into the large end of the straw that is coming to an end. Try to stagger these joints so that they are not readily visible.

Ornaments from milliner's straw plait. Joints are stapled or sewn. Straw plait is available in hobby and craft stores; it should be soaked before being shaped.

Pinecones dangle from a wreath of braided straw. The pinecones are shaped from strips of straw worked in the Tyrolean plait. Sweden.

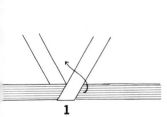
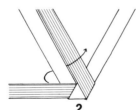
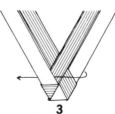
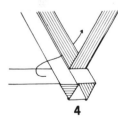

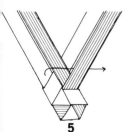
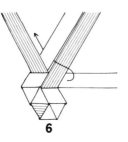

Tyrolean (or fishtail) plait. Use long lengths of dampened straw, and plait according to the diagrams, adding new straws at staggered intervals.

The finished plait is coiled, while still damp, in widening circles from the bottom up. Use needle and thread to stitch back and forth through the center of the coiled shape to secure. Force the edges down and together at the top; secure with needle and thread and add a bow.

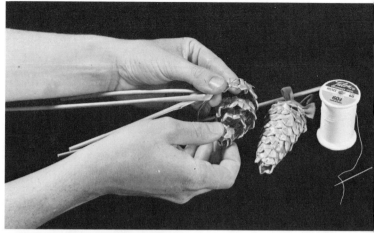

Plaited Czech ornaments. This type of plaiting is often seen in Europe, and most particularly in England, where it forms the basis of many "corn dollies" or harvest ornaments.

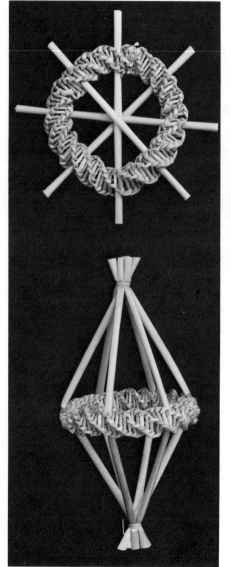

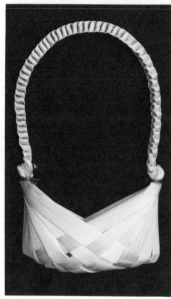

Polish basket combines a woven base with a catstep handle.

Woven ornament from Sweden. *Photo courtesy of the Swedish Information Service.*

Madonna. Mexico. Note the number of different plaits and weaves used to make this figure.

Woven Christmas tree in colored straw. Ecuador.

Animals and Figures

As with most other constructions, straw used for animals and figures must be worked damp, and all joints must be tied as tightly as possible with crochet cotton or other strong thread. In the few cases where a loose weave is desired (see the wings of the Mexican bird, for example), a long straw or piece of raffia can substitute for the thread.

If you encounter difficulty fastening a number of straws together, try inserting a needle through the straws to secure them at the point where they are to be joined, or (in the case of a large number of straws) secure the bundle with a rubber band before tying.

Crèche scene from natural and colored woven straw. Ecuador.

Angel mobile, from Sweden. Ribbons attached at three equidistant points along the wreath are threaded through a wooden bead to form a loop for hanging and for adjusting the balance.

To keep straws from slipping when tying in a fan shape, insert a needle through the straws near the point where they are to be fastened. Tie with strong thread or crochet cotton and slip out needle. For a larger bundle, secure the dampened straw with a rubber band before tying.

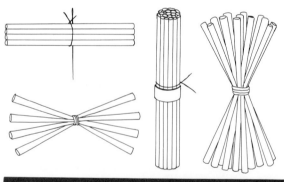

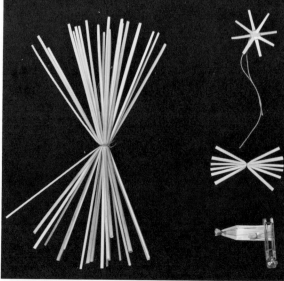

For an angel about four inches tall:
1) Bind a bundle of 15 to 20 dampened 9-inch straws together tightly in the center. Fold all the straw ends above the tie downward, and bind about ½ inch from the top to form the neck.
2) Weave four 1¾-inch straws over and under with thread to make an 8-point star for the halo.
3) Tie six 3-inch straws together in the center, and trim the ends to make the wings.
4) For the arms, take six 3¾-inch straws, tie about ¼ inch in from either end, and trim the ends close to the tie. While still damp, bend at the elbows and hold the crease by securing with a clothespin or hair clip.

Lift four straws at the back of the figure and insert the wings; lift four to six straws in front and insert the arms. Tie tightly at the waist. Use needle and thread to sew the halo to the back of the head, bringing the excess thread up through the top of the head to form a loop for hanging.

The completed angel.

Mexican bird. The body and tail are formed in one piece; the wings are shaped separately.

Mexican bird:
1) Insert a needle through the center of nine or ten 6-inch-long straws, and tie together so that the ends fan out. Bend both sides back from the center to make the wings.
2) For the body, use seven 9-inch straws, bundled together and tied in the center. Pull two straws out from the bundle below the tie and bend over the fingernail to form the beak. Bend the top straws down over the tie, and fasten securely below the beak to make the head.
3) Insert the wings below seven of the body straws, and tie together behind the wings, about 1½ inches back from the tie at the neck.
4) Use a piece of raffia or a long flattened straw to weave over and under the tail straws, taking two at a time. Use a second piece to weave the wings in the same manner. Trim tail and wings to desired shape.

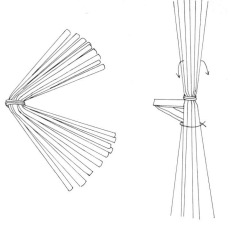

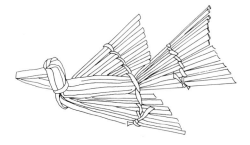

Scandinavian-style straw figures, including a goat, a woman, a small angel, and two elves.

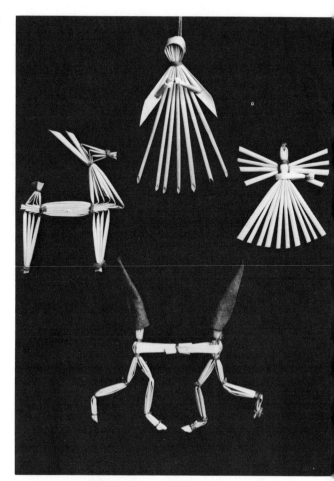

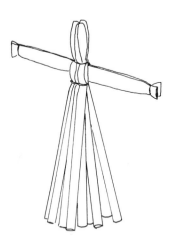

Straw elves:
1) Start with a bundle of four or five 8-inch straws, tie in the center, and pull the top straws down. Tie ½ inch down from the top for the neck.
2) Lift the two back straws and insert arms made of two 3½-inch straws. Tie at the waist below the arms.
3) Bend and tie at the knees (½ to ⅝ inch below waist) and ankles (¾ inch below knees). Bend the remaining straw forward to form the feet, tie at the toes, and trim off excess straw. Glue on a small cap cut from red felt.

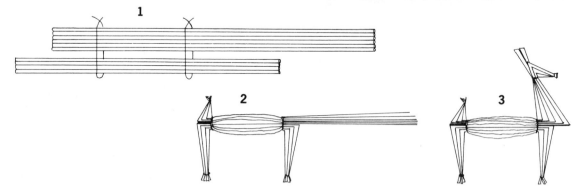

Small straw goat:
1) Start with 10 long straws and arrange according to the diagram, with four on the bottom (to become legs), and six on the top (for head and tail). Tie at the two points indicated to form the torso.
2) Starting with the lowermost straw, bend the leg straws down one at a time, making each bend slightly farther from the tie than the last. Tie at the desired length to form hooves.
3) Fold four of the six tail straws up in the same manner, and trim the remaining two with scissors. Similarly, bend upward each of the six neck straws, starting at the top and working down and outward. Tie at the neck, and bend four of the remaining straws to form the head, leaving the two uppermost straws straight to protrude as horns. Tie at the nose.

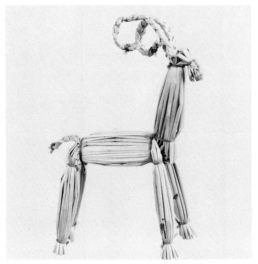

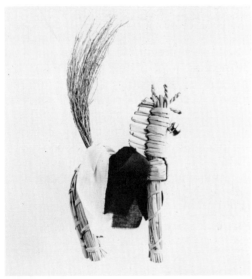

Top, left: The *julbuk,* or Christmas goat, so often seen during the holidays in Scandinavian countries. This is a larger version of the goat diagrammed, requiring more straw but formed in a similar manner except that the leg straws are divided into two sections and placed along either side of the torso, and six straws are allowed for the two horns so that each can be braided.

Top, right: A giant Christmas goat from straw. The figure incorporates the whole grain stalk rather than just segments. *Courtesy of the Swedish Information Service.*

Center, right: Acorn-eating squirrel has a tail formed of fluffy seed heads. *Courtesy of the Swedish National Tourist Office.*

Center, left: Japanese horse of twisted and bound rice straw.

Bottom: Mexican angels.

Simple shapes made by threading straw triangles.

Geometric Constructions

A wide variety of geometric shapes can be made by threading lengths of dry straw into triangles, and joining the triangles into three-dimensional constructions. An ordinary needle and sewing thread can be used for small shapes, but larger projects will require making a needle from wire somewhat longer than the longest straw to be used.

Start a construction by passing the thread through three straws, and tie off the ends to form a triangle. Thread two more straws onto the long end of the thread, and tie these off at the nearest joint of the first triangle to form a second triangle. Continue adding straws, rethreading the needle through the finished shapes whenever necessary to reach a new point for adding on straws.

Since straw has a tendency to split, it is important not to make the ties too tight. To strengthen the straw against splitting, it is a good idea to dip the ends of the cut pieces in diluted white glue, allowing the glue to dry before threading. (Make sure, however, that the glue does not dry in such a way as to close off the ends of the straw).

Although they lack the sheen of natural straw, paper or cellophane drinking straws can be used very successfully for geometric constructions, and there is no worry of splitting.

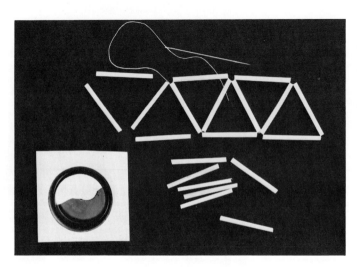

Threading segments of straw. Use a needle (or length of wire) slightly longer than the longest straw in the construction. Do not pull the thread too tight when threading or knotting or the straw may split, weakening the stability of the whole structure. To strengthen the straw, dip the ends in diluted white glue, then blow on the ends so that the glue does not dry, closing the opening.

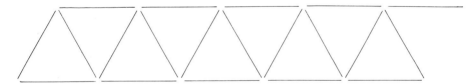

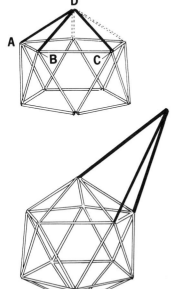

Threading an icosahedron (a geometric solid with 20 triangular faces). Cut 30 straws of equal length, and arrange 20 of them according to the diagram. Starting in the upper left corner, thread the first three straws and knot to form a triangle. Thread the next two straws, and tie into a second triangle, then continue down the row. Draw the last straw around to the first and tie to make a circular band of 10 triangles.

To form the top of the icosahedron, add five straws in the following manner: Thread two straws onto the thread remaining where the last join was made (A) and tie at B. From B pass the thread through the straw to C, then add on another straw and tie at D. Add two more straws in the same manner, knotting and repassing the thread through existing triangles whenever necessary. Repeat with the remaining five straws on the bottom of the figure.

A geometric shape can be stellated (have points attached) if straws are added to each of the faces. To stellate an icosahedron, 60 straws are required (three for each of the 20 faces).

An icosahedron and a smaller stellated icosahedron.

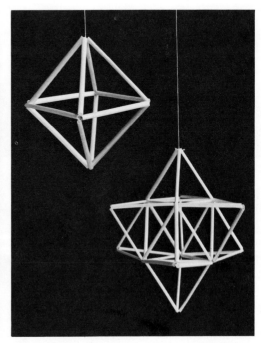

An octahedron, and the same figure stellated.

The top figure is made like an icosahedron, but when the top and bottom domes are added they are collapsed inward instead of being brought out to form a point. At the bottom is the same shape with points added to the 10 outward facing planes.

A geometric ornament from Poland, with puffs of colored paper tied at some of the joints.

Straw marquetry plaque from the Soviet Union. Dyed and natural straw is dampened, split, and ironed flat, then glued onto a painted wooden plaque.

Cornhusks

Colonists arriving in the New World from Europe in the seventeenth century were confronted with a formerly unknown crop: maize, or corn. From the Indians they soon learned uses for all parts of the plant: the kernels as a nutritious food for man and animals, the cobs as kindling and for smoking that other New World discovery, tobacco, and the husks or shucks for braiding baskets and rugs, and shaping into playthings for children.

The tradition of making figures from cornhusks, which passed from the Indians to the colonists, is carried on even today in the Ozark Mountains of Missouri and in the Southern Appalachians. In addition, the craft has spread to Europe, where the Czechs, in particular, have become known for their meticulously crafted dolls of corn.

Three Czech dolls in celebration dress. The two larger figures wear garlands braided from red, yellow, and green embroidery thread.

Left: Mother and child. Cornhusk dolls from Czechoslovakia.

Cornhusk dolls from the southern Appalachians. Both natural and dyed husks are used. *Photo by Michael Daniel. Courtesy of the Southern Highland Handicraft Guild.*

Collecting and Drying Husks

Cornhusks or shucks—the outer foliage that protects the ear of corn—can be purchased already cleaned and dried from hobby suppliers, or from several firms selling the bleached husks for wrapping tamales.*

Collecting the shucks from fresh corn requires more time, but there is an advantage, since corn silk, not included with the commercial husks, can be gathered at the same time. Note that there is a difference between the husks of sweet corn (that sold in the supermarket) and those of field corn (that fed to animals): the former is lighter in color and more pliable, the latter larger and tougher, with more prominent veins and greater color variation. Most, but by no means all, workers in corn prefer the softer husks of sweet corn.

Husks will have to be dried before they can be used. Green corn should be shucked carefully to keep the husks from tearing—cut off the base and peel off the layers rather than pulling them down from the top. Spread on newspapers or a cloth and let dry in a warm place until shriveled and creamy in color. Gather the corn silk when the corn is shucked, and dry along with the husks.

Field corn can often be harvested in late autumn when it has dried on the stalk, after which no further drying is needed. Sometimes the corn silk can be salvaged when dried corn is shucked, but often it is too brittle and powdery to use.

Bleaching and Dyeing

If the dried corn husks are spotted, mildewed, or discolored, they should be bleached before use. Place the husks in a bowl of water to which a half-cup of household bleach has been added, and soak from fifteen minutes to an hour or so, or until the discoloration has disappeared. Bleaching has the added advantage of softening the corn fibers, making it easier to substitute field corn for sweet corn, but the process can go too far—husks will actually disintegrate if left too long in the bleach. Always rinse the husks in clear water before proceeding.

Husks (and corn silk) can be dyed using ordinary household or other dyes. While any shade can be used, colors in the gold-rust-brown range are particularly attractive. Dye according to package directions, rinse in clear water, and spread out on newspaper to dry.

Dampening

Like straw, cornhusks are generally worked damp. Place the husks you will be using in a bowl of water, adding a teaspoon or so of glycerin if the husks seem especially brittle. Three or four minutes is usually adequate for softening, but allow more time for especially thick husks. When softened, remove the husks, shake out excess water, and wrap in a damp towel until ready to work. Damp husks are preferable to those that are soaking wet, as there will be less shrinkage and curling as they dry.

---

* See *List of Suppliers.*

Hair

Hair for cornhusk dolls can be made from twine (flax, jute, or sisal are possibilities), assorted yarns, or embroidery thread, as well as from corn silk. Use a straight pin or a needle to unravel the strands of twine or yarn, then tie loosely in the center to form a part. For a boy's figure, make this tie very tight so that the hair spreads out into a circle. Glue in place, then trim with scissors.

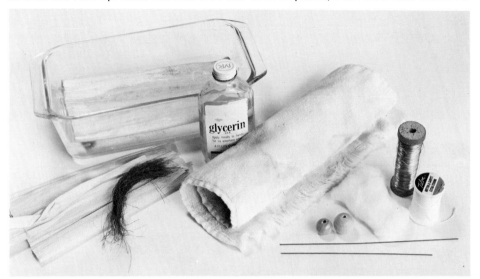

Materials for making cornhusk dolls. Soak the dried husks in water, adding glycerin if the husks are brittle. When softened, wrap in a damp towel. Wooden or Styrofoam beads are used for heads, wire for the arms, cotton for padding, and spool wire or thread for tying.

Materials for hair include *(left to right)* jute fiber, unraveled with a straight pin and tied in the center, jute before unraveling, sisal, yarn, 6-strand embroidery floss, and dried corn silk.

MAKING A CORNHUSK DOLL

Insert a piece of wire in a ¾-inch wooden or Styrofoam bead, cover the bead with white glue, and place in the middle of a strip of cornhusk approximately two inches wide and six to seven inches long. Wrap the husk around the bead. (The inside or shiny side of the husk should now be facing out). Tie tightly just above the bead, bring the top of the husk down over the bead, and tie again at the neck.

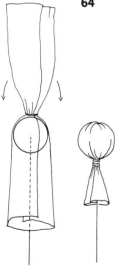

For the arms, place a 4½-inch length of wire along the grain of a strip 5½ inches long and 3½ inches wide; roll to form a cylinder. Trim the ends so that the total length is about five inches, and wire or tie ¼ inch in from each end to form hands.

Gather a 3-inch-by-3½-inch piece of husk (right side in) around one arm about ½ to ¾ inch above the wrist and tie securely, overlapping the ends. Pull this husk back toward the center to form a puffed sleeve and tie near the center. Repeat with the other arm.

The completed head and arm pieces.

Insert the arms between the neck pieces and tie below the bust.

Select two strips of dampened husk about 1½ to two inches wide and five inches long; place them in front of and behind the head. Tie just above the arms and pull the back husk down to the waist. Lay a small piece of cotton at the bust, pull the front husk down, and tie front and back strips at the waist.

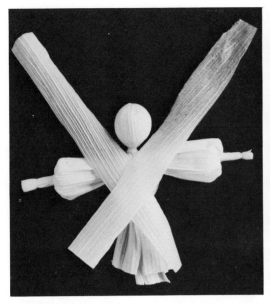

For the bodice, lay two ⅝-inch-by-5-inch strips to form an X across the bust. Bring these strips down and across behind the doll, and tie at the waist.

Bend the arms upward and lay a number of poorer quality husks around the body. Tie firmly at the waist, then pull the tops of the strips down to form the underskirt. Trim to ¼ inch shorter than the desired skirt length, and secure with a rubber band.

Cut a strip for the apron and lay at the waist, right side in, extending upward. Choose four unblemished husks about five inches wide (use more if the strips are narrower) and place one in front, one in back, and two at the sides. Pull these layers down carefully, bringing the apron down last, and trim to the desired length. Tie a narrow strip around the waist and add a bow for the apron at the back.

Encircle the skirt loosely with a rubber band to hold in place until the husks dry. Hair, features, and accessories such as a scarf or basket can now be added.

Three Czech dolls. The figure at left carries a goose home from the market in a basket of braided strips. The babe in the center, bundled in a folded piece of husk, takes a ride on a wooden sled. At right, a woman brings in hay for fodder.

Two girls celebrating a holiday. Czechoslovakia.

Czech flower girl. Use a smaller bead for a child's head, and reduce the other proportions accordingly. Flowers are made from dyed strips folded in half and knotted.

MAKING A CORNHUSK BOY

Form the head and arms as for the woman, but use a smaller bead and trim the arms to 4¼ inches. Wrap the arms loosely in a second husk and trim at the wrists to form sleeves. For legs, roll a 3½-inch piece of wire in a long husk 4 inches wide. Make two, join at the top, then attach to the arms.

Join head and body as for the female doll, but eliminate the cotton padding at the chest. Add the cross strip bodice, but trim all excess strips after tying at the waist, and add a wide waist band, gluing in back. For hair, tie unraveled flax or jute cord tightly in the center, and spread out the strands in a circle. Glue onto the head and trim.

Two small boys on a seesaw. Czechoslovakia. The overblouse is made like the bust of the female doll *(lower left photo, p. 64)*, but is trimmed rather than being tied off at the waist. Glue front and back strips together under the arms.

Cornhusk angel with flute. Czechoslovakia. The angel is constructed as for preceding little boys, but the overblouse is lengthened to form a robe. Wings are two husks glued together for stiffening.

Cornhusk angel with hair of corn silk and a halo shaped from dried grass.

Boy with lamb.

MAKING A CORNHUSK LAMB

Insert a wire in a ball of cotton, then wrap with a piece of husk. Tie at the nose, bring the top husk down, and tie again at the neck. Insert a second piece of cotton for the body, and tie at the tail. Wrap wire with cornhusks for the legs, leaving enough wire exposed to insert into the body. Roll up narrow strips of damp husk, secure with a hairpin until dry, then stretch these coils out and glue all over the body.

Egg basket in the shape of a goose. Czechoslovakia.

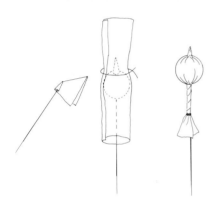

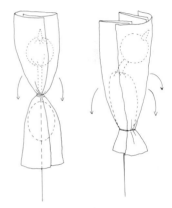

MAKING A CORNHUSK GOOSE

Start with a ¾-inch square of cornhusk, fold on the diagonal, and roll around a length of wire. Insert the wire through the hole of a wooden bead (or substitute a ball of cotton). Wrap and glue a strip of cornhusk around the head and tie at the beak; pull the top layer down and tie at the neck. Wrap the neck with a narrow strip of husk.

Wrap a husk around the neck, overlapping the ends, and tie about one inch below the neck tie. Insert a little cotton padding, and bring the top of the husk down over the cotton to form the bird's breast. Fold two strips of husk in half, and place these facing upward at either side of the breast; add a third fully opened strip in the front. Tie all these at the base of the breast, then pull them down and back to form the body.

Pull back the three body strips and join to form the tail. Before tying, insert a number of curled strips cut from a husk which has been rolled while wet and secured with a hairpin until dry. Make a long braid from three husks, shape into an oval, and sew or glue to the bottom of the goose.

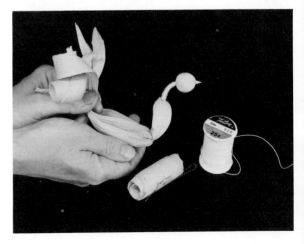

Cornhusk flowers from dyed and natural husks. Some of the flowers have seedpods as centers.

ZINNIA

Zinnia. Cut a number of ½-by-3-inch strips. Fold each in half, gather at the base, and secure with spool wire. Wire a number of these shapes together to form a flower of the desired fullness.

TULIP and FIVE-PETAL FLOWERS

Tulip and five-petal flowers. Cut five strips of cornhusk into 1-by-4-inch pieces. Twist each strip once in the center, then fold in half. Secure with spool wire at the base, and round out the petal by grasping the edges at the widest point and stretching outward. Assemble with the petals cupped inward for the tulip, outward for other flowers.

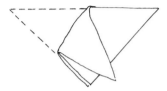

ROSE

Rose. Form the bud from a square of damp cornhusk folded in half diagonally. Bring the left and right points down to the base, overlapping slightly, and wire securely. Cut petals in a wedge shape, rounding the corners, and curl over a pencil or knitting needle. Wire smaller petals around the bud, then add additional larger petals until the desired fullness is reached.

Basket of flowers from southern Appalachia. *Photo by Michael Daniel. Courtesy of the Southern Highland Handicraft Guild.*

Wreath of split cornhusks and baby's breath. Gina McCormack. Husks are cut into ⅝-by-8-inch strips, wired four at a time to wooden picks, and inserted into a Styrofoam wreath form. About 120 bunches were required for this 12-inch-diameter wreath.

Swedish elf has a beard down to his toes, a gray felt jacket, and knitted cap and mittens. 7 inches high.

From the Forest: Wood and Wood Shavings

Working with Wood

No elaborate workshop is needed for working with wood. A simple saw, a vise or clamp, some sandpaper, and perhaps a hand drill—these are the basics. The committed woodworker, naturally, will be tempted by an endless variety of specialized tools, each designed to make a specific task easier: planes, chisels, gouges, punches, drills, not to mention a whole range of power saws, drills, lathes, sanders, and so forth. But specialized equipment should be acquired only as the need arises, when it is clear that the anticipated amount of use will justify the investment.

Using Available Wood Shapes

There are available so many different kinds of preformed wood pieces that often a project can be completed with few or no woodworking tools. Spools, cigar boxes, golf tees, hors d'oeuvre picks, clothespins, beads, and discarded toys are some of the materials you may already have on hand. A visit to the lumberyard or hardware store will add such items as dowels, molding, curtain rings, drawer pulls, spindles, and table legs. In addition, hobby stores and mail-order firms can often supply such specialized or hard-to-find shapes as doll bodies, boxes, candleholders, wooden eggs, bowls, trays, and buttons.

Once a collection of wooden shapes is assembled, it is easy to join the pieces into interesting arrangements. Glue is usually all that is required to hold the parts together, though once in a while you may want to drill a joint and insert a dowel, or substitute a screw or nail. Most preformed wood pieces are cut from clear, fine-grained wood, so they should need little more than light sanding to prepare them for finishing. Suggestions for both adhesives and paint are discussed below.

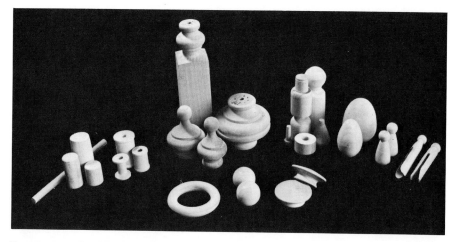

Few or no woodworking tools are needed if you use preformed wood pieces. From left: dowel segments, spools, spindles, assorted wood turnings from a selection for children, eggs, doll bodies, clothespins. Front: curtain ring, wooden beads, doorknobs.

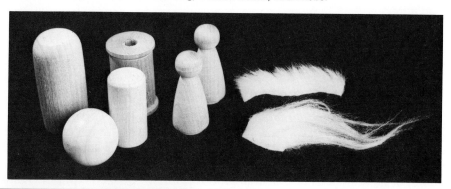

Wood turnings and scraps combined with a bit of fake fur easily become Christmas elves. The wood pieces are glued together, then painted with poster colors.

After painting, the shapes are sprayed with a clear sealer, and beards and noses (from air-drying clay) glued in place.

Assorted Scandinavian elves assembled from simple parts.

Wooden soldier made from dowels. A skewer is inserted in holes drilled in the arms and body, so that the arms are movable.

Swedish dolls in native costume are painted on turned wooden pieces. Ingrid Dixelius. *Courtesy of the Swedish Information Service.*

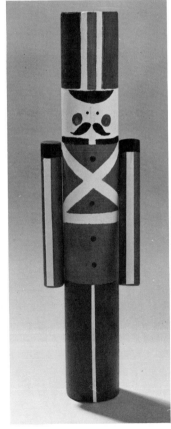

Tiny (1-inch-high) Italian angels are painted in glossy enamels.

Wooden angel. 2 inches high.

Angel on horseback. Enamel and poster color. Italy.

Painted bird. The body is notched to make room for the wings and tail, which are cut from a single piece of flat wood. Denmark.

Wooden birds from Taiwan have clamps glued to the underside so that they can be clipped onto a tree branch.

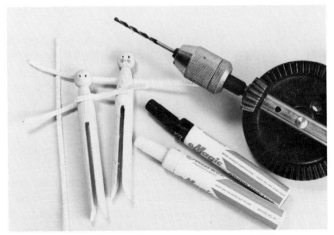

To give arms to a clothespin doll, drill a hole sideways through a wooden clothespin and insert a pipecleaner or (if a drill is not available) wrap the pipe cleaner around the body. Paint on the features or draw with felt marking pens.

Three clothespin dolls: old-fashioned doll, Scandinavian miss, and colonial lady. The dolls are dressed in lace-trimmed scraps, and have hair of 6-strand embroidery floss.

Clothespin dolls in colonial dress, from a tree celebrating the American Bicentennial. Awa Lau Wahine Officers' Wives' Club, Pearl Harbor.

Adhesives for Wood

A number of adhesives are suitable for wood. White glue, an emulsion of plastic resin in water, is milky-looking and water soluble when wet (thus spills clean up easily), but becomes strong, transparent, and water resistant when dry. Not actually waterproof, it should be limited to indoor use. The thicker craft version of white glue (variously labeled "tacky," "sticky," or "thick") is especially convenient for use with small wood pieces since it grips better and dries faster than its more liquid household counterpart.

Where greater rigidity is desired (white glue remains flexible even when dry), clear household cement is a good choice. Transparent and quick-drying, household cement has only one drawback: it contains solvents that are flammable and produce irritating fumes. As a precautionary measure, always work in a well-ventilated area away from heat and flame. Different brands of household cement are of different consistencies, and colors range from waterclear to amber, so experiment to find the product you prefer.

If a wood assemblage is to be subjected to considerable stress, or is intended for display outdoors, consider using epoxy, an adhesive consisting of two components (resin and hardener) that must be mixed before setting takes place. Costly and a bit messy, epoxy is best saved for those projects where its strength and water resistance are called for.

Contact cement is what the name implies: an adhesive that grips immediately on contact. It is thus perfect for joints which cannot be clamped. The process is to apply the adhesive to both of the surfaces to be joined, allow the glue to dry, then press the pieces of wood together. Once the coated surfaces touch, no further adjustment is possible, so work carefully.

A final choice for joining small wood objects is the glue gun, an electric device that applies a line of melted glue which bonds and dries almost instantly. The adhesive is strong and waterproof, but also rather expensive and somewhat messy. The use of the glue gun is illustrated in Chapter 2 (see Attaching with Adhesives).

Coloring Wood

Wood has a natural warmth and beauty of its own, and there are times when its appeal is greatest if left unfinished. At other times, however, coloring with either stain or paint will be needed to bring out the desired characteristics. Stains are transparent or semitransparent coatings which are applied and wiped off, leaving the grain of the wood visible, while paints are designed to cover the wood grain with colored pigment. Most paints can be converted to stains if they are thinned with the appropriate solvent, brushed on, and then wiped with a cloth to remove the excess.

Both paints and stains come in water-based and non-water-based forms. Water-based colors include poster and watercolor paints, felt pens (the nonpermanent variety), many inks and dyes, and latex and acrylic paint. Latex and acrylic (along with some inks and dyes) dry to a permanent finish, but other water-based colors require a protective coating (shellac, varnish, lacquer, or spray glaze) if they are to receive much handling or will come in contact with water.

Non-water-based colors include enamels, lacquers, artist's oil paints, most wood stains, and waterproof felt pens. These colors are permanent when dry and require no protective coating. For thinning, they require turpentine or paint thinner rather than water, and brushes must be cleaned in a solvent. When used as stains, they are generally applied directly to raw wood, but if the color is to be opaque the wood should usually be sealed. For a sealer use shellac, varnish, or several coats of latex paint or gesso. To achieve a water-smooth finish, apply several coats of gesso, sanding between coats, then spray-paint.

Types of Wood

For most decorative projects you will want to use wood that is fairly soft, has a straight grain, and cuts and paints well. Pine is an excellent choice. If clear pine is not available, substitute the resin-free segments of a piece of knotty pine, or salvage strips of wood from discarded fruit boxes and storage crates.

Basswood, poplar, mahogany, and cedar all have their adherents—basswood in particular works easily and takes paint well. If not available locally, these easily worked woods can be ordered from woodworking companies in thicknesses of ⅛ to ¾ inch and up. Fir, though easy to obtain, is resinous and hard to finish; try to find more suitable wood even if it means a search. Note that the measurements given for lumber represent the rough and not the finished dimensions, so that a "1-inch" board is actually closer to ¾ inch in thickness, and so forth.

Plywood, which consists of thin sheets of wood glued in layers, is handy in the ⅛- and ¼-inch panels, but thicker sheets are often difficult to cut without power tools. For very thin ornaments, aircraft plywood is an excellent choice. Designed for use in model airplane construction, it is light and sturdy and has smooth top and bottom layers that finish easily. Thin sheets (1/64- to 1/32-inch thick) can actually be cut with scissors; thicker sheets (up to ¼-inch thick) require a knife or saw.

One other useful hobby material is balsa wood, available in assorted sizes ranging from thin sheets to large blocks. Exceptionally soft and lightweight, it cuts easily with a knife. Though balsa is appealing because of its availability and ease of handling, its open grain structure makes it very hard to paint or finish, and completed projects are not very strong.

Saws

Probably the most useful tool for decorative wood projects is the coping saw. The coping saw has a blade that is very thin and narrow, perfect for cutting intricate curves in wood that is not too thick. The blade is removable, so that inside cuts can be made by drilling a hole, inserting the blade, and then attaching the C-shaped saw frame. If you plan to do much work with a coping saw, consider making yourself a V-notched support to stabilize the work and make the cutting go more smoothly.

A keyhole (or compass) saw is also used for cutting irregular wood shapes, but because the blade is thicker and stronger than that of the coping saw, it can be used for boards of greater thickness. In addition, the depth of the cut is not restricted as with the coping saw, where the C-shaped frame limits the distance the blade can travel in from the edge. Though not as versatile when it comes to intricate curves, the keyhole saw is still an extremely useful tool.

If you plan to do a lot of decorative work in wood, consider investing in a table-model jigsaw. These versatile tools handle intricate cuts quickly and easily, and many come with handy attachments for sanding, drilling, and other woodworking tasks. Like the coping saw, the electric jigsaw has a removable blade, so that inside cuts are no problem.

Assemble toothpick stars on a piece of circular graph paper covered with plastic wrap or wax paper. Use thick white glue or clear household cement to attach the parts. Circles punched from cork sheeting, wood veneer, or cardboard help to strengthen the centers.

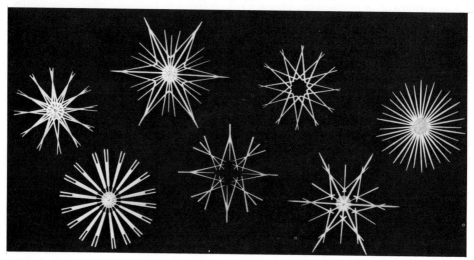

Toothpick stars.

A large (12-inch) star. Use household cement rather than white glue for large pieces where rigidity is desired.

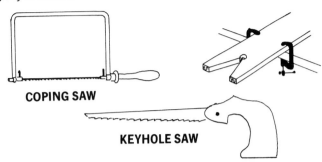

COPING SAW

KEYHOLE SAW

Both the coping saw and the keyhole saw are useful for decorative wood projects. To make a support for inside cuts when using the coping saw, V-notch the end of a board and clamp to a working table. Drill a hole in the wood to be cut, insert the coping saw blade, and reattach the blade to the saw frame.

MAKING A PUZZLE

Use carbon paper to transfer a design onto wood. Tape the drawing in place so it will not slip.

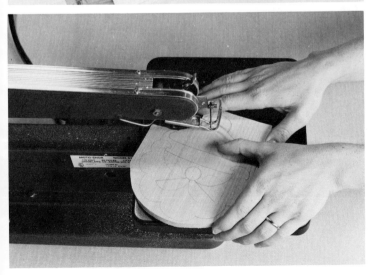

A coping saw could handle this job easily, but an electric jigsaw greatly speeds the work. If using a coping saw, make sure the blade is kept vertical, or the puzzle pieces will not fit together well.

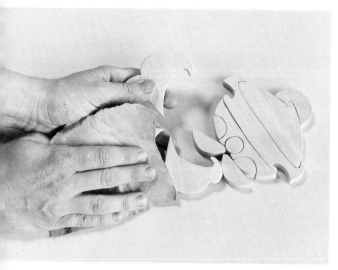

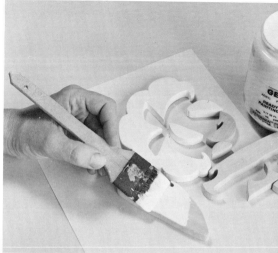

Sand all parts well. If the puzzle is to be kept natural, keep the edge sanding to a minimum or the pieces may be too loose. Painting, on the other hand, will make the fit too tight unless the edges are well sanded to begin with.

Acrylic gesso is applied to seal the wood and fill the pores. The first two coats are thinned slightly, the last coat is applied without thinning.

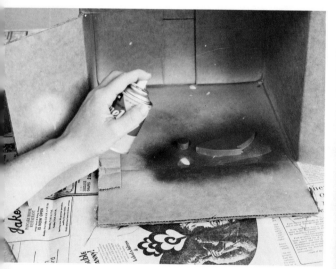

Spray paints give the smoothest finish. Use a box as a spraying chamber to avoid overspray. Work outdoors, or in a well-ventilated area.

Santa puzzle from ½-inch-thick basswood, gessoed and enameled. The pieces interlock so that the puzzle can be suspended without falling apart.

To MAYA. Linda von Geldern. The parts are cut from cedar, then spray painted.

Painted animals. Acrylic paint is brushed directly onto unprimed basswood.

BUTTERFLY PUZZLE. Linda von Geldern. When puzzle parts do not interlock, they can be held together with a frame backed with hardboard. Acrylic paints, brushed on and wiped off, have been used to stain this butterfly.

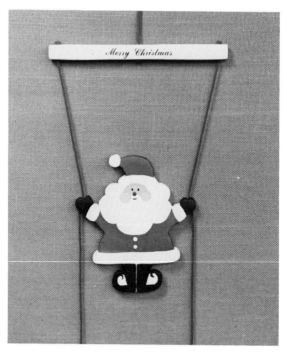

UPWARDLY MOBILE SANTA. Santa is cut from ½-inch basswood, painted with poster colors, and sprayed with matte-finish acrylic spray. Pressure-sensitive transfer lettering is used to spell out his greeting. Holes are drilled in each hand and threaded with velvety nylon cord. Pulling on the cords causes Santa to climb upward.

Enameled wooden rooster. Sweden. *Courtesy of the Swedish Information Service.*

The rooster is a popular Easter figure in European folk art. These examples from Sweden show some of the ways in which wood can be treated. *Courtesy of the Swedish Information Service.*

SPRING. Linda von Geldern. Painted wood puzzle in a cedar frame.

JOY. Linda von Geldern. Painted and stained cedar puzzle, cut on an electric jigsaw.

Painted Christmas ornaments from West Germany. Similar shapes could be cut with a knife from aircraft plywood, wood-veneer sheets, or thin balsa wood.

Wood Shavings

In the Scandinavian countries, craftsmen make beautiful ornaments from wood shavings, a material discarded as scrap in most of the rest of the world. Delicate and lacy, the decorations are at their best suspended from a Christmas tree branch or hung from the ceiling where they turn slowly with the breeze.

Wood shaving ornaments are inexpensive, easy to make, and require no special tools. The raw materials can be obtained from hobby shops, lumberyards, and mail-order companies, or—with a sharp plane and a little practice—you can make your own.

Curlicue wood shaving ornaments are delicate and lacy.

Homemade Wood Shavings

Select a piece of 1-inch clear pine 2½ to 3 or more feet in length (use a clear section of knotty pine if clear pine is not available), and soak the board in a tub of water for twelve to twenty-four hours, weighting to keep submerged. When the wood is well saturated, secure the board edge up in a sturdy vise.

Adjust a well-sharpened smooth or jack plane to a medium opening, then make a few sample cuts, placing the plane squarely on the end of the board and moving steadily forward with constant downward pressure. If the cut is too deep the plane will catch in the wood and the shavings will be too thick; if the cut is too shallow the plane will skip over the wood and the shavings will be thin and broken. Adjust the gap accordingly, and practice until you can produce long, smooth shavings.

For flat ornaments, dry the strips under a weight; for curls wind the damp shavings in coils and secure with a rubber band until dry.

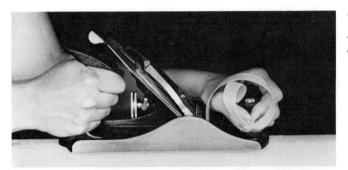

Cutting wood shavings from a soaked pine board. Move the plane smoothly forward with a steady downward pressure for long, even shavings.

Types of wood shavings include *(from left)* Finnish wood tapes in assorted widths and colors, veneer plywood edging, a homemade shaving, wood curls manufactured in the United States, thin wood filigree curls imported from Finland.

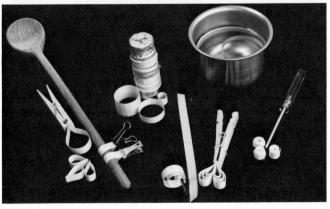

Soak wood shavings to make them flexible, then wrap around jars, bottles, etc., to get an assortment of shapes. Circles within circles are made by winding a continuous strip in ever bigger revolutions. A mark is made each time the tape passes the starting point, so that the strip can be unwound to use as a pattern. At the right, a paper quilling tool is used to roll very tight coils.

When the shapes are dry, they can be combined into ornaments.

Large ornament combines flat wood strips, firm wood shavings, and thin wood curlicues. Finnidee of Finland. *Courtesy of Finn-Matkos, Inć., Stamford, Connecticut.*

Hanging design uses flat wood strips, beads, and shavings. Sheets of balsa or aircraft plywood could also be cut to provide a framework. Finnidee of Finland. *Courtesy of Finn-Matkos, Inc.*

OLISH PAPER CUTS. Designs in glazed paper from
ne Łowicz region of Poland.

DECORATED EGGS. Appliqué, resist, and painting are among
the techniques used.

WREATH. Fresh fruits wired to a
circle of evergreens.

FILIGREE STRAW STARS. Split and flattened straws are inserted into the ends of hollow straws.

MADONNA. Mexico. Pleated and woven straw.

CASTLES. Baker's clay shaped and baked around removable cardboard cores.

CORNET STARS. Wood shavings, wooden beads, and toothpicks.

BUSHEL OF VALENTINES. Linda von Geldern. Puzzle of stained and enameled wood.

SUGAR SANTA. 5 inches high. The figure is piped with thinned royal icing.

YARDSTICK ROSES. Made from tissue paper "creped" around a ruler.

WOOD SHAVING ANGEL. 4 inches tall. West Germany.

CHRISTMAS HANGING. Marge Hastert. Batik squares sewn to a burlap backing, edged with ribbon.

ROYAL ICING ORNAMENT. 3½-inch diameter.

BATIKED ORNAMENTS. Fine lines waxed with a kistka and a tjanting.

STUFFED ORNAMENTS. Felt pen on cotton sheeting.

HICKETY-PICKETY, MY BLACK HEN. Marsha Anne Isoshima. Elegant hen sits on a black satin pillow.

PYSANKY. Luba Perchyshyn. Ukrainian-style wax resist eggs. Photo by Slawko Nowitsky. Courtesy of the artist.

HIS GLORY FILLS THE WHOLE EARTH. Sister Helena Steffensmeier. 6 feet 8 inches by 3 feet 11 inches. Stitchery and appliqué on black homespun.

SHEAF OF WHEAT. The bow is of glue-stiffened fabric.

NUT WREATH. 10-inch diameter. A glue gun is used to attach the nuts to a plywood backing.

EMBOSSED ORNAMENTS. Tooled aluminum foil (36-gauge) colored with felt markers and glass stains.

HEART. Stephen Blumrich. Batiked fabric sandwiched between leaded glass. Courtesy of the artist.

CLOTHESPIN DOLLS. Colonial lady, Scandinavian miss, and girl in bloomers.

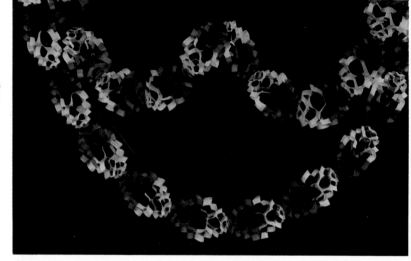

TISSUE PAPER GARLAND. Circles of tissue cut so that they expand when joined in a chain.

Commercial Wood Shavings

Commercially produced wood shavings are not a widely known product in the United States, so it may be necessary to search to find a local supplier. Some hobby shops carry shavings, and nearly all lumberyards stock a wood veneer tape which is similar enough to be almost interchangeable. If you cannot track down what you want locally, it is easy to order by mail from the firms that manufacture or import high-quality wood shavings.*

Several varieties of wood shavings are available. Finland, the primary European supplier, exports two types to the United States. One, variously called hobby strip, wood strip, or simply wood shaving, is a fairly firm material that comes in rolls of ten strips, each strip approximately thirty-two inches long. The rolls are available in four widths (.4, .8, 1.2, and 1.8 inches) and eight colors (natural birch, red, blue, green, purple, yellow, orange, and brown). In addition, the Finns export boxes of "wood filigree," thin curlicues in widths of .4 and .8 inches.

American suppliers are also entering the field, and there is at least one company manufacturing commercial wood shavings. The curled shavings come clustered in a box, and fall between the two Finnish products in thickness.

The thickest product available is the veneer tape sold at lumberyards. Designed as an edging for plywood panels, it comes in 6- to 8-foot lengths in assorted widths (generally ¾ to 2 inches) and various woods (fir, birch, oak, teak, walnut, mahogany, ash, etc.). The tape has a thin paper backing which is almost invisible on the lighter woods such as birch and ash, but which detracts from the appearance of the darker woods. (When used as edging, of course, the paper-backed side is invisible.) Though veneer edging is not quite as flexible as the other types of wood shavings, it can be used interchangeably in many projects that do not require tight coiling.

Flat veneer sheets, though not thin enough to be curled like shavings, are often used in conjunction with wood curls. Veneer sheets, which are available in numerous woods, are generally about $\frac{1}{28}$-inch thick, and can be cut with scissors or (preferably) a sharp craft knife. To avoid splintering the veneer, dampen before cutting, or else cut through tape placed along the front and back of the cutting line. Thin aircraft plywood (discussed above) can also be substituted for wood veneer—it cuts easily with scissors, and has little tendency to splinter.

Coloring Wood Shavings

Wood shavings can be purchased colored, or they can be colored at home with fabric dye, food coloring, watercolors, acrylics, felt pens, wood stains, and so forth. If using a water-based dye or paint, first dampen the shavings so that they take the color evenly. Then either immerse the shavings or brush the color directly onto the wood. (Note that the color will dry a shade or two lighter than it appears when wet.) Oil- or alcohol-based dyes and stains should be brushed directly on the dry wood, and the excess wiped away with a cloth. When dampening colored shavings before working, always soak the colored strips separately to avoid any bleeding.

---

* See addresses in the List of Suppliers.

Working with Wood Shavings

Wood shavings are generally moistened before using, since they become much more flexible when damp. Immerse in warm water and soak until pliable—just a few minutes for thin shavings, and up to thirty minutes or more for thick veneer edging. (Filigree curls or wood strips to be shaped into circles over one inch in diameter may need no dampening.) Do not allow the shavings to remain in water for extended periods of time, or the wood may become brittle when dry.

To make circles, ovals, teardrops, and most other shapes, wrap damp strips around objects of the desired shape (bottles, dowels, wooden spoon handles, etc.) and secure with rubber bands or clamps until dry. If you want to glue the strips while damp, use water-soluble white glue and cover the molds with foil or plastic wrap so the glue does not stick. Otherwise, allow the shapes to dry fully, then secure the ends with fast-drying clear household cement.

To make circles within circles, start by winding up a long strip, making each succeeding revolution larger than the last. If you mark the point where each circle passes the starting point, you will be able to unwind the strip and use it as a pattern for making other shapes of exactly the same size. Make "teardrops within teardrops" the same way, but crease the tape firmly over a knife blade each time it passes the starting point. Use white glue if you want to secure the strips while they are damp, clear household cement if you wait to glue them until they are dry.

To make very tight coils, allow the shaving to soak for longer than usual (15–45 minutes depending on thickness), then roll around a toothpick or a paper quilling tool (a metal rod with a slit in the end) and wind. Needle-nose pliers can also be used for winding up the shaving. Gently slide the completed coil off the toothpick, quilling tool, or pliers, and encircle with a rubber band to maintain the shape until dry.

For straight strips, allow damp shavings to dry while weighted with a book or other flat, heavy object, or press until dry with an iron set at medium heat.

Assembling the Parts

When all the parts for an ornament are dry, assemble using white glue or clear household cement. If you want to experiment with other joining methods, try sewing or stapling the parts together.

For symmetrical ornaments it helps to work on a piece of circular graph paper (see Appendix) covered with wax paper or plastic wrap. Place this in turn on a sheet of corrugated cardboard or composition board and you will be able to hold the parts in place with straight pins while they dry.

Hang the ornaments by piercing the wood with a needle and threading with nylon fishing line, or by attaching wooden beads or small coils of shavings (through which a thread can be strung) to the top of the ornament.

OPPOSITE PAGE: *Top, left:* Large (18-inch) ornament is designed to hang on the wall. *Right:* Shaped and dried wood shaving circles can be punched (use a revolving leather punch for neat, small holes) and threaded onto skewers. Finnidee of Finland. *Courtesy of Finn-Matkos, Inc. Bottom, left:* Wood shaving Christmas tree. The ends of the wood shavings fit into a framework made of four sticks. Finnidee of Finland. *Courtesy of Finn-Matkos, Inc. Center:* Wood shaving circles, flat wood strips, and notched dowel segments. Finnidee of Finland. *Courtesy of Finn-Matkos, Inc. Right:* Though wood shaving ornaments originated in Scandinavia, they are now being imitated in other parts of the world. This Taiwanese import, though attractive, lacks the precision and care that characterize the Scandinavian examples.

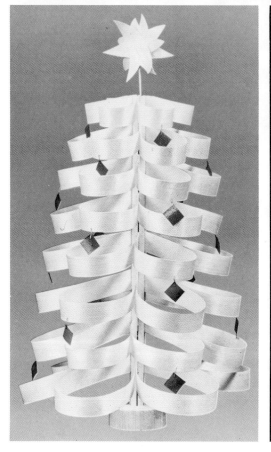

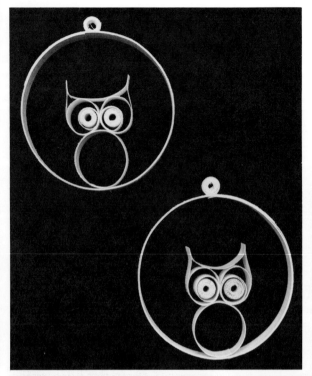

Wood shaving owls from Denmark. The outer circle consists of a double layer of wood tape. Note the tight coil glued to the top to serve as a hanger.

Wood shaving balls. Shape damp shavings around a jar or cylinder, but make each circle slightly looser than the last. When dry, glue the second largest circle inside the largest, placing at right angles, and add the other two circles on the inside. Adjust the seams so that they do not all meet at the same point.

Three wood shaving angels. West Germany. The heads are wooden beads, the hair is unraveled thread. Note the extra-wide shaving that forms the body of the middle angel.

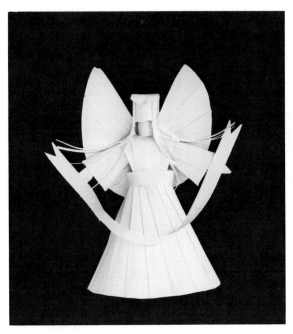

Also from West Germany, this wood shaving angel is very different in design from the three angels on opposite page.

A Swedish ornament from wood shavings and wood veneer. The red "flowers" are dyed or stained.

Left: Delicate snowflakes are cut from thin wood sheets. West Germany.

Right: Wood shaving ornament from Japan is used to decorate ceremonial jars of sake.

Dove in a circle. Sweden. Similar shapes could be cut from thin aircraft plywood or from wood veneer. Note how the wings and tail are notched to fit the body.

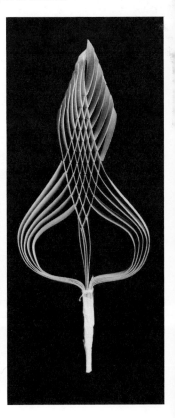

Cornets

To shape wood shavings into cones, or "cornets," start by cutting a paper pattern of the same width as the wood stripping, then cross over the ends as diagrammed and trim off the excess. Note that you can change the size of the cornet by adjusting the angle at which the strips cross each other—the tighter the ends are pulled the smaller the cornet. No matter what the size, always keep the tip of the cone closed and pointed, not open and loose.

Once you have decided on a sample shape, use the paper pattern to cut a number of strips from wood shavings. Soak the shavings briefly in warm water, then draw over a knife blade to produce an even curl. Overlap the ends so that the tips match, then secure with thick white glue and clamp until dry (wooden clothespins with the ends reversed make the best clamps). Drying can be speeded by placing the cornets in the sun or in a slightly warm oven, but do not leave too long or the wooden clothespins may become stuck in place. It is also possible to dry the cornet before gluing—in this case release the clothespin clamp, apply a little clear household cement to the overlapping ends of the cornet, and reclamp briefly until the glue sets.

When a number of cone shapes are completed, assemble using white glue or clear cement. Slices of doweling or circles of wood shaving or cork sheeting can be used to strengthen the center of star shapes; beads, skewers, and toothpicks can all provide decorative accents.

To make a pattern for wood shaving cornets, shape a strip of paper the same width as the wood shaving into a cone, then trim the ends as illustrated. Note that the size of the cornet changes depending on whether the strips are overlapped loosely or pulled tight.

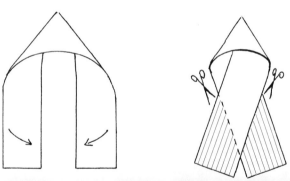

Use the paper pattern to cut a number of wood shaving strips, then soak the strips and curl each over a knife blade. Shape into cornets, gluing the ends and clamping until dry.

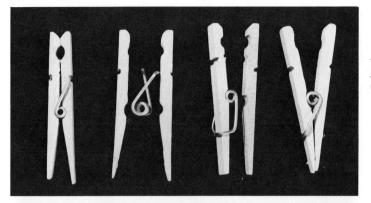

To make pointed clothespin clamps, take apart a wooden clothespin, turn the spring upside down, and reassemble.

Glue completed shapes together with thick white glue or (for greater rigidity) clear household cement. Use circular graph paper (see Appendix) to make the ornaments symmetrical.

Three simple cornet stars. The star at the left has a wooden bead in the center; the other two have centers made by slicing a small cork crosswise.

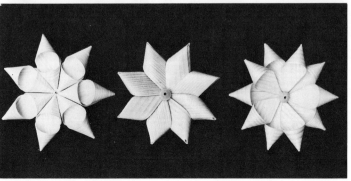

Three star variations. Each point of the left star is made from a double cornet, with the base of one cornet slipped inside the cone of another.

Variations are possible if the cones are glued at an angle, or on their sides.

Two 10-point stars made in two layers.

Three larger stars made by joining inward- and outward-pointing cornets in assorted patterns.

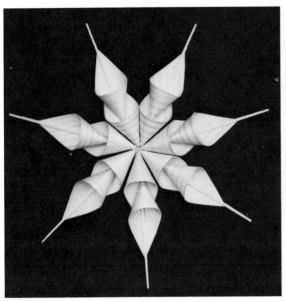

Front and back view of a 6-spoke, 12-cornet star with toothpick spokes. A small circle cut from veneer tape strengthens the back.

Front and back of three elaborate stars made from cornets, toothpicks, hors d'oeuvre picks, beads, and circles of wood veneer.

Five cornet stars are glued onto the spokes of a center star. To make the ornament rigid, join the parts with clear household cement rather than white glue.

Wreath of simple stars.

Bird in flight. Sweden. The wood for the wings and tail is notched, then split and twisted in such a way as to produce a fan.

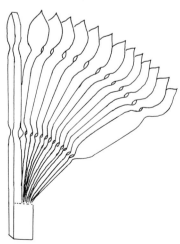

After soaking, a notched block of pine or basswood is carefully split, and each slice twisted to lock into the adjoining piece.

Whittling a pine tree from a cone of wood.

Swedish filigree cross. The carving begins at the center and continues out toward the end of each beam. *Courtesy of the Swedish Information Service.*

Whittled Fans and Curls

This is a technique that requires some practice, but the results are invariably striking. The trick is to use a suitable knife (a sharp pocket knife with a thin blade is ideal) and to choose straight-grained softwood (such as pine or basswood).

For a bird, a body is first whittled from a block of wood, then separate pieces ½ to 1 inch wide are selected for the wings and tail. With the grain running lengthwise, the wings and tail are notched in several places (the notches must be symmetrical for the pieces to interlock).

The blanks are soaked for twelve to twenty-four hours (or boiled for perhaps twenty minutes) to soften the wood and reduce the tendency to crack. After soaking, the splitting begins, with the aim being to make each slice as thin as possible. As the feathers are split they are twisted to interlock in the adjacent notches, so that the finished wing opens out like a fan.

Similar whittling skills are involved in making wood-shaving crosses and Christmas trees, but in these cases smooth rather than notched wood is used, and the cuts are made progressively shorter (or longer, depending on whether you are carving toward or away from the end of the wood).

Blown eggs decorated with tissue paper cutouts. Clear acrylic glaze is used as both adhesive and gloss coat.

Decorated Eggs

The egg was esteemed as a symbol of creation and resurrection long before it was associated with the Christian celebration of Easter. According to the legends of ancient Egypt, India, Phoenicia, and Persia, the earth was produced by the breaking or hatching of an enormous world-egg. The phoenix, that fabulous creature of Hindu mythology that was later taken to symbolize Christ, was said to die at sunset in a blaze of flame, only to leave behind an egg from which to be reborn. As a sign of fertility and the regenerative power of nature, eggs were colored and eaten at the time of the spring festivals in places such as Egypt, Persia, and Greece.

Whether or not the egg as a symbol of the Christian Easter grew out of these early beliefs and practices is not clear, but it is thought that both the egg and the hare were considered emblems of the Anglo-Saxon goddess of spring, *Eostre,* whose festival was celebrated at the vernal equinox. According to the eighth-century historian known as the Venerable Bede, it was from *Eostre* that the word Easter derived. Although Bede's view has been challenged, eggs did come to be linked with spring in the Christian world because they were forbidden during Lent. After the scarcity of winter and the fasting of Lent, eggs were looked upon as prized possessions which the generous could give and the grateful could receive. Such generosity was reflected in the account book of the late thirteenth-century English monarch Edward I, which recorded that four hundred eggs were purchased to be boiled, stained, or covered with gold as gifts for the royal household.

As eggs became more intimately associated with the Easter celebration, customs surrounding the decoration of Easter eggs became increasingly elaborate. In Eastern Europe, and in the Ukraine in particular, egg decorating developed into a fine art, with the creation of multicolored designs incorporating both pagan and Christian symbols. In Germany, the tradition of the Easter hare laying colored eggs flourished, and a book of the late sixteenth-century admonished children not to fret if the hare himself escaped, for there would still be eggs in the nest. In Switzerland and Germany, the device of using a pin to scratch designs in dyed eggs became popularized, and in Poland colorful cut-paper designs began to be used to embellish eggs. Perhaps the most elaborate egg decoration took place in Russia, where imperial factories were set aside to create egg-shaped momentos of porcelain, crystal, and gemstone, and where the tsar and tsarina saw fit to patronize the jeweler—Peter Carl Fabergé—whose gem-studded eggs have since become museum pieces.

Today egg decorating is enjoying a renewed popularity, but interest is no longer confined to the Easter season. A number of artists and craftsmen are so intrigued with the egg as a surface for decoration that they work almost exclusively with this shape. Some exploit and adapt traditional methods, others bring new and different techniques to the craft. Along with an introduction to the traditional approaches, this chapter explores some of the interesting work being done by contemporary craftsmen.

About Eggs

Types of Eggs

Eggs suitable for decoration come in a variety of sizes, shapes, and colors. On the small side are quail, pigeon, and banty eggs, ranging from about ¾ inch to 1¾ inches in length. Chicken eggs, generally 2 to 2½ inches long, are most widely used because of their easy availability. A step larger are duck eggs, whose smooth and durable shell makes them a favorite of egg decorators. Goose eggs, with their showy proportions (generally 3½ to 5 inches in length) and thicker shell, are considered by some to be an even greater prize.

Quail, pigeon, and banty eggs, along with duck and goose eggs, can sometimes be purchased from local hatcheries, farmers, or farmers' markets, but if you live in an urban area or seek more exotic specimens (such as ostrich, emu, rhea, or swan) you will probably have to deal with the mail-order companies that specialize in supplying eggshells.

You should be aware that there are restrictions governing the taking of wild bird eggs, so if you plan to do your own collecting, make sure to restrict yourself to the eggs of domesticated fowl.

Preparing Eggs for Decoration

Mail-order eggs will usually arrive clean and blown, but if you use fresh eggs, your first problem will be how to prepare them. The decision rests mainly on the manner in which the eggs will be decorated. If they are to be dyed, handle them as little as possible, do not use bleach, detergent, or other harsh cleaners, and avoid abrasive cleaning pads. Fingerprints, bleach marks, and scratches, even if invisible on the undyed egg, will resist the dye and show up as blemishes on the finished egg. If cleaning is absolutely necessary, rinse the egg in lukewarm water, and pat away dirt spots with a soft cloth dipped in vinegar.

If the shells are not to be dyed, they can be cleaned with more vigor, using detergent, bleach, and scrubbing pads. (Note, however, that bleach may remove the natural spots on some eggs, and change the color of others, so proceed cautiously.)

Eggs to be decorated can be left raw and whole, boiled, or emptied by blowing. Contrary to common expectation, an unblown egg will not spoil or begin to smell. Instead, the contents will slowly evaporate and eventually turn to dust. The speed of this process is dependent on a number of variables, including the size of the egg, whether or not it is varnished, climate, and storage conditions; altogether it may require several years. During this time the egg should be kept away from sources of strong heat (direct sunlight, a hot attic) and displayed or stored in such a way as to allow for air circulation. If the eggs are to be stored in an egg carton, make sure the carton is cardboard, not plastic.

Boiling is a second possibility, and the usual procedure if the eggs are to be eaten. In the case of eggs intended for consumption, make sure that only materials known to be nontoxic are used for decoration, since the seemingly hard shell is in actuality a very porous membrane. Furthermore, do not leave hard-boiled eggs at room temperature for any length of time, especially if there are even small cracks in the shell, or you will be inviting spoilage.

If boiled eggs are to be preserved, rather than eaten, the usual cooking time must be extended to a minimum of two hours. Anything less and you are likely to find that the boiled eggs begin exuding a sticky, foul-smelling liquid. Anyone familiar with the penetrating smell of rotten eggs will know that these will have to be discarded as quickly as possible. There are certain techniques (such as scratch eggs) requiring the use of eggs boiled for a long period of time, but since the results of boiling are not always predictable, it is a good idea to use a fresh or blown egg whenever possible.

A third method, blowing the eggs, has several advantages: the eggs cannot spill, even if dropped; the insides cannot rot; and the egg itself can be salvaged for cooking.

To pierce an egg for blowing, use a needle, a knife blade, or (especially for larger, thick-shelled eggs) a small electric drill. If a knife point is inserted carefully and rotated slowly, a very neat and perfectly round opening can be made. Make holes in both the top and bottom of the egg, insert a needle or skewer to break the yolk, and shake to loosen the egg and mix yolk and white. Place the egg over a bowl, and blow through the top hole until the contents have been emptied. Optionally, the rubber bulb of a baster or a similar device sold by egg decorating supply companies can be used to expel the contents. If the aim is to mass-produce blown eggs, consider investing in an airbrush and cans of propellant (or a compressor). Although costly, the airbrush with its controlled pressure makes fast work of emptying eggs. Ordinary canned air (the kind used by photographers for dusting negatives) will unfortunately not work; the pressure cannot be controlled and the egg explodes.

It is also possible to blow an egg using only one hole instead of two, an advantage if the bottom of the egg can be concealed on an egg stand. For this method only the bottom is pierced, and the hole sufficiently enlarged with scissors to accommodate a drinking straw and to permit the contents to come out. Bend the straw so that one end can be inserted in the hole, and blow into the other end. Air pressure buildup inside the egg will cause the contents to empty quickly.

After emptying eggs by either the one-hole or the two-hole method, blow a mouthful of water into the shell, shake to rinse the inside, and blow the water out. If the holes in the egg are small the membrane often dries closed, trapping residual moisture or yolk in the shell, so it is important to bake the shells in a 200° oven for 10 to 15 minutes. If this is not done, the trapped liquid is likely to seep out at some later time, staining and spoiling the design.

To blow out the contents of an egg, make a small hole at each end using a needle, knife point, or small electric drill. If using a knife, rotate the point in the hole to make a neat, round opening.

Insert a toothpick or skewer to break the yolk, then blow the contents into a bowl. Rinse with a mouthful of fresh water.

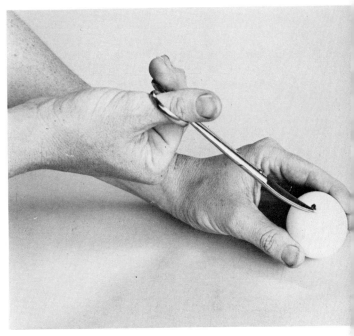

The rubber bulb of a baster (or similar gadget sold expressly for emptying eggs) can also be used to expel the contents.

For single-hole eggs, make one opening only, and enlarge slightly with scissors.

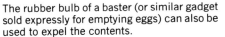

Make a bend in a length of drinking straw, insert the short end into the egg, and blow to build up pressure and force out the contents. Rinse with clear water.

To dry the egg and harden any remaining yolk (which might seep out later to spoil the design), bake the blown eggs in a 200° oven for 10 minutes. Stands can be improvised to keep the eggs upright.

Eggs from Other Materials

Alternatives to real eggs include wood, Styrofoam, plastic, and plaster. Wooden eggs, often available in hobby shops or by mail order, need only to be sanded before they are painted. Styrofoam eggs, lightweight yet sturdy, are good for covering with fabric, string, or yarn, which can either be pinned or glued in place. Some glues dissolve Styrofoam, so be sure to choose a compatible adhesive, such as white glue. Plastic egg shapes, either from stocking containers or from craft supply stores, are popular for beaded and decoupaged designs.

Plaster eggs can be made by pouring plaster of Paris into a blown egg, then chipping away the shell when the plaster is dry. Mix plaster according to package directions (put one part water into a plastic bowl, sift two parts plaster through the fingers, and mix gently), then place in a plastic measuring cup or plastic squeeze bottle and pour or squeeze into a one-hole blown egg. Allow to dry for about two days, then gently crack and peel away the shell. Fill any holes or defects with fresh plaster or spackling paste. When fully dry, sand lightly and paint with acrylics or enamels.

Another option when making plaster eggs is to leave the plaster in the shell. This can be an advantage, since the egg has a smooth and less porous surface which is easier to decorate. Since the fast setting of ordinary plaster may generate enough heat to make cracks in the shell, however, it is a good idea to switch to slower-setting casting plaster if the aim is to keep the shell unblemished.

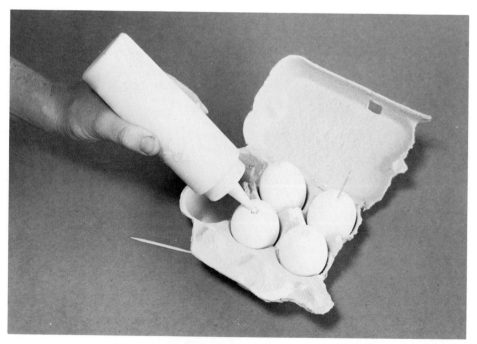

A squeeze bottle is handy for forcing freshly mixed plaster into an emptied egg. Work quickly before the plaster begins to set. Tap the egg several times after it is filled to release any air bubbles, and insert a wooden skewer or toothpick if a handle will be needed.

Decorating the Surface of an Egg

All sorts of materials—paper, decals, straw, flowers, seeds, etc.—can be used to decorate the surface of an egg. Keep in mind that the adhesive chosen should be compatible with the material being applied. Colored tissue paper, for instance, will run if applied with a water-based adhesive such as polymer medium or white glue; lacquer or clear acrylic glaze should be used instead.

If a final gloss coat is desired, check that this also can be used in conjunction with the adhesive chosen. Often the same product can be used for both glue and glaze—this is true of white glue, polymer medium, acrylic and other resin glazes, and lacquer. Lacquer can also be used over the water-based adhesives, which are not affected by the strong solvents it contains, but it would be likely to lift any decoration glued with clear acrylic or other glazes. If in doubt about the compatibility of any two products, consult with the staff of the hobby, art, or paint store where the supplies are to be purchased. (Labels are often purposely misleading, since manufacturers—especially those in the hobby field—generally try to make their product seem different from any other). If you do not want a yellowish cast in the gloss coat, avoid shellac and most products labeled as varnish, and check for the words "water-clear" or "colorless" on the label.

Chicken egg with violets cut from colored tissue paper. Water-based glues would cause the tissue paper to bleed; clear decoupage lacquer is used instead.

Leather punches in assorted sizes are good for cutting circles from stacks of tissue paper. Use a wooden or rubber mallet, and a rubber or end-grain wood pounding board.

Twelve to twenty pieces of tissue paper can be cut at one time if the layers are stapled together with a piece of typing-weight paper on the top. Nail scissors or curved surgical scissors, such as those shown here, are good for cutting curves.

Use water-clear acrylic glaze or brushing lacquer to apply tissue paper shapes. Brush on a little of the lacquer, use the brush to pick up and apply the paper cutout, then brush the top again with lacquer.

A final brushing or dipping in acrylic glaze or lacquer gives a clear gloss coat. Do not use lacquer over acrylic glaze, as the acrylic may crackle and lift. Bristle-type pipe cleaners make good handles for dipping if the holes in the egg are kept small.

Tissue-decorated eggs. The designs look almost embedded.

Black tissue paper does not run when wet, so it can be applied with water-based adhesives such as thinned white glue or polymer medium. Brush on more of the same adhesive to seal the design, or use lacquer or acrylic glaze for higher gloss.

MAKING DECALS

Choose a print of suitable size from a magazine, greeting card catalog, gift wrap paper, etc., and coat several times with transfer medium according to the instructions on the label. Transfer mediums are water-based resin emulsions chemically similar to white glue and polymer medium; milky-white when applied, they dry to a clear, insoluble plastic film.

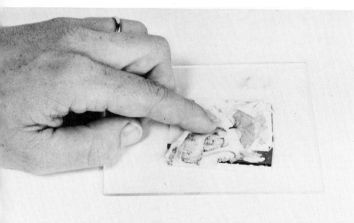

After the coats of transfer emulsion have completely dried, soak the print in warm water, and place face down on a piece of glass or a smooth countertop. The printing ink will have been absorbed into the plastic film, so that the backing paper can be gently rubbed away, leaving a clear decal.

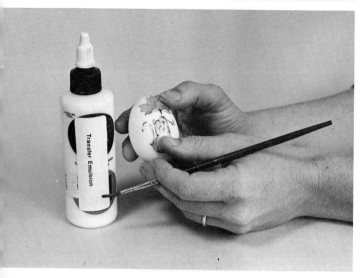

Allow the decal to dry, then trim to within ⅛ inch of the design. Paint the surface to be decorated with one coat of transfer emulsion, smooth the decal in place, and coat once more with emulsion. If desired, further coats of transfer emulsion, acrylic glaze, lacquer, or acrylic spray can be applied to embed the decal.

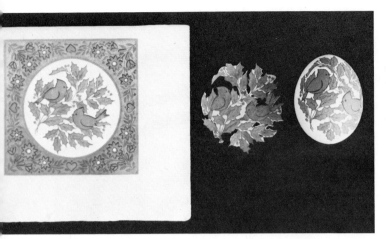

Paper napkins are a good source of designs to use on eggs. Cut away as much of the excess white area as possible, then glue to the eggshell with thinned white glue or polymer medium. Strong colors sometimes run; if this is the case spray the napkin lightly with fixitive or spray acrylic before gluing.

To embed designs in wax, first melt candle wax or paraffin in a double boiler or can placed in boiling water. When the wax has melted (it should have lost all cloudiness, but not be so hot as to smoke), submerge the egg and then lift slowly and evenly out of the melted wax. The empty egg will want to bob to the surface, but it can be controlled with a pipe cleaner "handle" and tweezers held just above the top of the egg. If the wax is too hot only a thin layer will be deposited; if too cold the layer will be too thick.

To add sheen, plunge the egg in cold water immediately after lifting from the hot wax. Gently pull out the pipe cleaner, or cut off at the top of the egg.

Eggs decorated with transfer decals.

Wax-dipped egg ornaments have designs cut from paper napkins.

Sparkle can be added to the surface of an egg using glitter, glass beads, "diamond dust," or other such finishes. Holding the egg on a skewer or pipe cleaner handle, paint one side with diluted white glue.

Sprinkle the glitter directly onto the wet glue, then allow to dry thoroughly. Repeat on the other side of the egg.

When the egg is thoroughly dry, use a soft brush to remove excess glitter.

Napkin-decorated eggs with four different finishes *(left to right):* wax, "diamond dust" glitter, glass beads, brush-on resin glaze.

Pressed flowers are glued into place on a plaster-filled egg, which is then dipped in hot wax.

Straw appliqué eggs. Straw, dampened and split according to the directions given in Chapter 3, is cut into decorative pieces and glued to the surface of dyed, blown eggs.

Dyed Eggs

About Eggs to Be Dyed

Eggs to be dyed require special handling (see Preparing Eggs for Decoration), since scratches, oil, and even fingerprints may resist the dye and produce blemishes. Use room-temperature eggs (cold eggs will not take dye well), and check for hairline cracks before starting. Patting the eggs with vinegar will clean them and prepare the shells for dyeing; if further cleaning is needed, soak briefly in warm water to which vinegar has been added, then blot dry with a clean cloth.

Whole fresh eggs are the easiest to dye since they sink and can be left undisturbed in the dyebath for the required length of time, whereas blown eggs float and will have to be weighted or to have the dye spooned over them. Dye liquid may also enter the holes of blown eggs; make sure this is expelled before the egg is put in a second color dyebath. One way to avoid the inconvenience of blown eggs is to dye fresh, whole eggs, then blow out the contents after decoration is complete. If nonedible colors are used, make sure to discard the contents.

Edible Dyes

If eggs are to be eaten, they should be dyed only with natural plant dyes or with certified food colors. The food colors come in several forms: tablets (such as those in Easter egg kits), liquids (used for cooking), and paste (sold for cake decorating). The paste colors are the most intensive and come in the widest range of color, and though they may seem expensive when compared to tablets and liquids, each jar goes a very long way. The general procedure when using food colors is to dissolve the desired amount of dye in a cup of hot water, then add a teaspoon or so of vinegar to help set the color. Colors can be mixed to produce intermediate shades.

Natural dyes are generally made by boiling plant materials (such as onion skins or carrot tops) in water to cover until the color is extracted. Most any plant which stains the hands can be considered for experimentation; often the color produced will be totally unexpected. (Red cabbage leaves, for instance, produce aqua.) The eggs to be colored can be boiled in the dye along with the plant material, or the dye can first be strained and then reheated. If the eggs are meant to be eaten, simmer in the dyebath for ten to twenty minutes, remove and cool, and polish with a bit of salad oil or bacon grease. (Remember to refrigerate these eggs promptly.) To produce boiled eggs meant for preservation, simmer in the dyebath until the desired color is reached, then transfer to a pan of clean hot water and continue boiling until the total cooking time is at least two hours. Blown eggs can also be colored in natural dyebaths, but they will either have to be weighted (a vegetable steamer works well) or filled with water (use a squeeze bottle or hold them under water until they fill) to keep them submerged.

Recipes for natural dyes are not always specific, so experimentation is necessary. Some homemade dyes worth trying are:

Plant	Color
onion skins	warm yellow to dark brown
black walnut husks	dark brown to black
spinach, carrot tops, lily of the valley	yellow-green to green
marigold petals, goldenrod blossoms, orange peel	yellow to gold
beets, beet juice, poke-berries, cherry or raspberry powdered drink mix	pink to wine
grape juice	steel gray
huckleberries, grapes	violet to purple

To help the dyes "take," experiment with adding salt, vinegar, alum, or cream of tartar to the dyebath.

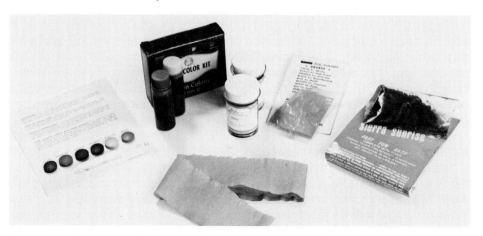

Types of egg dye include *(left to right)* tablets from an egg-decorating kit, liquid food color, jars of paste food color, powdered egg dyes, and fabric dye. In front is a strip of crepe paper, which can be soaked in warm water to produce a dye solution. The last three dyes are *not* edible.

Nonedible Dyes

Assorted fabric dyes, powdered egg dyes, and dye extracted by soaking crepe or tissue paper in hot water all expand the range of colors available to the egg decorator if edibility is sacrificed. The most rewarding to use are the powdered aniline colors sold in small packages expressly for dyeing eggs.* Intense and brilliant, the colors resist fading and come in about fifteen different shades. Each inexpensive packet makes a pint or more of dye,

*See the List of Suppliers for addresses.

enough for several dozen eggs, and if the dyes are fresh when mixed the solutions can be stored in glass jars and used for more than one season. Mix the dyes according to directions, adding vinegar where called for, and allow to cool to room temperature before using.

Resist Methods of Dyeing Eggs

A resist is something that blocks the absorption of dye, leaving undyed areas to contrast with the areas that are colored. Resists can be made from a number of materials, including glue, leaves, paper, adhesive tape, string, rubber bands, wax, and so forth.

Some of the most beautiful resists are done in wax, using a technique similar to batik. The wax can be applied with the head of a pin, with the nib of a drawing pen, or with a "kistka," a special tool used in Ukrainian-style egg decorating. Beeswax is generally chosen as the wax, since it adheres to the eggshell without chipping off. White areas of the shell are covered first, then the egg is dyed in yellow or some other light color, and the areas to remain this color waxed. The procedure of alternately waxing and dyeing is continued, working from light to dark, until the desired number of colors is achieved. Only then is the wax removed to reveal the finished design.

Pysanky, or Ukrainian-style eggs, are by far the most elaborate of the wax-resist eggs. Though customs centering on the egg date to the pre-Christian era, the spread of Christianity to the Ukraine in the tenth century led to the decorated egg's becoming an important religious symbol. Stories abound in Ukrainian folklore linking the *pysanky* with biblical figures, telling how Mary's tears,falling on an offering of eggs, turned to brilliantly colored spots, or how a peddler (Simon of Cyrene) had his wares turned to elaborate *pysanky* when he went to the aid of a man struggling with a heavy burden (Jesus).

Great ceremony accompanies the dyeing of *pysanky.* The procedure invariable begins with the appropriate prayer, and ends with the completed eggs being presented at the church for the priest's blessing. The blessed eggs can then be distributed as talismans and signs of devotion to friends and loved ones.

Pysanky are traditionally decorated in secret, with no two alike, though certain recurring patterns tend to differentiate one region from another. Designs tend toward the geometric, and though predominately pagan in origin, they often incorporate Christian symbols such as the fish and the cross. Common motifs, often so stylized as to be unrecognizable, include stripes or bands (symbolizing eternity), the sun (growth and renewal), the comb or rake (harvest), pine needles (eternal youth), and the hen or rooster (fertility).

Most communities with a Ukrainian population will have a local source of supply for egg decorating equipment, or the necessary materials can be purchased by mail. The kistka, or implement used to apply the wax, can be made at home from a small piece of copper or brass, or the tools can be purchased in small, medium, and large sizes. There is even available an electric kistka, which some professional egg decorators use almost exclusively.

Gently handle eggs to be dyed, since scratches and blemishes show up vividly once the egg is dyed. Clean in a vinegar and water solution, or pat (not rub) with a soft cloth dipped in vinegar.

A resist using rubber cement. Dye the eggs a light color, then dribble with rubber cement in a random pattern. Let the cement dry, then dye in a darker, contrasting color.

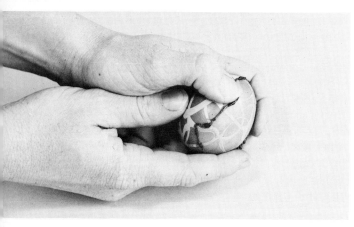

Remove the egg from the second dyebath and pat dry. Peel off the rubber cement to reveal the two-tone design.

Eggs dyed using rubber cement as a resist.

Plant-resist eggs dyed with food colors. This is a fast and easy technique, suitable for hardboiled eggs to be eaten and for blown eggs.

Choose leaves and flowers with a distinct outline to create a clear silhouette. If the leaves are especially stiff, dip in hot water to make them limp. Hold the plant against the egg, then wrap tightly in squares of cheesecloth or nylon stocking, securing with rubber bands or freezer ties. Dip in food color dye until the desired color is reached.

Small cutouts of tissue or typing paper resist the dye in the same way plants do. If working with many small pieces, secure them to the egg with spray adhesive or a little rubber cement before wrapping the egg in a nylon stocking; remove them later with cleaning fluid or rubber cement thinner (do not scrape off or the dye will be scratched). If colored tissue paper is used for the resist, the imprint will be in color.

Blown eggs dyed with onion skins. The colors range from light yellow (under some of the leaves) to dark golden brown. Polish the eggs with a cloth dipped in salad oil.

Place several cups of tightly packed onion skins in a saucepan, cover with water, add a little salt or vinegar, and boil to extract the dye. Nylon- or cheesecloth-wrapped eggs can be boiled along with the onion skins, or the dye can be strained before using. Blown eggs should be held under water until they fill enough to stay submerged, or else they should be weighted (a collapsible steamer works well). Remove eggs from the boiling solution when the desired color is reached.

PINHEAD WAX-RESIST EGGS

Materials for pinhead eggs include straight pins with heads of assorted sizes, a cork (or eraser) to serve as handle, an old spoon stuck in clay and bent to shape over a votive candle (or use a small metal bowl over a candle warmer), bits of wax (beeswax, or half-and-half beeswax and paraffin), and egg dye (mixed and allowed to cool).

Melt small pieces of wax in the bowl of the spoon. (If the wax smokes, turn the spoon away from the flame and allow to cool.) Dip the pin in the hot wax and apply the flat surface of the head of the pin to the egg. Lifting the pinhead leaves a dot, drawing it down slightly makes a teardrop shape. Place the egg in the cooled dye solution (heat would melt the wax); remove when the desired color is reached and pat dry. Repeat waxing and dyeing if more than one color is desired.

Some shapes that can be produced with the head of a pin.

To remove wax, place the egg in a warm oven until the wax begins to melt, then wipe with a paper towel. Wax can also be removed with solvents such as cleaning fluid, rubber cement thinner, or denatured alcohol, or by holding the egg to the *side* of a candle flame (soot is deposited above the flame).

Wax-resist pinhead eggs, dyed in vivid chemical dyes.

Left: A penholder with metal nib can be used to "draw" wax on the egg. Dip the pen point in melted wax, using a spoon or candle warmer arrangement such as that suggested for pinhead eggs. Alternatively, the pen can be heated directly in the candle flame, then put in the wax. Use a brush to wax large areas which are to remain undyed.   *Center:* The same egg with the wax removed.   *Right:* A wax-resist design drawn with a metal nib pen.

PYSANKY: UKRAINIAN-STYLE WAX-RESIST EGGS

Materials for *pysanky* include a candle, kistka for applying the wax (both ordinary and deluxe versions are shown), a cake of beeswax, wide rubber band, fresh raw egg at room temperature, pencil for drawing the design, and powdered chemical egg dyes. Dissolve the dye in hot water and allow to cool before using.

To make a kistka, cut a piece of copper foil or thin brass in the shape shown. Roll into a cone, leaving a tiny hole in the tip. Bend the tabs down at right angles to the cone, and attach to a dowel using fine copper wire. To enlarge the hole, rub the tip back and forth across fine sandpaper.

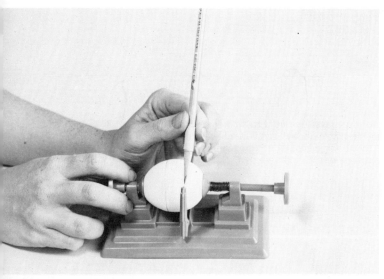

Draw the design in pencil, but never erase. (Pencil lines come off when the wax is removed, but erasures block the dye, creating blotches.) The device shown* is very useful for drawing lines horizontally and vertically around the egg. Wrap a pencil with masking tape so that it fits into the plastic holder designed for felt pens.

When you are ready to begin waxing, heat the kistka in the candle flame...

Decoregger, a product distributed by Spearhead Marketing Company, is usually available in shops around Easter time (see List of Suppliers).

...and press into the cake of beeswax. If the kistka is sufficiently heated, melted wax will be sucked up into the cone. Test the flow of wax by drawing on your fingernail.

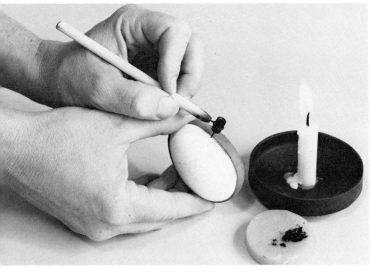

For straight lines, draw along the edge of a wide rubber band. Note that soot from the candle darkens the wax, making the lines easy to see. If a blob of wax accidently drops on the shell, try to incorporate it in the design, or let it harden, then gently scrape away as much as possible with your fingernail. It will be almost impossible to remove all traces, however.

Colors such as green or blue, which may not fit into the planned dyeing sequence, can be painted on with a toothpick or tiny brush. Let the dye dry, then cover with wax.

Dip the egg into its first dyebath (usually yellow), and allow to remain until the desired color is reached. Remove and pat dry with paper towels. Next wax over all lines that are to remain the first color.

Continue waxing and dyeing, working from light to dark colors. A typical progression might be yellow, orange, red, brown, black. Each succeeding dyebath may require more time for the color to "take." By the time you are ready to dye the last color, the egg may be almost completely covered with wax.

One way to melt the wax is to hold the egg to the side of a candle flame, then wipe with a clean cloth. Other methods are to heat the egg in a warm oven, or to wipe with a cloth dipped in a solvent such as cleaning fluid or rubber cement thinner.

For gloss, apply a coat of shellac, lacquer, varnish, or acrylic using a spray can, a brush, or your fingers. Support the eggs while drying on a rack made by pounding nails into a board in a triangular pattern.

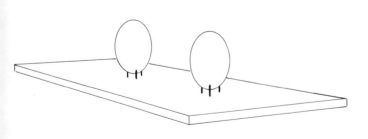

Opposite: A beautiful assortment of *pysanky*, made by one of America's most distinguished egg decorators, Luba Perchyshyn. *Photo by Slawko Nowitsky. Courtesy of the artist.*

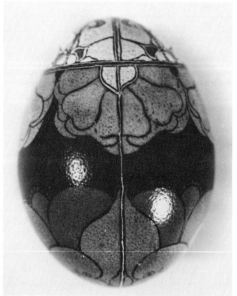

Duck eggs from Czechoslovakia, decorated with wax-resist designs. Red, traditionally an auspicious color, predominates.

PEACOCK EGG. Waxed and dyed by batik artist Stephen Blumrich.

EASTER CHICKEN AND EGGS. Stephen Blumrich. Both chicken and eggs are dyed using wax-resist techniques.

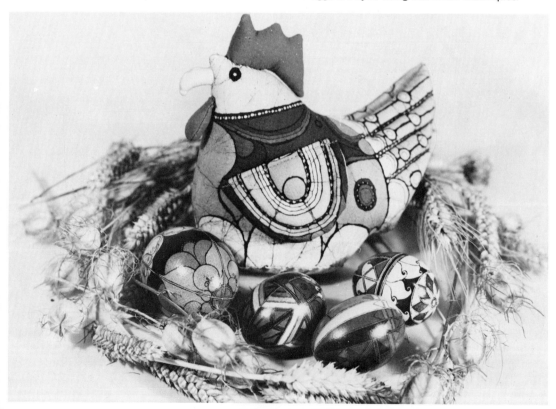

Scratch Eggs

In contrast to resist-dyed eggs, which use wax or some other material to hold back the dye and produce white areas, scratch eggs are made by first dyeing an egg a dark color and then scratching away the dye to reveal the white shell underneath. Traditional in Germany and Switzerland, the technique of scratch eggs was carried to the New World by early immigrants. As early as 1781, a British lieutenant imprisoned near Frederick, Maryland, reported: "The young people have a custom, in this province, of boiling eggs in logwood, which dyes the shell crimson and though this color will not rub off, you may, with a pin, scratch on them any figure or device you think proper. This is practiced by the young men and maidens, who present them to each other as tokens."* The German settlers who came to be known as the Pennsylvania Dutch popularized the craft of scratch eggs, incorporating the folk-art motifs that were typical of their art: tulips, thistles, hearts, butterflies, and birds. Today the tradition is still kept alive in some Pennsylvania Dutch communities, as well as in certain areas of Europe.

Eggs colored by natural dyes, especially onion skins, are customarily used for scratch eggs. Chemical dyes can be substituted, but the color is much more tenacious, and requires more work to scratch away. Boiled eggs have an advantage, since they can support the pressure of the knife or needle against the shell, but if the shell is accidentally pierced the egg will certainly spoil. Blown eggs can be used, but the etching must be done with a light hand. A good compromise might be to dye a one-hole blown egg in the boiling onion bath, then fill the egg with melted paraffin to provide support when working on the design.

An ordinary needle, inserted in a cork or eraser if desired, can be used for scratching the pattern, although many feel that a stencil knife, with its combination of point and blade, makes faster work of a project.

---

*Priscilla Sawyer Lord and Daniel J. Foley, *Easter the World Over* (Philadelphia: Chilton Book Co., 1971), p. 29.

A Victorian example of scratch-egg art. Illustrated in *Household Elegancies* by C. S. Jones and Henry T. Williams, published in 1875.

SCRATCH EGGS

Eggs dyed with onion skins are traditionally used for scratch eggs, though food colors or chemical dyes can be substituted. Use white charcoal or a dressmaker's pencil to sketch the design on the dyed egg.

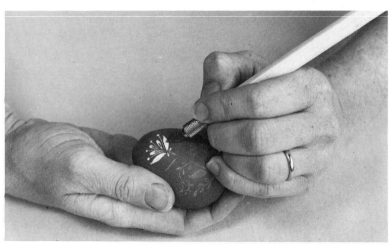

Cradling the egg in one hand, use both the tip and the side of a penknife or stencil knife to scrape away dye until the white shell shows through. Work gently, both to avoid puncturing the shell and to produce gradations of color.

Completed scratch eggs. Spraying with lacquer or clear acrylic will help protect the design.

RAM. Lisa Chock. Sanskrit writing in felt pen on a goose egg dyed in coffee grounds.

BLACK AND WHITE EGGS. Allen Emura. The designs are drawn in India ink with a technical drawing pen.

Drawing and Painting on Eggs

Eggs can be decorated with almost any of the drawing and painting media used on paper. Possibilities include pencil, felt markers (water-based and permanent), India ink, colored drawing inks, watercolors, poster paints, acrylics, and oils. If the smooth surface of the egg seems to reject the coloring, try spraying the shell with a workable fixative or (especially before painting) brush on a coat of acrylic gesso or white latex paint. Polymer medium, shellac, varnish, lacquer, or clear acrylic glaze, either brushed or sprayed on, can be used as a final top coat, but test beforehand to make sure the product selected will not lift the design underneath. (Water-based polymer medium, for instance, would dissolve a design drawn with ordinary felt markers, and permanent felt pens would be adversely affected by lacquer and some spray glazes.)

Beautiful craftsmanship coupled with a sense of fantasy characterize the eggs of Anne Byrd Easley of Boulder Creek, California. The artist works on a variety of eggs, ranging from quail and chicken to duck, turkey, and peacock. *Photo by Mona Helcermanas-Benge.*

THE LION AND THE LAMB. Anne Byrd Easley. Designs are drawn on the eggs with India ink, then painted and glazed. *Photo by Mona Helcermanas-Benge.*

Beverly Marchese and Valerie Forwood specialize in painted eggs. They use the single-hole method of emptying the eggs, then apply several coats of acrylic gesso, sanding between coats. Designs are drawn with a pencil.

Water-based acrylic paints, kept moist on a damp paper towel, are painted on using very fine (#0000 to #0) artist's brushes. Two coats of lacquer are applied for a high-gloss finish. Note the stand used for supporting the eggs when they are not being worked on.

PAINTED EGGS. Valerie Forwood. The completed eggs are glued to ceramic egg stands, hiding the holes used to empty the eggs.

ANIMALS. Painted in acrylics by Beverly Marchese.

TAPA EGGS. Beverly Marchese. Abstract designs in rust and brown suggest the tapa cloth patterns of the Pacific.

Edie Johnstone uses china painting techniques on eggshells. China paints, traditionally used on porcelain to be fired, are prepared by grinding powdered pigments in oil. Subtle shading, achieved by repeated applications of paint, is characteristic of this type of work. *Photos courtesy of the artist.*

Two sketches by Edie Johnstone demonstrate the techniques used in china painting. Base color is applied using the square shader brush, and while this is still wet a darker shading color is painted on top. Fine details are added only at the end, using a fine-pointed sable brush. Brushes are cleaned in turpentine.

CHRISTMAS EGG. Edie Johnstone. *Photo courtesy of the artist.*

Papier-mâché egg from India. 2 inches high. Reds and greens with gold accents.

Papier-mâché egg, blue with gold. Kashmir. *Collection of Cynthia Sudholz.*

Painted egg from Hungary. Silk cord, drawn through circles of felt, provides a hanger.

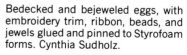

Wooden egg from Germany opens to reveal a hiding place for trinkets. 3½ inches high.

Bedecked and bejeweled eggs, with embroidery trim, ribbon, beads, and jewels glued and pinned to Styrofoam forms. Cynthia Sudholz.

Hand-painted wooden eggs from India. 3½ inches high.

Enameled wooden eggs from Poland.

STONEWARE EGGS. Karen Jennings. 6
inches long. The decorative elements
are built up using a wax-resist
technique. The lightest glaze is applied first, then waxed, and the process is repeated until the desired
number of colors is achieved. After
firing, gold and platinum glazes are
applied, and the firing repeated at a
low temperature.

Fabric-covered Styrofoam eggs. Cut embroidered trim into strips the length of the egg, taper the ends, and adhere to the Styrofoam with white glue. Cover the seams with velvet ribbon in a contrasting color.

Hand-painted wooden eggs from Sweden. Nylon thread is glued into a hole drilled in the top to form a loop for hanging.

Skillful brushwork characterizes these Oriental designs. Taiwan.

Styrofoam eggs wound in glossy pearl cotton.

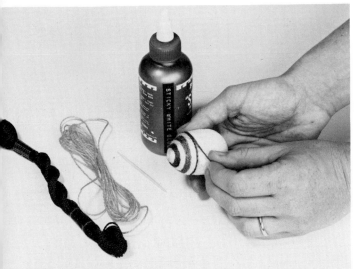

Wind yarn, string, embroidery floss, etc., around Styrofoam egg shapes, starting at the narrow end and holding in place with tacky white glue. When ending a color, snip thread at an angle and use a toothpick to poke the ends under the wound section. When the widest part of the egg is reached, you have the choice of continuing (the winding will go more slowly and there will be a tendency for the thread to slip off) or starting again at the other end and meeting the design at the center.

In Eastern Europe, as well as in certain parts of the United States, the inner stalk of a rush-like plant is wound around or applied in wavy patterns to the surface of an egg. The rush is gathered in spring, and a stick used to push the pith from the long, hollow stems. It is applied while fresh and pliable. In this Polish example, brightly colored yarn is used to contrast with the creamy pith.

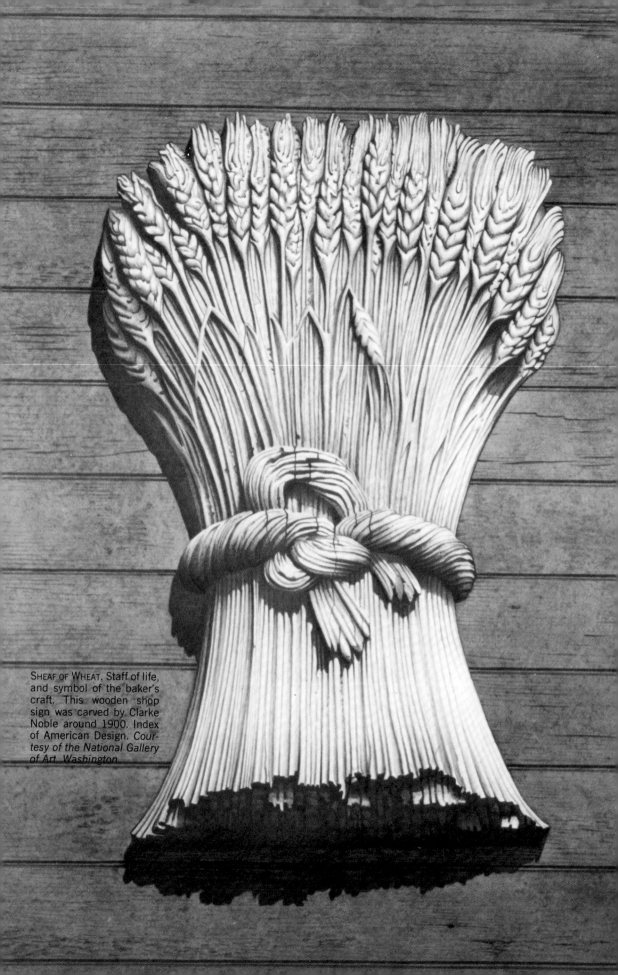

SHEAF OF WHEAT. Staff of life, and symbol of the baker's craft. This wooden shop sign was carved by Clarke Noble around 1900. Index of American Design. *Courtesy of the National Gallery of Art, Washington.*

Kitchen Crafts

Although its treasures are often overlooked, the kitchen is a storehouse of craft materials. Flour, salt, sugar, eggs—the ingredients are ones most any cook feels comfortable dealing with. Working in the familiar environs of the kitchen, the artist/cook is free to experiment and improvise, unfettered by the need for specialized equipment or the requirements of an established "Art" form. This probably explains why kitchen art tends to be so uninhibited, spontaneous, and expressive.

The Baker's Art

The art of the baker has an ancient and fascinating history. Remains of Swiss lake dwellers, who lived about ten thousand years ago, show that even at that early date man had developed skill in grinding and baking grains. It was the Egyptians, however, who discovered the use of leavening and created what might be considered the first true bread. Egyptian bakeries not only turned out over thirty different kinds of bread, they also produced symbolic forms such as birds, flowers, and animals, which served as ritual offerings to the gods and the cult of the dead.

Leavened bread is believed to have passed to the Greeks as early as the sixth century B.C., and by the fifth century public bakeries were in existence. As in Egypt, bread acquired a religious significance, with devotees of the grain goddess Demeter fashioning honey cakes—often in the shape of a plow—to present at the temple of Elesius as an offering to ensure the fertility of the fields. The worship of Demeter was also to influence the Romans, who identified their deity of the fields, Ceres (from whose name the word "cereal" derives), with the Greek goddess of bread.

Although leavened bread was acquired more slowly by the Romans (public bakeries appeared only around 170 B.C.), it eventually played a more important role in Rome than in Greece. The wealthy were quick to exploit the decorative potential of bread. If entertaining a poet, they could order bread in the shape of a lyre; if celebrating a wedding, the bread would be formed into joined rings. In addition, bread assumed an important political significance when grain and later loaves were distributed as part of the public dole—a tradition immortalized in Juvenal's *panem et circenses* (bread and games).

During the years following the collapse of the Roman Empire, baking skills suffered a relapse, but with the rise of towns baking again assumed importance. A great variety of fancy breads and pastries were baked for fairs and religious holidays, some—perhaps carry-overs from earlier sacrificial shapes—in the form of animals and humans. Decorative molds, which had been used by the Romans but which had disappeared in the chaos of the early Middle Ages, reappeared in the fourteenth century, and by the sixteenth century picture cookies were extremely popular. Elaborate breads and cookies were often intended more as ceremonial gifts than as foods to be eaten, and it was common for the recipients of molded gingerbread, springerle, or *tirggel* to

Christmas cake of anise dough from Switzerland, made with a wooden mold carved in the seventeenth century. *Courtesy of the Swiss National Tourist Office.*

Tirggel, the traditional Christmas biscuit made in the Zurich region and dating from Roman times. This interesting example, which shows a view of the city of Zurich, was shaped in a wooden mold carved in 1706. *Courtesy of the Swiss National Tourist Office.*

save and display the baked masterpiece. In Russia, where gingerbread was offered at births, weddings, and even funeral feasts, a record may have been set by the number and size of the examples received on the occasion of Peter I's birth. Among them were representations of the Kremlin, with its turrets and horse guards; a gingerbread in the form of a badge, weighing 125 pounds; and two loaves of 100 pounds each bearing images of enormous double-headed eagles. In addition to such elaborate breads, the popularization of baking led to the development of numerous local variations, so that hardly a region existed without its own specialty: hot-cross buns in Britain, oversized pretzels in parts of Germany, *Grättimaa,* or Saint Nicholas, figures in Switzerland, challah among the Jews.

The contemporary revival of interest in baking as a decorative art, encouraged in part by an exhibit at the Museum of Contemporary Crafts in New York ("Cookies and Breads: The Baker's Art," Winter 1965–1966), has led to the popularization of recipes of items that are frankly ornamental. Two of these, both inedible, and both referred to as "bread dough," have become particularly well known. One consists of bread and white glue, and is an adaptation of a traditional South American dough used to make brightly colored figures for All Souls' Day. The second, a mixture of flour, salt, and water, is a more recent improvisation. To avoid confusion when referring to these doughs, the first will be called "bread clay," the second, "baker's clay."

Bread dough turtle from Ecuador, baked for the celebration of All Souls' Day, November 2. 3½ inches long. An adaptation of the recipe used in South America has led to the development of a popular craft dough consisting of white bread and glue.

Grättimaa—a Swiss version of Saint Nicholas. These pastries, traditionally baked in Austrian, German, and Swiss households in time for Saint Nicholas Day (December 6), are representative of the kind of folk-art figures that appeared with the popularization of baking. *Courtesy of the Swiss National Tourist Office.*

Bread Clay

If you have ever taken a piece of soft white bread and squeezed it into a ball, you will recall how supple and pliant the resulting mass was. Bread clay, made by mixing white bread with white glue, has the same claylike pliability. The addition of synthetic glue, however, adds tremendous strength, and finished pieces dry to an almost porcelain hardness. Though traditionally this dough is allowed to air-dry, it can also be baked, resulting in a product that looks like bread but is considerably more durable.

Mixing Bread Clay

The basic recipe for bread clay is:

8 slices white bread
8 tbsp. (½ cup) white glue

Remove the crusts from the bread (do not drop crust crumbs into the bowl—they will show up as spots) and tear the slices into small pieces. Pour the white glue over the bread, and mix with the hands. At first the mixture will be extremely sticky, so make sure to remove all rings and other jewelry. Knead the dough vigorously for about five minutes, or until smooth and velvety. At this point the dough should no longer stick to the fingers, but if it does, carefully clean and wash the hands, apply a little lubricant (glycerin, hand lotion, liquid detergent) to the fingers, and return to the dough. If properly kneaded, the mixture should now form beautifully into a smooth ball. Stored tightly wrapped in a plastic bag in the refrigerator, the bread clay should keep for several months before becoming moldy.

Some hints on mixing:

—"Day-old" bread from discount stores is fine for making bread clay. Bread fresh from the bakery is often too moist; it should be allowed to air-dry for several hours.
—As long as the ratio of one slice of bread to one tablespoon of glue is maintained, the recipe can be varied, but eight slices is about the most that can be kneaded by one person at one time.
—Depending on the size of the loaf, freshness of the bread, and other factors, the dough may be too dry or too sticky. In this case, add a little more glue or bread (or water/flour) to get the right consistency. Decide this only *after* kneading for a full five minutes, since the texture of the dough can change dramatically in a short length of time.
—Some recipes call for adding small amounts of a lubricant to the dough. Experiment, if you like, with glycerin (from the druggist), hand lotion, liquid detergent, or fabric softener.
—For large quantities (sixteen to twenty-four slices), an electric mixer of the single-beater heavy-duty type can be used to mix the dough. Use the regular beater (not the dough hook) and start the mixing slowly. It is not a good idea to use an ordinary two-beater mixer, since the strain could easily lead to a burnt-out motor.

Coloring the Dough

Any substance that will mix in with the dough can be used for coloring. Break off the piece of dough to be colored, add the coloring material, and knead until well blended. (Make the color a little on the light side, since it will dry somewhat darker.) If the dough becomes sticky, knead in a little flour. Make a number of different-colored balls and store in small plastic bags until ready to use.

Poster paints are easily worked into the dough, and make a good choice, but it is important not to use too much water when joining pieces of different colors or the colors may run. This is not a problem if acrylic paints are used, but it will take considerably longer to knead the paint into the dough (probably because the plasticizer used in the paint reacts with that used in the white glue). Liquid food colors make the dough quite sticky, but paste colors are useful—though more subject to fading than regular paints. Experiment also with watercolors, shoe polish, powdered dyes, instant coffee, etc.

Working with Bread Clay

Bread clay is a delight to work with—it cuts easily, holds impressions well, and is perfect for detailed work. The dough dries out quickly, however, so always remember to keep tightly sealed in a plastic bag. Work in progress should also be covered with plastic wrap if it must be left for a while.

When rolling out bread clay, always lift and turn the dough between each roll so that it does not stick to the tabletop (a little flour sprinkled on the surface will also help). Transfer the dough to a piece of aluminum foil before rolling for the final time. The foil provides a temporary backing and a way to lift the design in and out of the oven, and it will peel off easily when the item is dry.

Cut the rolled dough with a knife, cookie cutters (lightly floured), pizza wheel, scissors (including pinking and scalloping shears), or a needlepoint stylus. This latter tool is especially good for trimming the dough away from patterns cut out of heavyweight paper—the method most often used to repeat designs when a cookie cutter is not available.

Impressions can be made in the dough using all sorts of household items: string, buttons, bobbins, cake decorating tubes, nuts and bolts, and so forth. To allow for shrinkage when the dough dries, always make the impressions a little deeper and more distinct than seems necessary. A few gadgets may be worth purchasing, including a garlic press (for hair and fur), a clay gun (a versatile tool that works like a miniature cookie press), and miniature heart and flower cutters (although some small cutters can be shaped from drinking straws). Don't overlook the possibility of taking impressions from cookie or candy molds or from other carved items you may have. Just dust the mold with cornstarch, press the bread clay in place, then shake or lift out the dough and allow to dry on a flat surface.

When building up layers of bread clay, wet the underside of each new piece so that it will adhere well. If extra support is needed for larger pieces, insert toothpicks or lengths of wire (preferably aluminum), or, for bulky shapes, wrap the dough around an aluminum foil core.

There are several ways to provide for hanging bread clay ornaments. One is to simply punch a hole in the dough, then thread with cord or ribbon when the ornament is dry. Another is to insert a loop of wire into the dough, and allow this to dry or bake in place. Since hairpins, paper clips, and florist's wire may eventually rust, aluminum wire is usually recommended (or use aluminum pull tabs from soft drink cans). If you are not sure where the balance point of a hanging ornament will be, wait until the item is dry, then attach a cord to the back of the piece with a spare piece of bread clay.

MAKING BREAD CLAY

Remove the crusts from eight slices of white bread and tear into small pieces. Combine with ½ cup white glue, adding a little glycerin if desired.

Mix ingredients with your hands for about five minutes. The dough will be very sticky at first, but will become more supple and claylike as the kneading continues.

Add poster paints, acrylic paints, or other coloring directly to the dough and knead until the color is evenly distributed. Keep unused dough tightly wrapped in a plastic bag to keep it from drying out.

Roll the dough out on aluminum foil and cut with floured cookie cutters, with a knife, or with a needle-pointed stylus (here used for tracing around a paper pattern). The foil provides a means for lifting the ornaments; it will peel off when the dough is dry. This bread clay has been colored brown in order to make mock gingerbread.

An assortment of household items (including buttons, cake decorating tubes, a scalloping comb for frosting) can be used for making impressions in the clay. Make the imprint deeper than you think necessary, since it will become less distinct as the clay dries.

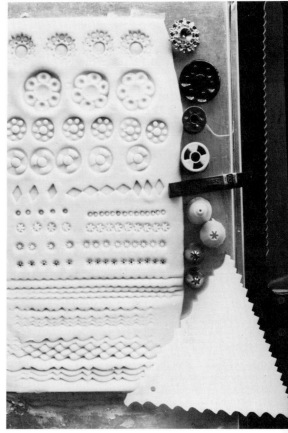

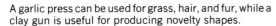

A garlic press can be used for grass, hair, and fur, while a clay gun is useful for producing novelty shapes.

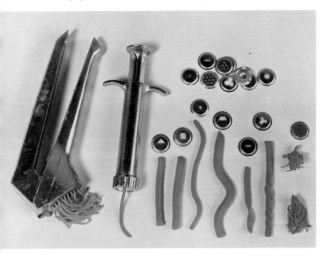

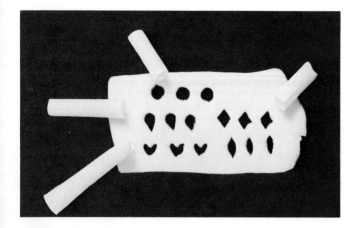

Miniature cutters can be purchased, or they can be made by bending paper drinking straws into assorted shapes. Dip the cutters in flour before using; if the dough sticks in the straw, blow from the opposite end.

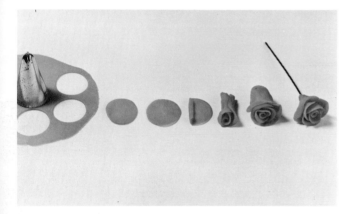

Making roses. Roll the dough very thin, then cut out circles using a cake decorating tube. Flatten the edges of the first circle between thumb and forefinger, then roll up to form a bud. Wrap with additional circles until the rose reaches the desired fullness. Trim off excess dough at the bottom, and insert a length of wire.

A wooden mirror frame decorated with roses and leaves. Ecuador. The filigree work is probably produced with a tool similar to a clay gun.

MAKING KUMQUATS

Color dough light orange (it will darken a shade or two as it dries), then wrap around an aluminum foil core. The foil core means that less dough is required and that drying is speeded.

Roll the kumquat around in a strainer to produce the characteristic citrus texture. Place in a spoon or other curved-bottom implement and insert a wire stem.

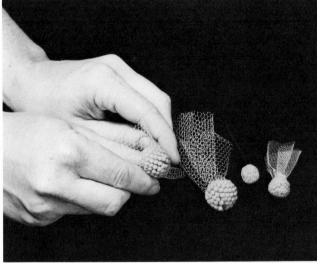

Stand the stems in a block of Styrofoam to dry. For sheen (and to minimize cracks and shrinkage), coat the fruits several times while drying with a half-and-half mixture of white glue and water. For illustration showing the use of bread-clay kumquats in a holiday wreath, see Chapter 2.

To make berries, force dough through a square of nylon net. Gather the excess net at the bottom and trim off, leaving the rest of the net to dry in the dough.

Assorted miniature fruits. Apples at left have clove centers, and have been dipped in lacquer. Poppy seeds accent the berries, which are coated with white glue and water. The peach is rolled in hands dusted with cornstarch to produce bloom, and a little red paste food color is patted on with a damp tissue for blush. The orange is textured in a strainer, then dabbed with cinnamon. For more distinct texture, as for the lemon, roll the dough between your palms along with some salt.

Basket of miniature fruit. 3 inches high.

Brightly colored dough ornaments from Ecuador, of the type usually produced for All Souls' Day.

South American Santa Claus. 4 inches high. For the sake of economy, the core of the figure is made of natural dough; colored dough is used only on the front surface.

These 1-inch-diameter Indian ornaments are of resin, not dough, but similar designs could be created by pressing beads and wire into balls of colored bread clay.

Heart ornaments. Metallic thread hangers are inserted in the dough before drying. Tiny roses are made by cutting a thin strip of dough with scalloping scissors, then winding up from one end.

Various finishes can be applied while the dough is baking. From left: no finish, canned evaporated milk, mayonnaise, egg white (applied to raised area only).

Drying and Baking

Bread clay can be either air-dried or baked. Air-drying is generally called for if colored dough is used, since oven heat would cause the colors to scorch and darken. Uncolored dough is not particularly attractive air-dried—if white or cream color is desired, white pigment should be added to the dough. Air-drying will require anywhere from several hours (for small decorations, roses) to several days (for large items), and can be hastened by placing the objects in a warm location.

To minimize shrinkage, prevent small cracks from developing, and produce a ceramiclike finish, bread clay sculptures can be coated several times while drying with a half-and-half solution of white glue and water. If the item has detailed impressions, let the surface harden somewhat before applying the first coat (otherwise the impressions will "melt"), and allow the glue to dry before each subsequent coat. After the final coat (three are usually sufficient), place the item briefly (three to five minutes) in a 350° oven to develop sheen. Finally, set the sculpture aside until it is fully dry.

Uncolored dough is generally baked to give the impression of "real bread." There are no set rules on time and temperature, since much will depend on the effect desired. To achieve a puffed look, with the uneven color characteristic of bread, bake at 350° to 400°. Generally about half an hour is required for ornaments, an hour or more for wreaths or thicker items. If some parts seem to be darkening faster than others, cover those parts with aluminum foil to help retard browning. Since there is no need to bake sculptures until "done" (they will continue to air-dry out of the oven), remove whenever you are satisfied with their appearance.

Use a lower oven temperature (200° to 300°) and a longer baking period for items that you want to brown lightly and evenly, without puffing.

Once in a while there is a problem with ornaments, especially thin ones, curling. Counteract this by placing the items face down on a countertop as soon as they come from the oven, and weight with a pie pan or plate while they are still warm and flexible. They will usually cool flat.

Baking: Special Effects

During the last half of the baking period, a number of finishes can be brushed on bread clay sculptures to produce interesting effects. A single coat of canned evaporated milk produces a beautiful sheen; several coats basted on at intervals cause faster browning and deep brown highlights. Repeated coats of mayonnaise make the dough look like real bread—good for producing imitation rolls and dollhouse-size loaves of bread. Egg white acts as a glaze, while egg yolk darkens the dough—first to yellow-orange, then, with further baking, to dark brown. Try adding food color to an egg yolk and apply near the end of the baking for touches of color.

Sweetened condensed milk and sugar water also aid browning and add sheen, but they leave the surface sticky and are unsuitable for sculptures meant to be preserved.

Finishing: Paint and Glaze

Most any type of coloring material can be used to color bread-clay sculptures once they are dry. Possibilities include poster paints, watercolors, oils, acrylics, enamels, colored inks, felt pens, metallic waxes, and antiquing solutions. If the whole piece is to be colored, it is sometimes helpful to apply a coat of white latex paint or acrylic gesso. This provides a good ground for painting, and will make the colors stand out with greater brilliance.

If a natural look is desired, there is no need to glaze the sculptures. But for added sheen, or for protection against insects, consider any of the following clear finishes (listed in the approximate order of increasing thickness):

Sprays. Matte- or gloss-finish acrylic, assorted resin craft sprays. Not thick enough to provide a barrier to insects unless several coats are applied.

Thinned white glue, polymer medium. Do not use over finishes (poster paint, water-based felt markers) that would be dissolved by water.

Clear acrylic glaze, clear lacquer, nail polish, assorted craft glazes. Some of these are not compatible with enamels, oil colors, or permanent felt markers; check the labels and experiment.

Polyurethane varnish. Satin or gloss finish. The slight yellowish tint adds warmth to baked pieces.

Two-part resins. Mixing the two parts produces a syrupy liquid designed to be poured over the sculptures. Results in a heavy-bodied, glasslike surface.

If you are not familiar with the characteristics of the glaze you have chosen, test it out on an inconspicuous part of your sculpture, since some of the clear finishes listed may be incompatible with certain paints and dyes.

A Note on Insects

Some authors advise adding borax or crushed mothballs to inedible doughs in order to discourage insects. I do not advise this—the sculptures look so much like real cookies that it is almost inevitable a child or pet will one day chew on one. Since the basic ingredients are nontoxic, no particular harm is done, but it would be courting danger to incorporate hazardous chemicals in any item that looks edible.

Instead, if there are indications that insects have taken up residence inside dough sculptures (small holes and bits of "sawdust" will be visible), try freezing the items for forty-eight hours or sealing them in a closed container along with plenty of moth crystals (paradichlorobenzene) for a week or so. Lacquered items are admittedly a bit more troublesome, since freezing shatters the lacquer and contact with paradichlorobenzene causes the lacquer to melt, but mothballs (naphthalene) can be used. If an item is properly lacquered in the first place, however, there should not be a problem with insects, since the lacquer acts as a barrier.

Bread clay angel. 5 inches long. Her hair is extruded from a garlic press, the ribbons on her dress are cut with scalloping shears, and the flowers are punched with a miniature cutter. It is hard to know how this type of ornament will balance, so add a hanger ("glued" on with a piece of dough) only after the figure is dry.

Joy. Use floured cookie cutters to cut out the letters, then make impressions with assorted tools.

Christmas ornaments. The gloss on some of the figures comes from evaporated milk painted on toward the end of baking. The lion's mane and whiskers were coated with beaten egg yolk.

Ornaments by Jane and Sonia Dart, aged 10 and 9. Children love working with bread clay.

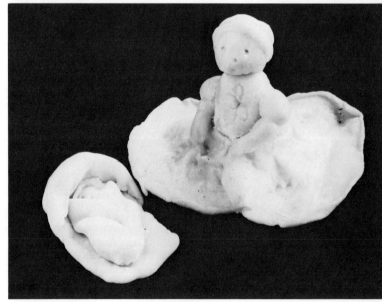

Mother and Child. Jane Dart, aged 10. Sheen is provided by a coating of egg white.

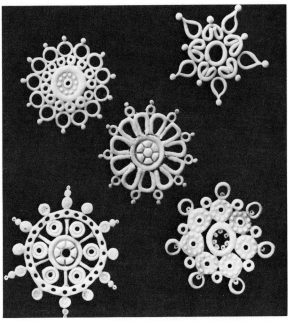

Christmas wreath. 8 inches diameter. Baked at 325° for about one hour.

Ornaments. Coils of dough, rolled between the fingers, are combined with pieces cut with cake decorating tubes, drinking straws, etc. The dough shrinks considerably as it bakes, so make sure all joints are tight.

Carolers. 2½ inches high. Bodies are shaped from a single piece of dough, with toothpicks forced up each leg for added support. Arms were supported during baking with balls of aluminum foil to keep them from sagging. The even color comes from long, slow baking—225° for approximately five hours.

MAKING A WREATH

Before beginning to assemble a wreath, make all the leaves and place them under a piece of plastic wrap. If the leaves are put in place as each is made, the first ones will dry out before the circle is complete, and baking will be uneven.

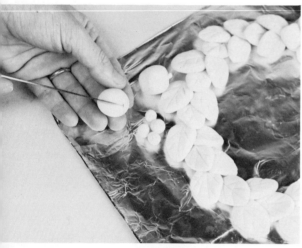

Draw a circle on a piece of aluminum foil and arrange the leaves, moistening wherever the pieces overlap. Shape larger fruits around foil balls. Use scissors or a knife point to add distinguishing characteristics.

Below, left: Make a bow from three strips of rolled dough. The aluminum foil supports keep the bow full; they can be removed after baking.

Below: A large (10-inch diameter) wreath.

Slightly thinned vinyl spackling paste makes a good mock frosting for imitation gingerbread. If desired, the spackling can be colored with food colors or water-based paints.

"Gingerbread." Dark brown bread clay and vinyl spackling.

"Gingerbread" hearts. Holes punched in the dough with a drinking straw provide for hanging.

Baker's Clay

Baker's clay, a mixture of flour, salt, and water, is much cheaper to make than bread clay, and is ideal for large projects such as candle holders and baskets. It is more doughlike than claylike, holds impressions only moderately well, and cannot be shaped with the same precision as bread clay, but the resulting sculptures often tend to be even freer and more spontaneous.

Baker's clay does have one distinct drawback. Because of the large quantity of salt in the dough, fully dried items tend to draw moisture from the air, soften, and even disintegrate. The softening is not a problem in dry areas or in artificially heated rooms, but anyone living in a damp climate will have to take measures to preserve the dough sculptures. Sealers such as lacquer or varnish are helpful—apply one or two heavy coats by brushing or dipping (sprays are ineffective)—but they do not guarantee permanence. If an item starts to soften, it can often be rehardened in a low oven, but if the softening has gone too far, cracks are certain to develop. The only foolproof way to counteract persistent dampness is to store items in tightly sealed plastic bags whenever they are not on display.

Making Baker's Clay

    4 cups flour
    1 cup salt
    1½ cups water (or less)

Stir dry ingredients together in a large bowl, then add water and mix. Turn out onto a lightly floured surface and knead for approximately ten minutes, or until the dough is smooth and pliable. Store in a sealed plastic bag in the refrigerator.

Since the moisture content of flour varies with the weather, it is a good idea to start with a little less water than called for, then add the extra only if it is needed. (Firm dough is easier to work with than soggy dough.) The recipe can be halved, but do not double it unless there is someone to share the kneading—it makes a lot. Some instructions call for whirring the salt in a blender or dissolving it in hot water before adding to the flour, but these steps make little difference in the final result. It is best to avoid the recipe popularized by a prominent salt company if you live in a moist area, since the instructions call for twice as much salt and the finished sculptures are even more susceptible to dampness.

Baker's clay does not store as well as bread clay, so if possible use it up within several days. Dough that has either softened or hardened in the refrigerator, however, can be reused if flour or water is kneaded in before beginning work.

COMPARING BREAD CLAY AND BAKER'S CLAY:

	BREAD CLAY	BAKER'S CLAY
QUANTITY (one recipe):	Enough for several small ornaments.	Enough for many ornaments; one bread basket; one or two "castles."
COST:	Moderately expensive. For significant savings, buy glue in large containers, bread at "day old" stores.	Inexpensive.
STORAGE:	Dough keeps several months in refrigerator in plastic bag.	Dough begins to get soggy in refrigerator after several days (but still useable).
CHARACTERISTICS:	Like clay, fine textured, holds imprints, good for detail.	Like bread, uneven texture, good for large pieces. Corrosive (be sure to wash cookie cutters carefully).
COLORING:	Mix colors directly into dough, or paint later.	Same. Eliminate powdery effect by glazing.
DRYING:	Air-dry, or bake until desired appearance is achieved.	Baking usually required. Air-dry if weather is very dry.
PERMANENCE:	Sturdy, no softening in humid weather. Insects like this recipe.	Softens in humid weather. Insects do not seem as attracted to baker's clay as they do to bread clay.

Working with Baker's Clay

Most of the instructions for working with bread clay apply also to baker's clay, with the following exceptions:

Coloring: It is better to paint finished pieces of baker's clay than to try to work color into the dough. The culprit is the salt—it dries on the surface to produce a powdery, whitish coating, obscuring the true color of the dough. Still, this effect may be desirable, so experiment for yourself. (Do not use food colors, however—they bake out at temperatures over 200°.)

Impressions. Make impressions much deeper than you would with bread clay, since this recipe tends to expand more in baking.

Hangers. In addition to attracting rust-causing moisture, the salt in baker's clay is extremely corrosive, so make sure to use only nonrusting wire for hangers. Better yet, punch a hole and hang with ribbon when dry.

Air-drying. Air-drying is successful only if the weather is very dry; on a damp day the sculptures will just turn soggy. Air-dried dough looks whitish—almost like limestone.

Baking. It is best to bake baker's clay sculptures until they are fully dry. As a general rule, count on baking for one-half hour in a 350° oven for every ¼-inch thickness of dough. (Average pieces require about an hour.) Remember that oven temperature is variable—move to a higher range (375° to 400°) for greater puffiness and faster browning, or try a lower temperature (200° to 300°) to minimize expansion and even out the browning.

Baker's clay figures, each about 4 inches high.
Note the difference in texture between these and
figures shaped from bread clay.

BUTTERFLY. 5 inches wide. Sunny Aigner. The artist first shapes and bakes the dough, then draws on the surface with India ink and paints on a design with acrylics.

Miniature wreath. 3½ inches in diameter. The mottled color comes from painting the dough with evaporated milk during baking.

SHEEP. Caroline Gale.

PAINTED FIGURES. Caroline Gale. The artist paints her figures with bottled enamel paint, then varnishes them with a glaze made by the same manufacturer.

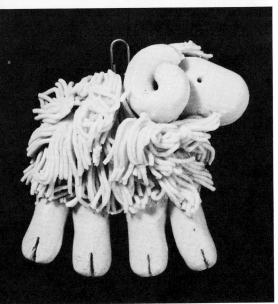

PUDGY ANGEL. Jenny Choy.

CHRISTMAS ORNAMENTS. Sunny Aigner. Note how the "lumpiness" of baker's clay contributes to the character of these whimsical figures.

ELVES. 2½ inches high. Jenny Choy. The baker's clay figures are painted with acrylic paints, then dipped in polyurethane varnish to add gloss and provide a barrier against moisture.

VALENTINES. Sunny Aigner. India ink and acrylic paint on baker's clay.

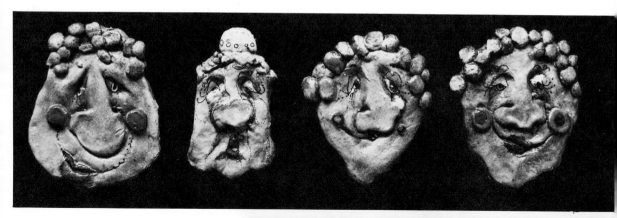

MOTHER'S DAY. Sunny Aigner.

Castles. Candle-lit towers make a striking centerpiece. Make sure to provide holes at both bottom and top for air circulation.

Castles in the daytime. Baker's clay is wrapped around an assortment of foil-covered cardboard cylinders, then baked for several hours. A firm dough is best for a project such as this, so add extra flour to the recipe if necessary.

Edible Doughs

Many cookie recipes can be adapted for making ornaments which are both decorative and edible. Use any dough that bakes without too much puffing or spreading, and which cuts easily into sharp, clean shapes. Recipes for rolled or molded cookies such as gingerbread, sugar cookies, and springerle are all suitable. You may have to cut down slightly on the shortening and increase the proportion of flour in order to produce a dough that holds impressions well.

For decorating the cookies, use edible materials such as raisins, candies, nuts, spices, and frosting. Baked and cooled cookies can be painted with food coloring (this is particularly attractive over a glaze of smooth white icing), or "paint" made of egg yolk and food coloring can be applied during the last ten minutes of baking.

Cookies which are to be kept for more than one season should generally be backed with a piece of cardboard cut to size and "glued" on with royal frosting (see below).

The following recipe is one developed by Evalynn Quisenberry, who often makes sculpted cookies on a grand scale (her dragon, illustrated, is four feet long). She uses intriguing ingredients to color the dough: tomato paste (for orange), curry powder or turmeric (yellow), cocoa (brown), and powdered ceremonial green tea (deep green). The sculpture is rolled out and worked on wax paper, then cut in sections that will fit the oven. The wax paper pulls off easily after baking.

Evalynn Quisenberry's Basic Art Cookie Dough

½ cup butter or margarine

½ cup white granulated sugar

½ cup brown sugar

2 eggs

1 tsp. cardamom

1 tsp. cinnamon

1 tsp. ginger

½ tsp. cloves

½ tsp. nutmeg

2½ cups loosely packed all-purpose white flour

Coloring as desired

Using an electric beater, cream the butter, white sugar, and brown sugar until fluffy. Beat in eggs. When thoroughly blended, add spices.

Combine desired coloring agent with flour and stir enough of the flour into the egg-butter mixture to make a stiff dough. Cover and chill twenty-four hours.

Roll out on wax paper to a thickness of about ⅓ inch, and cut out desired shapes with a pizza roller (a knife tends to tear the dough). If the design is too big for the oven, cut into sections (cutting through the wax paper), and place each on a baking sheet. Bake at 325° for twenty to thirty minutes, or until the edges of the cookie begin to brown and the cookie looks dry and feels "set." Handle carefully while hot.

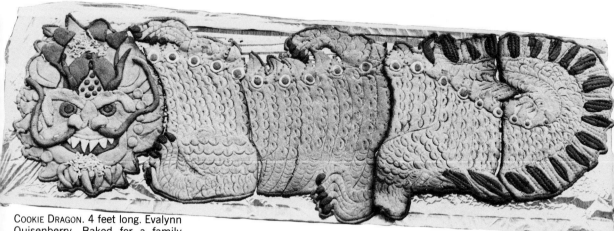

COOKIE DRAGON. 4 feet long. Evalynn Quisenberry. Baked for a family birthday, this royal dragon ("royal" because he has five toes, not the usual four) is made completely of edible dough. Note how the cookie is divided into segments to fit the oven. *Courtesy of the Honolulu Star-Bulletin.*

Cookie mold of the Europen type, used for molding springerle and other holiday treats. Missouri, nineteenth century. Index of American Design. *Courtesy of the National Gallery of Art, Washington.*

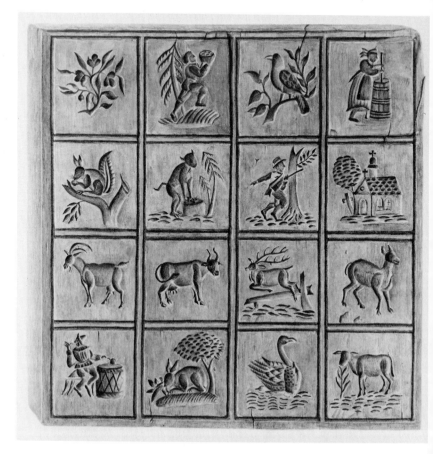

Tirggel. Holiday biscuit from the Zurich region of Switzerland. From a nineteenth-century mold. *Courtesy of the Swiss National Tourist Office.*

Tirggel. Nineteenth-century mold. *Courtesy of the Swiss National Tourist Office.*

Tirggel celebrating the joys of winter travel. *Courtesy of the Swiss National Tourist Office.*

Handpainted clay bells. Mexico.

"Appenzell Beaver." A type of *lebkuchen* (biscuit with honey, spices, and fruits) with an impressed layer of marzipan. From a nineteenth-century mold. *Courtesy of the Swiss National Tourist Office.*

Mexican clay bird ornaments. Similar decorations could be made from either bread clay or baker's clay.

BIRTHDAY PARTY. Becky Patterson. Bisqued clay, gessoed and painted with acrylics. *Photo courtesy of the artist.*

ORNAMENTS. Marika Somogyi. The artist uses French clay, a partially polymerized resin clay available in a number of colors. After the clay is kneaded and shaped, the sculptures are baked in a 350° oven.

The Confectioner's Art

The art of the confectioner developed much later than that of the baker, mainly because the primary ingredient of sweets, sugar, was slow to come into general use. Sugar making was practiced in India as early as 3000 B.C. but was slow to spread; the sweetener was unknown to the early civilizations of the fertile crescent, and the Egyptians, Hebrews, Greeks, and Romans all went without it. Cultivation of the cane spread to Syria and Palestine with the Arab conquests of the seventh to ninth centuries, and it was there that Western Europeans, represented by the Crusaders, first saw and developed a taste for the white crystals. Although the product was not uncommon in Europe after the Crusades, it remained a scarce luxury that could be purchased only by the ounce, and was used more often as a medicine than as a sweetener.

Not until the sixteenth century—when production began to increase due to the expansion of cane plantations to the New World—did the price of sugar begin to decline. Only then did honey, the traditional sweetener, give way to the much more versatile sugar as the basic ingredient in confections, and only then was the way open for the development of the confectioner's craft. Nevertheless, sugar remained a luxury for a while longer (as late as 1736 it was listed with precious stones among the wedding gifts of Maria Theresa, Archduchess of Austria), and it was only in the late nineteenth century that confectionery manufacture began on a large scale. Chocolate, a product of the New World introduced to Europe by the Spaniards, came into general use as a sweet at about the same time. Today, booming consumption has turned both sugar and chocolate into major food industries.

Royal Icing

Royal icing provides the basis for nearly all decorative sugar work. A mixture of egg white and powdered sugar, it can be beaten to a stiff, fluffy consistency, or thinned to flow like a glaze. The icing pipes well, dries hard, and lasts indefinitely.

About the Ingredients

Although fresh egg whites can be used for royal frosting, a more versatile icing is produced by substituting meringue powder (dehydrated egg white). Icing based on powdered whites can be rebeaten to restore volume after storing, and piped decorations remain a brilliant white. In contrast, rebeating will not restore icing made with fresh whites, and piped items eventually begin to yellow. The powder is inexpensive considering the quantity of icing it makes, and keeps indefinitely if stored in a dry place.

Powdered, or confectioners', sugar should be purchased fresh (squeeze the package to make sure the contents have not hardened), since even small lumps can clog the decorating tubes. In a pinch, lumpy sugar can be whirled in a blender, then sifted through a fine mesh strainer. Do not expect the resulting icing to pipe as well, however.

Cream of tartar acts as a stabilizing agent that helps produce volume; it can be eliminated if it is already an ingredient in the brand of meringue powder selected. Gum tragacanth, a powdered vegetable gum with gelatinlike characteristics, can be combined with prepared icing to add strength and moisture resistance.

Preparing Royal Icing

It is essential that all utensils be clean and free from grease, since egg whites will not foam in the presence of oil. For this reason, plastic bowls (which attract grease) should be avoided in favor of glass, enamel, or stainless steel.

Royal Icing: Meringue Powder	*Royal Icing: Egg White*
3 tbsp. meringue powder*	3 egg whites (at room temperature)
1 pound confectioners' sugar	1 pound confectioners' sugar
7 tbsp. lukewarm water*	½ tsp. cream of tartar
½ tsp. cream of tartar	

Combine all ingredients, blending at low speed in an electric mixer. Then turn to high speed and beat for five to ten minutes, or until the icing stands in straight peaks and is stiff enough to hold a line when cut through with a knife or spatula.

This produces an icing of medium consistency, perfect for stars, shells, and borders. Flowers require a stiff icing, so longer beating or the addition of a little more sugar may be called for. For lines and writing, or where strength is particularly important, beat for a shorter period of time at slower speeds. The shorter the beating, the less air is incorporated; the longer the beating, the fluffier (and more fragile) the icing becomes.

Since royal icing dries out very quickly, keep the bowl covered at all times with a damp cloth. Icing based on egg white cannot be rebeaten to restore texture, so try to use immediately. Meringue-based icing keeps well, and can be restored to full volume by beating.

Equipment

For any kind of piped work, it is necessary to have piping bags and a selection of cake decorating tubes. Plastic and canvas piping bags are available commercially; they are convenient to use, but must be washed carefully between each use. Parchment cones are more often preferred by decorators; they can be made in varying sizes, one for each color icing, and

---

*The amount of meringue powder and water may vary with the product used; follow label directions to get the equivalent of three fresh egg whites.

discarded after use. Vegetable parchment (greaseproof paper) can be purchased in long rolls or in precut triangles; or butcher paper, heavy bond, or even wax paper can be substituted.

Before beginning to pipe, cut about ½ inch off the bottom of the cone you will be using and drop into it a metal decorating tube. The hole should allow about two-thirds of the tube to show; enlarge if necessary. An alternative is to cut a larger opening and insert a plastic coupler, then choose a decorating tube and hold it in place with the screw-on coupling ring. The coupler is a convenient device that makes it possible to change tubes without emptying the decorating bag, and although designed for use with a plastic or canvas bag, it can also be used with parchment.

Decorating tubes are available in well over a hundred different shapes, but only a very few are needed for most decorating work. Some of the more useful are round tubes (#1 through 12 according to one of the major numbering systems), open star tubes (#13 to 22), closed star tubes (#23 to 35), leaf tubes (#65 to 70), rose tubes (#101 to 104), and drop flower tubes (assorted numbers). A good basic collection, which would provide for nearly all decorating needs, might consist of two or three round tubes, one each of the open star, closed star, and drop flower tubes, and one rose tube.

Coloring Royal Icing

Paste food colors are preferred to liquid because they will not thin or change the consistency of royal icing. Sold in small jars, either singly or in sets, paste colors are extremely concentrated, and a single jar may last for years. Although a wide range of colors is available, there is no need to purchase more than a few, since these can be combined to produce intermediate colors. Paste colors tend to separate, so mix well before using.

Place the icing to be colored in a cup or bowl, and add a dab of paste color on the end of a toothpick. Mix this in thoroughly before adding more—a little bit may be sufficient. Colors darken slightly as the icing dries, so start with shades a little on the light side. Colors also intensify on standing, so if you have difficulty producing deep shades (red and black are particularly troublesome), mix and allow the icing to stand for twenty-four hours or more before using.

Hints on Piping

Use a metal spatula or kitchen knife to transfer icing into the decorating bag, but never fill more than half full. Fold over the top of the bag or twist tightly so that icing does not leak out the top when pressure is exerted.

Practice piping on a sheet of wax paper taped to a smooth surface. As long as the icing does not crust over, it can be scraped up and reused.

Most piping, including lines and borders, is done with the decorating bag held at at 45° angle. Squeeze with the right hand, using the fingers of the left hand to guide and steady the bag.

Dots, balls, and stars are made with the tube held perpendicular to the decorating surface. Barely touch the decorating tube to the wax paper, squeeze out icing, and raise the tube slightly (keeping the tip buried). Then stop the pressure and pull away. For drop flowers, rest the tube on the wax paper, then squeeze and turn the bag in a clockwise direction. Stiffen the icing slightly if the edges of the drop flower are not clean cut.

Leaves can be piped from slightly softened icing using metal leaf tubes, but a parchment bag gives even better results. Flatten the end of a parchment cone, and use scissors to trim a little off each side to make an inverted V. When pressure is exerted on the cone, the frosting will come out the sides of the V, while the point will produce the center rib.

Most flowers are piped with stiffened icing using a flower nail and the rose tube. The flower nail provides a good flat surface which can be rotated while the piping bag is held still. Attach a square of wax paper to the top of the nail with a bit of icing, then pipe directly onto the wax paper. This way each flower can be set aside to dry while another is being piped. For ideas and instructions on piping a variety of flowers, consult a cookbook or cake decorating manual.

Baskets make charming containers for floral "arrangements." Use a round, star, flat, or basketweave tube, and pipe the icing directly onto a paper cup or other suitably shaped foundation. When this is dry, place a Styrofoam ball in the basket and "glue" flowers to the surface with royal icing.

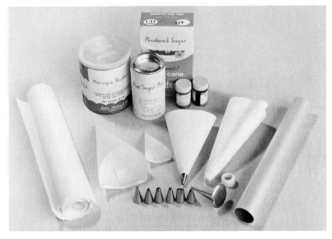

Equipment for piping ornaments from royal icing includes (front) six commonly used decorating tubes, flower nail; (second row) roll of parchment paper, large and small parchment decorating cones, parchment cone with decorating tube inserted, plastic decorating bag with coupler inserted, wax paper; (back row) meringue powder (dried egg whites), powdered run sugar mix (a substitute for thinned royal icing), confectioners' sugar, jars of paste food color.

For most work, you will want to beat royal icing until stiff peaks form and the icing will not fall from a spoon. Use a slightly underbeaten (or thinned) icing for writing and leaves, and a stiffer icing (beat longer and/or add confectioners' sugar) for most flowers.

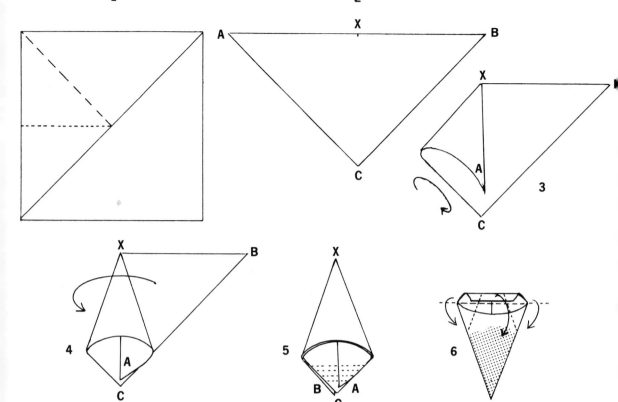

FORMING A PAPER DECORATING CONE:

1) Take a square of parchment, bond, or butcher paper and cut in half along the diagonal. Dotted lines indicate how to cut for medium and small size cones.
2) Make a tiny crease in the middle of the long side of the triangle at X.
3) Holding the thumbnail of the right hand at X, grasp point A and roll inward to meet C. Adjust so that there is no hole at X, only a sharp point.
4) Holding points A and C together in the left hand, bring point B around and behind the cone to C. Adjust so that points A, B, and C meet squarely, and so that X remains a sharp point.
5) Make a number of very small folds from A-B-C down toward X, creasing firmly each time. This will hold the cone securely without staples or tape.
6) After the cone is filled, fold the back flap over the front and the sides toward the center. This "diaper fold" will keep the icing from escaping out the top when the cone is squeezed. Continue folding down from the top as the icing is used.

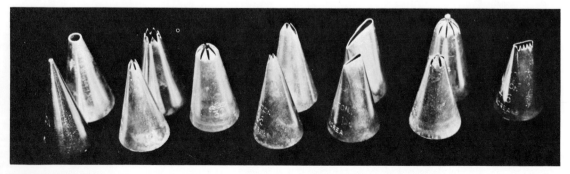

Often-used decorating tubes include (from left): round writing tubes, star tubes, closed star tube, leaf tubes, rose tubes, drop flower tubes, basketweave tube.

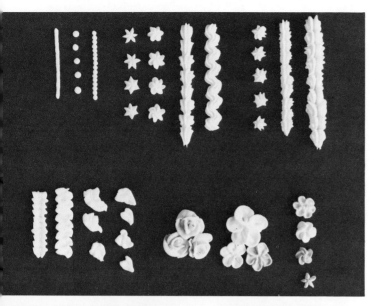

A selection of shapes piped with commonly used decorating tubes: (top) line, dots, and chain (round tube); stars, drop flowers, and borders (star tube); stars and borders (closed star tube); (bottom) borders and leaves (leaf tube); roses and flowers (rose tube); drop flowers (assorted drop flower tubes).

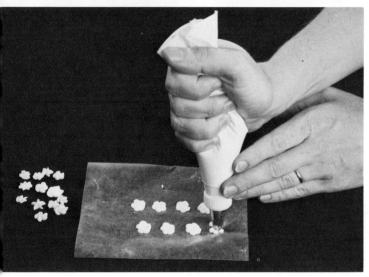

For drop flowers, hold the tube perpendicular to and resting on the decorated surface, then squeeze and turn clockwise at the same time. Make a selection of these flowers ahead of time and keep on hand.

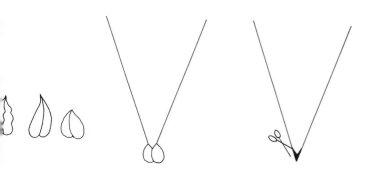

The best leaves are piped using a parchment cone with the tip cut in an inverted V. Use a slightly underbeaten (or thinned) icing. Fill the icing bag as usual, press the tip to flatten, and cut as indicated. Start to pipe with the bag touching the decorating surface, squeeze and pull the bag slowly until the desired size is reached; then pull away quickly to form a point. Move the bag back and forth while piping to produce a ruffled leaf shape.

Flower ball ornaments are made by "gluing" roses and drop flowers to Styrofoam balls with royal icing. Leaves are piped between the flowers to cover all unfilled spaces.

Small wreath of drop flowers used as a candle holder. Pipe a circle of green royal icing on wax paper, lay hardened drop flowers in place on the circle, and pipe leaves between each of the flowers.

Wreath of pink roses, 4 inches in diameter. Cut a circle from cardboard, lay on wax paper, and cover with green royal icing. Press piped and dried roses into the fresh icing, then pipe leaves between each of the flowers.

Miniature basket of flowers, 2½ inches high. Pipe icing in the basketweave pattern around the bottom of a paper drinking cup (from which the top half has been trimmed). Place a Styrofoam ball in the cup, glue on drop flowers with royal icing, and pipe on leaves.

For basketweave piping, use medium consistency icing and a round, star, or basketweave tube.
1) Pipe a vertical strip of icing.
2) Pipe short horizontal lines of icing across the vertical strip, leaving a space between each strip big enough to accommodate the width of the tube point.
3) Squeeze out a second vertical line a short distance from the first, and cover this with horizontal lines spaced to fit in the gaps created by the first row of horizontals.
4) The final result will look like a continuously woven basket.

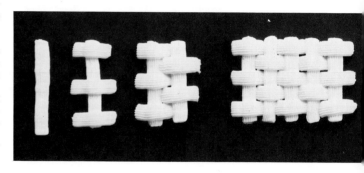

Filigree Ornaments

Filigree ornaments, though delicate and fragile looking, can stand up to season after season of use if made and stored properly. The ornaments are exceptionally easy to pipe, since only two decorating tubes (round and star) and three shapes (lines, dots, shell border) are required.

Combine the ingredients for royal icing, using either egg whites or meringue powder, and beat the mixture at low to medium speed for about five minutes. The object is to incorporate as little air as possible, yet still produce a mixture stiff enough to hold its shape. Although the volume of the icing will be less, it will be denser and stronger than if beaten for a longer time at higher speed. Test the consistency by piping a few sample lines. If the icing does not flow smoothly out of the tube it may be necessary to soften it slightly by adding a few drops of water.

Avoiding overbeating may be the only precaution necessary to ensure strong filigree ornaments. But if you live in a damp climate (high humidity does weaken royal icing), or think that the decorations are likely to receive much handling, you may want extra insurance. One trick is to pipe the design directly onto a piece of nylon netting—though practically invisible, the netting provides considerable added strength. Another help is to add gum tragacanth to the beaten icing—this gelatinlike powder makes royal frosting extra strong and much more resistant to moisture. The procedure is to stir ¼ teaspoon gum tragacanth (available from cake decorating suppliers) into two heaping table-spoons of icing, and allow to sit for about an hour before using. The mixture will eventually turn gummy, so prepare only as much as you intend to use in one sitting.

Pipe flat ornaments directly onto wax paper, or onto a piece of netting "glued" to wax paper with a dab of icing. If a pattern is needed, tape this in place on the underside of the wax paper. Allow the icing to dry thoroughly (this is important), then gently lift the design by sliding a knife or spatula underneath it. Turn and repipe on the back for added strength. If the ornament is to hang, make sure to add a loop of thread while the icing is still soft.

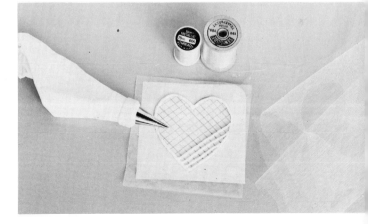

Filigree ornaments can be reinforced with nylon netting to provide strength. Cover the pattern with wax paper, then place nylon netting cut to size on the wax paper. Using slightly underbeaten (or thinned) royal icing and a round writing tube, pipe the design on top of the netting. When the top side is dry, turn and repipe the design on the underside. Insert a thread for hanging while the icing is still wet.

Filigree hearts. The heart at upper left is reinforced with nylon netting.

Barn and windmill. The barn is piped in flat sections on netting, then assembled using royal icing to cement the parts together. Note how the major joints are piped with a shell border for added strength. *Courtesy of Maid of Scandinavia.*

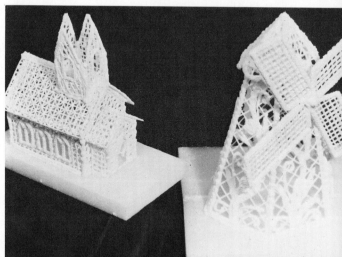

Church and Dutch windmill. A writing tube was used for the straight and curved lines, and a closed star tip for outlining the joints. In this case the excess nylon net was cut away after the design has been piped. *Courtesy of Maid of Scandinavia.*

Filigree ornaments. 3 to 4 inches high. Pipe designs such as these on wax paper, then turn and repipe on the back when dry. Items of royal icing may weaken in damp weather, so it is a good idea to incorporate netting or to strengthen the icing with gum tragacanth.

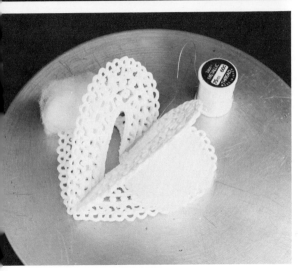

THREE-DIMENSIONAL FILIGREE HEART

Parts for a three-dimensional filigree ornament. Each pattern is piped on both front and back of a piece of netting.

Run a line of royal icing down the center of the large heart, lay on top of this a string for hanging, and press two of the half hearts in place. Support the structure with cotton balls until dry, then turn and repeat on the other side.

Filigree heart ornament. Notice how the nylon netting becomes almost invisible.

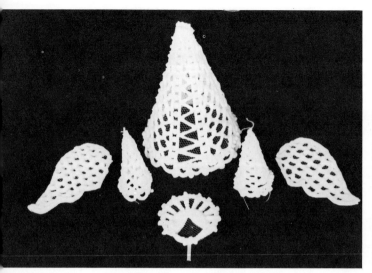

Parts for a filigree angel. Body and arms are piped on cardboard cones covered first with wax paper and then with nylon netting. A toothpick inserted at the neck will help attach the head to the body.

Filigree angel. 5 inches high. Parts are cemented together with royal icing and propped with cotton balls until dry.

Using Molds

For three-dimensional shapes, use plastic molds, metal tart pans, basket nails (miniature basket forms designed for cake decorators) or any other smooth-surfaced object without undercuts. Grease the mold with lard or vegetable shortening, then pipe an overall design, making sure that no large spaces are left open. For added strength, pipe some of the lines over lengths of thread laid on the mold, and/or go over the pattern a second time, and/or use a star tube to strengthen crucial joints. When the icing is completely dry (allow up to twenty-four hours), place the mold in a 200° oven for about thirty seconds, or just until the grease starts to melt. Hold the shape icing side down in the palm of the hand and gently lift out the mold. Repipe some of the lines on the inside of the mold for added strength, then (in the case of a two-part mold) use royal icing to cement the halves together, incorporating at the same time a thread for hanging.

PIPING OVER A MOLD

Use shortening to grease the mold so that the frosting shell releases easily when dry.

For added strength (optional), lay crochet thread along the major lines of the design. Secure at the end with a dot of icing.

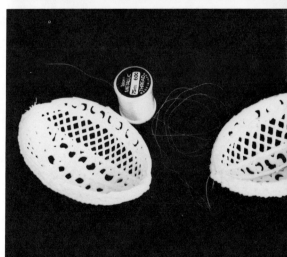

Place the mold on an overturned cup or bowl, and pipe the design using a round writing tube. Icing shrinks as it dries, so pipe thickly for durability. Repipe some of the lines for added strength. Allow to dry *thoroughly.*

Heat in a low oven just until the shortening begins to melt, then carefully invert the mold so that the icing shell falls into the palm of the hand. Repipe some of the lines on the inside of the shell, then pipe around the top edge of both halves. Lay a loop of thread around the edge of one of the halves, leaving some excess at the top for hanging, and press the sections together. Allow to dry, then repipe along the joint.

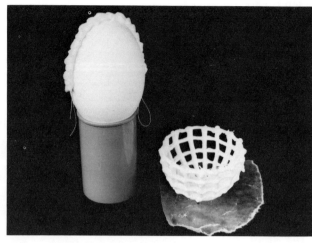

Filigree egg ornament. 3 inches high. Note how some of the lines are strengthened by being repiped in a chain of dots.

Even an eggshell can serve as a mold if properly greased. Make sure to pipe a strong handle reinforced with thread. Attach basket to handle with royal icing, propping the handle in place with cotton balls until dry.

Royal icing baskets, 2½ inches high, make attractive ornaments. Pipe a circle of icing at the base if you want the basket to stand upright.

Heart container. The two halves are piped on the outside of greased tart pans. To use as a candy dish, keep the top half separate.

Holiday ornament. 3½ inches in diameter. Piped with a #3 tube and reinforced with star tube borders, this ornament is quite sturdy. Wrap with tissue and store in a box or metal tin when not on display.

Run Sugar Work

Run sugar work (variously known as run-out, soft-sugar, and color flow) consists of outlining a shape with plain royal frosting, and then filling in the interior with softened icing. The filled-in areas dry smooth and hard, something like a sugar wafer.

Outlining

Begin by drawing a simple design on paper (children's coloring books provide good examples) and tape this in place on a smooth surface. Cover with wax paper, also taped in place; then outline the design using a round writing tube (#2 or 3) and plain royal icing prepared as for filigree work. Make sure that there are no breaks in the outline where softened icing might seep through.

For hanging ornaments, where greater strength is required, consider using a cardboard insert. Draw the design on both sides of a piece of thin cardboard (index card is good), then cut out. Attach a length of thread or nylon fishing line as a hanger, then pipe the outline on the upper side of the cardboard.

If the fill-in icing is of a contrasting color, allow the outline to dry for an hour or so; otherwise, proceed after a few minutes.

Filling In

The fill-in icing is made by thinning frosting to the proper "flow" consistency. Start with royal icing prepared as for filigree work, i.e., beaten at low to medium speed for about five minutes. (Overbeating can produce air bubbles that would show up in the finished work.) Place a portion of the icing in a bowl, add a few drops of water, and gently stir. To test the consistency of the icing, drop some from a spoon back into the bowl. When it takes a slow count of ten for the icing to sink back and nearly disappear into the mixture, the consistency is perfect. For small areas, flow icing will puff nicely if it is slightly on the thick side, but large areas require a fairly thin icing to flow in smoothly and quickly.

Fill a parchment cone half full with flow icing, and cut a very small hole in the tip. Starting at the edge of an outlined area, press out the icing, keeping the tip of the cone submerged. Flow icing crusts over quickly, so work smoothly and speedily to fill each area. Keep a pin handy to prick any bubbles that rise to the surface.

The run sugar design must now be allowed to dry thoroughly—generally for one to two days at room temperature. To achieve a glossy surface, place near a source of heat for the first several hours of drying time. Possibilities include an oven with the electric light or pilot light on, a cardboard box with a light bulb suspended from the top, or a heat lamp placed about two feet away from the frosting surface. Temperatures should not be too high (110° degrees is adequate) or the crust will expand and crack.

When the top side is completely dry, carefully turn over and repeat the outlining and fill-in on the back.

RUN SUGAR ORNAMENTS

Right: Run sugar ornaments can be piped directly onto wax paper, or onto a piece of thin cardboard or nylon netting. First pipe the outline using a round writing tube and slightly under-beaten royal icing. Attach a thread for hanging to the cardboard or embed in the icing.

Center, left: Fill a parchment decorating cone half full with royal icing thinned to the proper consistency (or use a commercial run sugar mix), and cut a small hole in the tip of the cone. Fill in the outlined areas, keeping the tip submerged so that the icing puffs slightly. Work quickly so that a crust does not form.

Center, right: Immediately place accent pieces (piped and dried) on top of the run sugar. When all the outlines have been filled, set aside until *completely* dry (one to two days), then turn and repeat the procedure on the back. For a glossy finish, place the run sugar ornaments near a heat source for the first two hours of drying time.

Bottom: Run sugar lovebirds. White lovebirds, outlined in blue, carry a pink heart.

Run sugar Santa. 5 inches tall. Eyes, nose, and buttons are piped in place after the surface has dried.

Fruits. These pieces were dried without heat, and thus have a matte finish.

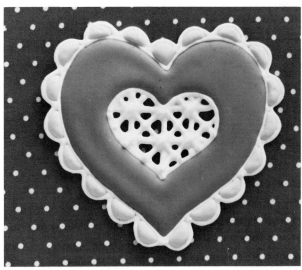

Sugar Valentine. Run sugar is combined with filigree work.

Butterflies. If a cardboard insert is used, it can be bent in the middle to raise the wings.

Sugar Molding

Elaborate old-fashioned panorama eggs, the kind with a wonderful fantasy world inside, seem to have all but disappeared, but they can be re-created by a technique known as sugar molding. Sugar molding involves packing moistened sugar in a mold, then hollowing out the interior to produce a shell. Though fragile in appearance, the shells are exceptionally strong and durable.

There are three different recipes for sugar molding, one using water, another egg white, and a third meringue powder. The egg white or meringue powder versions are somewhat stronger than the mixture based on only sugar and water, but if fresh egg whites are used the sugar shells may eventually yellow.

Sugar-Water

1 cup sugar
1 to 1½ tsp. water

Sugar-Egg White

5 cups sugar
1 egg white

Sugar-Meringue Powder

5 cups sugar
3½ tbsp. water
2½ tbsp. meringue powder

Use ordinary granulated sugar, or, for a very smooth surface, superfine (not powdered) sugar. Add the liquid to the sugar (mix food coloring with the liquid if tinted sugar is desired) and mix well with the hands or with a wooden spoon. Cover with a damp cloth until ready to use.

Molds are available in a variety of shapes (egg, ball, bell, flowers) from cake decorating suppliers and novelty stores, but suitable shapes may also be found among kitchen utensils (tart pans, gelatin molds) and children's toys (rubber balls cut in half, plastic containers). If the mold has an intricate surface, or if it will be used repeatedly, dust the interior with cornstarch to prevent sticking. Pack the sugar mixture firmly into the mold, level the top, and unmold by inverting onto a smooth surface (a cake pan or piece of cardboard covered with wax paper or aluminum foil is good).

Drying time will vary with the weather and the size of the molded item. Usually about two hours will be required for the surface to harden to the point where the item can safely be picked up and hollowed out. Drying can be speeded by placing the molded sugar in a 200° to 250° oven for five to ten minutes, but since the sugar hardens very quickly, this method often produces a thicker crust than desired. A thin shell not only looks daintier, it allows more light to pass and thus makes the scene inside easier to see.

Once the two molded sugar halves are hollowed and dried, the interior can be planned. Piped animals and flowers, cut-up greeting cards, artificial flowers, or miniature figures all make good choices. Before decorating the interior, it is a good idea to spread some untinted royal icing on the inside bottom of the mold. When this dries, it provides a base on which a scene can be piped (grass, pond, snow, etc.) and protects the sugar shell from colored icing seeping through. Set the figures in piped icing, using toothpicks for support if necessary, and allow to dry in place. Then "cement" the two halves of the mold together with royal icing, and pipe a design on the outside.

If the molded ornaments are to be hung (as in the case of Christmas balls and bells), make a hole in the top using an ice pick heated over the stove, and insert a wire hanger. The finished decorations may be rather heavy, so be sure to provide adequate support.

SUGAR MOLDING: PANORAMA EGG

Add water or egg white to granulated or superfine sugar and mix well. For larger quantities use an electric mixer at low speed.

Pack moistened sugar firmly into the mold, making sure there are no air pockets. If the mold is to be used repeatedly, dust with cornstarch.

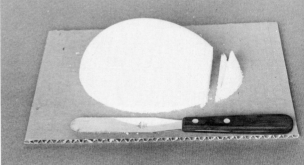

Place a piece of wax-paper-covered or foil-covered cardboard on top of the mold, then invert. Tap the mold lightly if necessary to loosen the contents, then lift off.

Cut away the tip of the egg where the window will be, and cover the cut end with plastic wrap so that it does not crust over. Air dry for approximately two hours (the time will vary with the weather and the size of the mold) or heat briefly (five to 10 minutes) in a 200° to 250° oven.

When the outer surface has hardened to the point that the egg can be handled without collapsing, scoop out the soft sugar interior. (The moist sugar can be reused so long as there are no hardened lumps.) Leave as thin a shell as possible (usually ⅛ to ¼ inch, depending on the size of the mold).

Interior scene of figures cut from a greeting card. Coat the inside bottom of the shell with white frosting and allow to dry, then add a layer of green icing "grass." Cut out the figures so that a paper tab is left at the bottom, and insert the tab in the moist icing.

Elaborate garden scene with piped flowers, trees, ducks, rabbits, and even a rainbow. The flowers are piped onto flat toothpicks, which are then embedded in the icing base.

Cement the two halves with a line of icing piped around the edge. The mound of icing at left will become a "cloud" into which the rainbow will disappear.

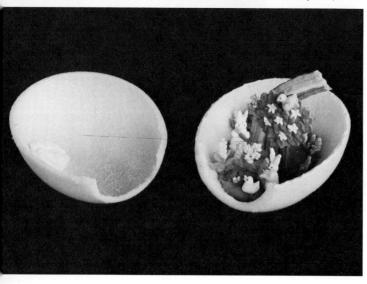

A round writing tube and several parchment bags are all one needs to pipe an assortment of rabbits. Experiment on wax paper, remembering to keep the tip of the tube submerged in the icing when piping circles and ovals. For details such as eyes, nose, and whiskers, prepare small parchment cones filled with colored icing; cut a tiny hole in the end of each and pipe the features directly from the parchment bag.

Birds or chicks. Start by piping a ball of icing, but keep the tip of the decorating tube close to the wax paper so that the ball flattens into a circle. With the tip still submerged, draw the tube down and to the right, then pull away to form a point. Repeat for the wings, and add a ball of icing for the head. Use a small round tube for the beak (just touch and pull away) and a parchment cone without a decorating tube for the eyes.

PANORAMA EGG. 5 inches long. Alice Loo. If desired, a piece of clear plastic wrap can be cemented to the "window" with icing before the opening is decorated.

Sugar eggs from Italy, with the designs piped directly onto the surface.

CHRISTMAS SUGAR BALLS. Lyle Janousek. Christmas doves and red poinsettias decorate the tops of these ornaments; borders are piped with a star tube.

Interior scenes just before the balls are assembled. Santa and the snowman sit firmly on icing snow.

Pipe a flat snowman from three circles of icing. To make a standup snowman instead, pipe a ball of icing, and let this become rather firm before adding a second and third ball on top. Pipe a toothpick-broom separately and allow to harden before placing in the snowman's arms.

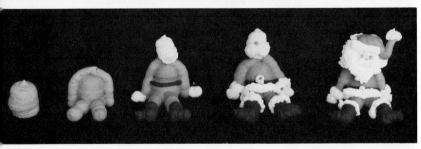

Piping a seated Santa. Do not try to pipe the figure all at once or Santa is likely to topple over. Let the base dry slightly, then add the head, and finally the details.

Pipe a Christmas tree directly onto a cone shaped from parchment or other paper. The "branches" are leaf shapes pressed from a parchment cone with the tip cut in an inverted V. Decorate the tree with garlands, balls, stars.

Chocolate Molding

Chocolate molding is more difficult than sugar molding, because chocolate itself is more temperamental. Once you learn its characteristics, however, you should not have too much trouble. Should you prefer to work with a more predictable material, try summer coating, a chocolate substitute also available in pastel shades.

Before being molded, chocolate must be tempered, i.e., heated and cooled. Heat water in the bottom of a double boiler to boiling, then remove from the heat and allow the steam to subside. Place cut-up pieces of chocolate in the top of the double boiler (use about one pound of sweet, semisweet, bitter, or milk chocolate), and set over the hot water. Stir the chocolate as it melts to eliminate any small lumps and to keep the cocoa butter from separating out (causing the "bloom" associated with overheated chocolate). Heat to 105° on a candy thermometer, then lift the pan from the heated water and cool the chocolate to about 80°, stirring occasionally. The chocolate is now tempered, but it will need reheating over hot water to bring it to the right temperature for molding—83° to 85° for milk chocolate, 85° to 88° for semisweet or bitter chocolate.

Summer coating does not have to be tempered, and the chocolate can be remelted and remolded without difficulty. Break pieces into the top of a double boiler and heat over a pan of hot water that has been removed from the stove. Stir until the chocolate melts and has a liquid look.

To make hollow forms, spoon melted chocolate or summer coating into the mold, spreading with the back of the spoon and pressing out any air bubbles. One application may be sufficient for small molds. For large shapes, repeat once or twice more, allowing the chocolate to solidify between each application, until the shell is between ⅛ and ¼ inch thick. Allow to harden in a cool place until solid (preferably overnight). Although some instructions recommend placing the molds in the refrigerator, this is not advisable for other than very short periods, since chilling can cause discoloration and loss of sheen.

Unmold the chocolate shells by inverting the molds onto a smooth surface, and join the two hollow shapes by heating the edges of the chocolate with a warm knife and quickly pressing the halves together. Handle the unmolded shapes (especially real chocolate) with a cloth or even gloves to avoid leaving fingerprints.

For molds with an intricate surface, apply the first coat of melted chocolate or summer coating with a paintbrush in order to penetrate all cracks and crevices. If the form is to be solid, fill both halves completely, then press the two sides together, keeping the edges even. Wipe off the excess chocolate, and secure with string or rubber bands until hardened. Unmold by inserting the tip of a knife between the two sides and twisting slightly.

Decorate molded chocolate forms with leaves and flowers piped directly onto the chocolate, or with prepiped icing shapes "glued" in place with a spot of icing. Scratching the smooth surface of the chocolate where the decoration is to be placed will help ensure better adhesion.

CHOCOLATE MOLDING

Temper chocolate by heating over hot (not boiling) water to 105° on a candy thermometer, then removing from the hot water and cooling to 80°. Stir often to keep the cocoa butter from separating out. (Summer coating, a chocolate substitute, does not require tempering.) Reheat the chocolate to about 85° and it will be ready for molding.

Fill the mold with a layer of melted chocolate, using the back of a spoon to press out any air bubbles. For large molds, build up several layers (allow chocolate to harden between each application) until the shell is ⅛ to ¼ inch thick.

For intricate molds, use a brush to paint on the first coat so that all crevices are filled. To make a solid figure, fill both halves of the mold and press together, then secure with string or rubber bands.

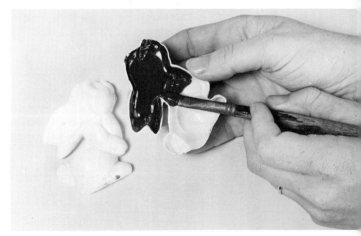

Hollow chocolate eggs. Two are of summer coating, a chocolate substitute that handles more predictably than real chocolate, and one is of semisweet chocolate. Icing decorations are applied just as for molded sugar eggs.

CANDY CLAY DOLL. Lois Nixon. Gum paste is shaped around a Styrofoam ball for the head; a Styrofoam cone is used for the body. Even the teddy bear is of candy clay painted with paste food colors. *Photo courtesy of the artist.*

CHOCOLATE EASTER HOUSE. Approximately 4 feet high. Pastry Chef Hans Weiler, Ilikai Hotel, Honolulu. Marzipan animals, molded sugar bunnies, and royal icing decorate the chocolate house.

SUGAR EGGS. Brenda Harrington and Jane Yelliott. The pastel-colored eggs are decorated with royal frosting, and hold arrangements of gum paste flowers and berries. The eggs sit on bases of sugar molded in tart pans. *Photo by Jane Yelliott.*

HINGED EGGS. Brenda Harrington and Jane Yelliott. Gum paste flowers arranged in molded sugar eggs. Superfine sugar is used to give the eggs a smooth, crystalline look. Note how thin and dainty the shells are kept. *Photo by Jane Yelliott.*

Gum Paste, Candy Clay, Pastillage

There are almost as many names for this claylike sugar mixture as there are ways to make it. Traditional recipes call for gum tragacanth, an elastic vegetable gum, while some adaptations favor the use of more easily available gelatin. All produce an edible clay that dries strong and hard and is ideal for molding flowers, braiding or weaving into baskets, or pressing into molds.

Below are two simple recipes for gum paste. Other recipes have slightly different working characteristics; they can be found in some cookbooks and most cake decorating manuals.

Gum Paste I

1½ tsp. gelatin

1/4 cup boiling water

1 pound confectioners' sugar

Dissolve gelatin in boiling water. Blend about half the sugar with the gelatin mixture. Gradually add remaining sugar, kneading until the clay is very smooth and pliable.

Gum Paste II

(For small quantities when royal icing is on hand.)

2 heaping tbsp. royal icing

¼ tsp. gum tragacanth

confectioners' sugar

Sprinkle gum tragacanth over icing; mix together, cover with a damp cloth, and allow to sit overnight.

Knead in enough confectioners' sugar to make a firm, smooth clay.

Here are some hints for working with gum paste:

—Gum paste dries out very quickly, so always keep unused portions covered with a damp cloth or plastic wrap. When not working with the clay, store well covered in a screw-top jar. Re-knead to restore pliability after storing.
—Gum paste becomes softer and more workable after a few days' "curing time," so try to make the clay ahead of time if it is to be used for flowers or other delicate items. Fresh gum paste, being firmer in texture, is excellent for molding.
—Tint the paste by kneading in food color. If an intense shade is desired, allow the mixture to rest overnight so that the coloring becomes fully dissolved.

—Sprinkle cornstarch on the pastry board, rolling pin, and hands when rolling or shaping gum paste. Avoid using too much, however, or the clay may become too hard.

—Use royal frosting to join pieces of gum paste (petals, sides of baskets, etc.)

—To glaze items made from hardened gum paste, brush on a mixture of ¼ teaspoon gum arabic to a scant ¼ cup of water. Let dry, then repeat for a higher gloss.

Storing Sugar Ornaments

Sugar ornaments, if properly treated, should last indefinitely. Since they tend to weaken somewhat in humid weather, however, they should be handled carefully at this time. In areas where persistent dampness is a problem, it is best to search out a warm, dry storage place (above the range, near a water heater, in the attic). An alternative is to keep the decorations in a metal cookie tin along with a small quantity of silica gel or other such drying agent. (If left in a damp closet with little air circulation for long periods of time, piped ornaments will actually disintegrate.)

Chocolate should be stored in a *cool*, dry spot, since temperatures over 80° may cause the cocoa butter to separate and rise to the surface, producing harmless but unattractive streaks. Do not use moth crystals (paradichlorobenzene), since the fumes seem to cause the chocolate to liquefy.

Popcorn chains. Chains of popcorn will last many years if the corn is popped without oil (keep the pan moving and the kernels will not scorch) and nylon thread is used instead of sewing thread. Popcorn is brittle just after it is popped, so wait until it picks up some moisture from the air before stringing.

PASTA ORNAMENTS

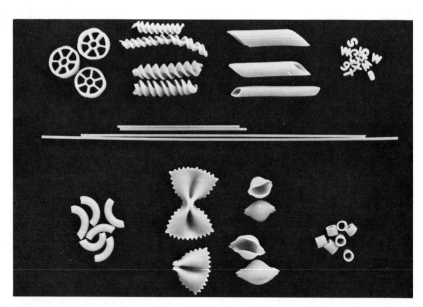

Assorted pasta shapes can be combined to make lacy ornaments. Some possible shapes include *(top, from left)* wagon wheels, corkscrew macaroni, mostaccioli, alphabet macaroni; *(center)* spaghetti; *(bottom)* elbow macaroni, bow ties, shell macaroni, and ditali.

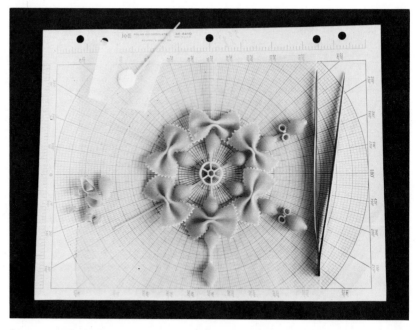

For symmetrical ornaments, work on wax paper placed over a piece of polar graph paper (see Appendix). Use white glue to join the pieces—the moisture in the glue "melts" the pasta, helping to make a strong bond.

Opposite: Pasta ornaments. The decorations are fragile, but damage is easily repaired if some spare pieces of pasta are kept on hand. Store with moth balls to prevent insect infestation.

Fabric

7

Fabric has traditionally played an important role in celebration art. Although the earliest textiles were doubtless created for utilitarian purposes—to clothe man and provide warmth and protection—it cannot have been long before fabric assumed a ceremonial value. Of the earliest surviving textile remnants, many incorporate motifs that tell of man's relationship to the elements, to the universe, and to the spiritual forces seen as ruling human life. Birth, marriage, and death; planting and the harvest; war and victory in battle; creation and resurrection—these are some of the universal themes illustrated in traditional fabric art.

The custom of using fabric to commemorate life's celebrations continues in contemporary life, though the form of expression is often very different than in the past. Today it is not unheard of to see a christening gown of denim, an altar cloth of patchwork, or a wedding dress done in batik. The drive toward experimentation motivating the contemporary fabric craftsman is in part explained by a rejection of traditional assumptions (which held, for instance, that embroidery was a woman's art, reserved for hearth and home) and in part by a newfound appreciation for the materials and techniques used by the folk artist or primitive craftsman. An added impetus has been the development of new materials—adhesives, nonwoven fabrics, bonding fibers, plastic and metallic threads and cloth—which often cannot be handled in the traditional manner. Consequently, fiber arts are in a ferment, with the distinction between the formerly highly defined crafts of embroidery, needlepoint, crewel, quilting, trapunto, and appliqué breaking down and new techniques and disciplines emerging. The resulting vitality and sense of experimentation are reflected in many of the works illustrated in this chapter.

Opposite: Batiked Wedding Dress and Shirt. Stephen Blumrich. A contemporary interpretation of a traditional garment. *Courtesy of the artist.*

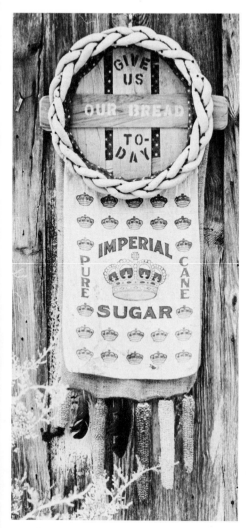

GIVE US TODAY OUR BREAD. Becky Patterson. Materials used for this imaginative Thanksgiving banner include an antique sugar bag, corncobs, feathers, and a vegetable crate lid. *Courtesy of the artist.*

NOT TO LOVE BUT TO BE LOVED. Becky Patterson. Tender rendition of a Mother's Day theme. *Courtesy of the artist.*

Stitchery

Stitchery is the term used to describe the embellishment of fabric with thread. Among the needle arts it incorporates are embroidery, crewel, needleweaving, cross-stitch, smocking, and canvas work.

Fabric

Any firmly woven fabric of moderately open weave is suitable for stitchery. Linen is the traditional choice for samplers and crewel work, and because the threads can be easily counted it is also suited for cross-stitch. Hopsacking, monk's cloth, homespun, muslin, denim, and certain drapery and upholstery materials also provide good backgrounds. Burlap (a jute fiber) is scratchy to work with and will eventually fade, but its open weave makes it attractive as a foundation for wool and other heavy yarns. Felt is easy to work with and comes in a brilliant range of colors. Like burlap it will fade in sunlight, and it may stretch and become misshapen if used on too large a project.

If washability is important, test wash a sample of the fabric before using. Even if the backing fabric is sturdy enough for machine washing, the finished project should be treated with care: use a gentle cycle, cool to lukewarm water, and a mild soap, and remove the item before the final spin cycle. Linen, felt, burlap, wool, silk, and some specialty fabrics should always be dry cleaned.

German pincushion/ornament (front and back). Counted stitch embroidery on an open weave fabric.

Thread and Yarn

The weight of the thread or yarn chosen should generally be in proportion to the thickness and weight of the background fabric. For easy care, remember to select washable yarns for use with fabrics that are to be hand- or machine-washed.

Cotton floss is probably the most widely available of the embroidery threads. Inexpensive, washable, and produced in a wide range of colors, the floss is composed of six strands of thread that can be used together or divided into smaller groupings. To keep embroidery floss from tangling when three or more strands are used, draw the thread through a cake of beeswax before beginning to stitch.

Pearl cotton is a twisted (not dividable) cotton thread with a shiny surface. Available in a wide range of colors, it is sold in balls or skeins in three sizes, #3, #5, and #8. (The largest of the sizes, #3, is not always easy to find.)

Crochet cotton and cotton string, though lacking the luster of floss and pearl cotton, can also be used for stitchery. Both take color well, so they are suitable for home dyeing with either natural or commercial fabric dyes.

Silk sewing thread and buttonhole twist (both sold on small spools), and silk floss (sold in skeins) all have a beautiful glossy surface, and though they are expensive there will be some projects which justify their use. Rayon floss is also good when a shiny effect is desired. Both silk and rayon floss tend to tangle, and benefit from an application of beeswax.

Yarns require a larger needle and more open weave fabric than do the cotton or silk threads. Crewel wool, traditionally used on linen, is sold in small

Stitchery yarns and threads include (clockwise from left) tapestry yarn (skein), tapestry yarn (single strand), nylon velour needlepoint cord, ball of crochet cotton, metallic cord, twisted metallic cord, metallic sewing thread, skeins of wool and acrylic yarn, three strands of novelty yarn; (center front to back) silk twist (Spain), silk buttonhole twist, 4-strand rayon floss (U.S.), 6-strand cotton embroidery floss, #5 pearl cotton, multi-strand rayon floss (Spain), cake of beeswax to prevent tangles.

packages of yarn wrapped on cards, and is slightly lighter in weight than tapestry wool. Both crewel and tapestry wool come in many colors and are available in needlepoint shops and department stores. Knitting yarns, whether wool or synthetic, are also useful for stitchery, though some of the fluffier varieties may not be suitable for sharply defined lines. Particularly bulky or nubby yarns can be sewn (couched) on the surface of the fabric rather than threaded through it.

Metallic threads are available in a number of different weights and textures. Traditionally used for ecclesiastical cloths and vestments, they provide a rich and ornamental look. Some of the metallic threads are not flexible enough to be drawn through the fabric; these will have to be couched onto the surface.

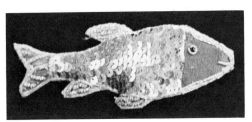

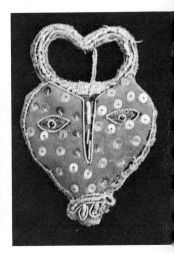

Sequins and assorted metallic threads embellish glittery ornaments from India.

Needles

The needle chosen for stitchery work must have an eye big enough to accommodate the thread. Sizes are measured by numbers; the smaller the number the larger the needle. Crewel or embroidery needles are of medium length, and have long slender eyes and a sharp tip. Commonly sold in assortments of sizes 3 to 9, they are suitable for embroidery floss (six-strand or divided) and pearl cotton. Chenille needles are also sharp, but have a larger eye to accommodate thick thread and tapestry wool. Tapestry needles, with the largest eye of all, can be used with most any thread or yarn. The tip is blunt, rather than sharp, which makes these needles particularly suited for loose weave materials and for whipped or threaded stitches worked on the fabric surface.

There are several methods for threading a needle. One is to moisten or wax the end of the thread so that the strands are straightened, and then push the tip through the eye. For wool, loop the yarn around the needle and pull tightly by pinching the thumb and forefinger up against the needle. Still grasping the yarn tightly, slip out the needle and bring the eye down over the top of the yarn loop, then pull the rest of the yarn through.

SOME COMMON EMBROIDERY STITCHES.

RUNNING STITCH

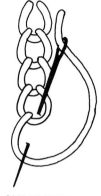

CHAIN STITCH

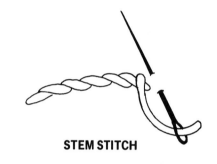

STEM STITCH

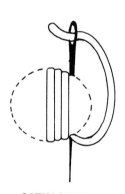

SATIN STITCH

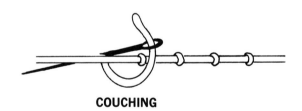

COUCHING

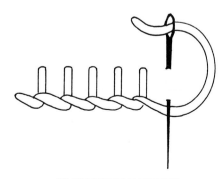

BUTTONHOLE STITCH

FRENCH KNOT

Hoops, Frames, and Supports

Fabric should generally be supported when being stitched. Wooden embroidery hoops with an adjustable outer ring, floor standing frames that allow both hands to be free, and artist's canvas stretcher frames to which the fabric can be stapled or tacked are all possibilities. Always straighten the fabric along the warp and weft (not the bias) and pull taut before securing.

Transferring the Design

The easiest way to mark fabric is to sketch a design freehand using pencil or tailor's chalk. Alternatively, a pattern can be traced using a light box or by taping both design and fabric to a window. If the fabric is too opaque for tracing, try using dressmaker's carbon, a special material available in light or dark colors to show up on any fabric. Place the carbon face down underneath the drawing and trace over the lines with a ball-point pen or tracing wheel. (Do not use ordinary carbon—it will smudge.) An alternative is to go over the back of the design with either a soft pencil or a special transfer pencil. The drawing is then placed right side up on the fabric and the lines traced (if pencil was used on the back) or ironed (if transfer pencil was used). One final method is to prick holes all along the lines of the design with a needle or tracing wheel, then use tailor's chalk or powdered charcoal to pounce through the holes. The advantage of this method is that the chalk can be rubbed away, while the lines made by pencil, dressmaker's carbon, and transfer pencil are all more permanent.

Hungarian felt ornaments. The design is embroidered on white felt using satin and stem stitch; the top layer is then attached to a red felt backing using chain stitch.

Stuffed horse ornament. Taiwan. Front and back pattern pieces are held together with the buttonhole stitch.

Left: Fish ornament. Taiwan. Machine zigzag stitching on red velveteen.

Right: Needlepoint hanging from a painting by Mads Stage, Denmark. *Courtesy of the Danish Information Office.*

Heart ornaments from Hungary. Rayon floss provides vivid colors.

HIS GLORY FILLS THE WHOLE EARTH. Sister Helena Steffens-meier. 6 feet 8 inches by 3 feet 11 inches. Scraps of wool, cotton, silk, lace, and patterned cloth are appliquéd to black homespun, then stitched in wool, acrylic yarn, silk floss, and gold threads. *Courtesy of the artist.*

HIS GLORY (detail). Note the combination of appliqué and stitchery.

MADONNA AND CHILD. Sister Helena Steffens-meier. 40 inches by 47½ inches. The background fabric is red with muted stripes. *Courtesy of the artist.*

ALLELUIA. Sister Helena Steffens-meier. 7 feet 6 inches by 3 feet. Sister Steffens-meier prefers to select a few stitches and use these with many variations to give unity to a project. *Courtesy of the artist.*

WE THE PEOPLE. Shirley Lewin. A bicentennial hanging using rug hooking techniques on canvas. *Courtesy of the artist.*

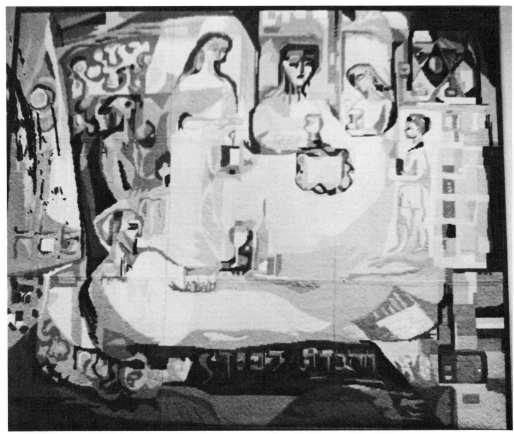

PASSOVER. Vivian Steinberg. The 6-by-7-foot mural, which depicts the ceremonial meal of the Seder, was stitched in nine sections on rug canvas using Persian rug yarn. Executed by the Miriam Auxiliary, Sisterhood of Oheb Shalom Congregation, South Orange, New Jersey. *Courtesy of the artist.*

SHAVUOT. Vivian Steinberg. The artist was inspired by the Three Pilgrimage Holidays celebrated in ancient Israel. She first created paintings the exact size of the finished work, then translated the design onto canvas. Stitching was done by members of the Miriam Auxiliary, using the basket-weave stitch only. *Courtesy of the artist.*

THREE KINGS. Needlepoint designed by Chris Faye, executed by Joyce Grady. Needlepoint is a form of counted-stitch embroidery worked on canvas.

SUKKOT (detail). Vivian Steinberg. The dancers represent the daughters of Shiloh, dancing to celebrate the joy of the harvest. The colors are delicate pinks, blues, and greens. Executed by the Miriam Auxiliary. *Courtesy of the artist.*

Felt is an easy fabric to work with since the edges need no hemming and will not ravel. Pin a paper pattern to the felt and cut out pattern and fabric together. Attach the layers using transparent nylon thread and a machine straight stitch.

ANGELS AND SHEEP. Machine-stitching through several layers of lightly stuffed fabric gives relief. Details (curls, bows) are glued on with white glue.

SANTA AND REINDEER. If nylon thread is used, the whole ornament can be machine-stitched without changing thread.

German elf, 3 inches high, is made of brightly colored felt circles spaced with wooden beads. Although scissors could be used to cut the circles, a mallet and leather punch would give faster results.

Appliqué

Appliqué (from the French verb *appliquer,* "to attach to") is the art of applying fabric cutouts to a background material. Stitchery is the traditional method used, though today adhesives and bonding fabrics often replace needle and thread.

Fabrics for Hand and Machine Appliqué

Most any kind of fabric can be used for appliqué, though materials that do not fray, stretch, or pucker excessively are best. For hand appliqué, where the edges are to be turned under, avoid bulky and loosely woven fabrics. Choose sturdy but lighter-weight materials instead. Firmly woven cottons and cotton blends (including denim, gingham, sailcloth, cotton broadcloth, kettlecloth, etc.) are excellent. Flimsy materials can often be backed with iron-on bonding fabric or interfacing, or stiffened with glue and water (see below) to give them more body and keep them from fraying.

Since machine appliqué requires no hemming, bulkier materials (corduroy, velvet, wool, brocade, upholstery fabric) can be added to the list of suitable fabrics. Sheers such as voile, organdy, and dotted swiss can be used as well, but avoid chiffon, crepe, and other loosely woven fabrics whose edges would be torn up by the action of the sewing machine needle.

Though it has to be dry cleaned, felt is an excellent choice for either hand or machine appliqué. The material does not fray, the edges do not have to be turned under, and intricate, crisp-edged shapes can be cut easily with scissors. Fading can be a problem with felt, however, so see that the finished piece does not get too much exposure to sunlight.

The fabric chosen for the foundation must be as heavy as or heavier than the cutouts used in the design, or puckering will result. If for some reason a lightweight material is called for, make sure to back it with a stronger piece of fabric. Be sure that all washable materials, whether used for appliqué or backing, are preshrunk, and iron carefully before work begins.

Thread

Mercerized cotton, polyester, and nylon thread, along with assorted embroidery threads and flosses, can all be used for appliqué. Polyester is recommended for washable items, since cotton thread may shrink and cause puckering. If you are not certain whether embroidery flosses or other threads are preshrunk, treat them to a thirty-minute hot water bath, then dry in a lingerie bag in the dryer. Transparent nylon thread is preferred for machine appliqué of felt, since it practically disappears in the thick fabric. Best of all, it is possible to outline one color and move immediately on to the next without the bother of changing the color of thread in the machine.

Transferring the Pattern

Transfer the pattern to the appliqué pieces and to the background fabric using any of the techniques discussed under Stitchery, or use paper patterns instead. For this method, copy the parts of the design on separate pieces of paper, then pin the paper to the material and cut through both paper and fabric together. (Allow ⅛- to ¼-inch margin if the edges are to be turned under.) An alternative approach is to cut out the paper pattern first, then pin it to the fabric and draw around it (allowing a margin if necessary), using pencil or white dressmaker's pencil. Keep in mind that fabrics have a horizontal and vertical grain, and that the warp and weft of the appliqué pieces should run parallel to the grain of the background fabric to minimize stretching or puckering. (Felt and other nonwoven materials have no grain, so these precautions do not apply.)

The paper templates can now be transferred to the background fabric and the outlines traced as a guide for attaching the cutout shapes. The advantage of the paper pattern method is that it allows you to play with and rearrange the pieces, making it more flexible than some of the other transfer techniques.

Hand Appliqué

Except on certain nonfraying fabrics such as felt and Pellon, the edges of material to be hand appliquéd are usually turned under. Start by clipping the outside curves and notching the inside curves. For circles or intricate shapes that are hard to turn under, run a line of machine stitching along the turn-under line (do this before the piece is cut out), then cut out and clip the curves to the stitching.

There are several methods for turning under the seam allowance. One is to replace the paper pattern on the underside of the fabric, and finger-press the clipped margin over the edge of the paper. An iron can be used, but most needleworkers feel that ironing flattens the shape too much, taking away the slight relief that is one of the attractions of hand appliqué. An alternative method is to pin or baste the appliqué pieces to the background, then turn under the edges as you work. (Corners must be folded or mitered; overlapping pieces do not have to be turned under.)

Any of a number of stitches can be used to attach the fabric pieces to the background. Possibilities include the blind hemming stitch, running stitch, whip stitch, slip stitch, and buttonhole stitch. Use matching thread, or, for a contrasting effect, use embroidery floss or pearl cotton in a different color. When all the pieces have been attached, remove the pins or basting thread, and add any embroidery detail desired.

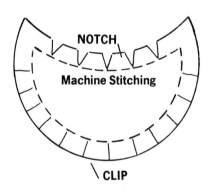

For hand appliqué, cut fabric shapes ⅛ to ¼ inch larger than the pattern all around, then clip the margin on the outside curves and notch on the inside curves. Fold or miter corners to make sharp points. To make intricate shapes easier to turn under, machine stitch along the outline, then cut the shape and clip the curves up to the stitching.

When cutting out the appliqué shape, plan so that the grain will run parallel to the grain of the background fabric. Pin or baste the shapes in place, then stitch.

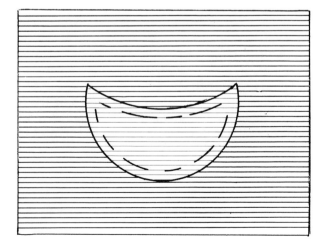

ASSORTED APPLIQUÉ STITCHES.

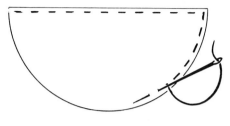

RUNNING STITCH

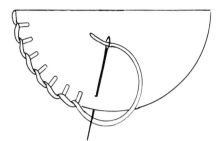

BUTTONHOLE STITCH

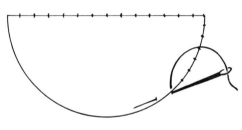

BLIND HEMMING STITCH

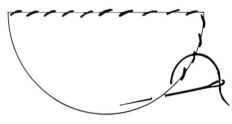

APPLIQUÉ STITCH

Machine Appliqué

Machine appliqué has two advantages: it is especially suited to projects which will be subject to hard wear, and it allows the use of thick, heavy fabrics whose edges would be too bulky if turned under for hand appliqué.

There are several possible approaches to machine appliqué. One method is to trace the design on the fabric to be appliquéd and cut out the shape, allowing an inch or so margin. Once pinned or basted in place, the applique is attached using a tight zigzag (almost satin) stitch following the traced outline of the design; the excess margin is then clipped away. A second technique is to cut the fabric piece to size, allowing no extra margin. After basting either by machine or hand, the piece is sewn down with a tight zigzag stitch set wide enough to cover the raw edge. When working with fabrics that will not fray—either because they have been backed with iron-on interfacing or because they are bonded to the background with fusible fabric or glue—you have the choice of using other stitches (straight stitch, open zigzag stitch, etc.) which do not completely bind the edges.

Although machine appliqué tends to be flatter than hand appliqué, the shapes can be lightly stuffed whenever more relief is desired.

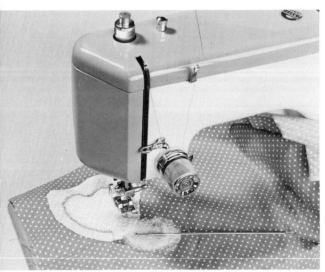

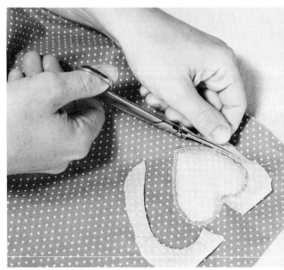

One method of machine appliqué is to trace the design onto the fabric and cut out, allowing a wide margin. Pin or baste to the background fabric, then attach using a tight zigzag stitch following the traced outline. The flatness characteristic of machine appliqué can be countered if a little stuffing is added before the design is fully stitched.

Clip away the excess fabric to the stitching line.

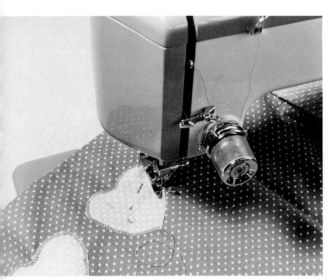

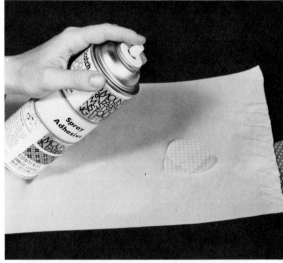

To cover the edge of the fabric more completely, cut the appliqué exactly to size, and fasten with a zigzag stitch set wide enough to cover the raw edge.

Spray adhesive can be used instead of basting to hold fabric in place while it is being stitched. The stronger varieties can also be used in place of stitching on pieces that will not be laundered or dry cleaned.

Other Bonding Methods

You can eliminate basting, and sometimes edge-stitching as well, if you use adhesives or bonding fabric to secure the appliqué pieces to the background.

Glue sticks and white school glue (not ordinary white glue) are temporary adhesives that can be used to hold a piece of fabric in place until stitched, and then laundered out in the first wash. White glue and fabric glue are permanent and do not wash out. Care must be taken not to apply too much of these adhesives, or they will saturate the material and show through on the front. (Often it helps to apply the adhesive to the backing rather than to the fabric piece to be appliquéd.) White glue and fabric glue are particularly useful when working with felt and other thick materials.

Spray adhesive, a glue resembling rubber cement in an aerosol can, is available in several strengths, with the heavier types generally considered most suitable for use with fabric. It is easy to use, less messy than white glue, and does not stain fabric, but it cannot be considered permanent if the piece is to be laundered or dry cleaned. Like many other aerosol products, spray adhesives are flammable and give off noxious fumes, so they should always be used in a well-ventilated area away from heat or flame.

Iron-on bonding fabric, a wispy material sold in tapes and by the yard, is used to fuse two layers of fabric. Most kinds must be cut to the size of the appliqué shape before ironing. Another type has a special backing paper that allows it to be fused first to the appliqué fabric; the shape is then cut, the backing paper removed, and the appliqué ironed onto the background. If you cannot locate fusible fabric with this special backing paper, you can usually substitute the nonstick paper that comes as a backing for self-adhesive shelf-lining paper, or use a special silicone-impregnated paper sold in photographic shops.*

Assorted appliqué techniques include *(top)* machine appliqué with a clipped margin, machine appliqué over a raw edge; *(center)* spray glue, machine stitched; *(bottom)* fusible web without stitching, hand appliqué with turned under edges.

Seal Release Paper, sold as a separation sheet for use in dry mounting and laminating presses.

Iron-on bonding fabric is cut to the size of the appliqué shape, then sandwiched between the appliqué and the backing and pressed with a steam iron. The bond will survive laundering and dry cleaning.

You can turn any fabric into a bondable fabric if you fuse it to bonding web. A silicone-impregnated backing sheet must be used to keep the layers from sticking to the backing.

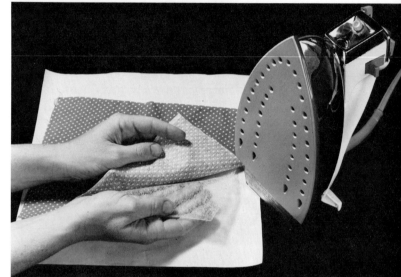

After pressing, peel away the backing paper, and cut out shapes from the web-backed cloth. These can now be fused to any background fabric. This method is especially good for cutting intricate shapes, or where it is important to keep the edges of the appliqué from raveling.

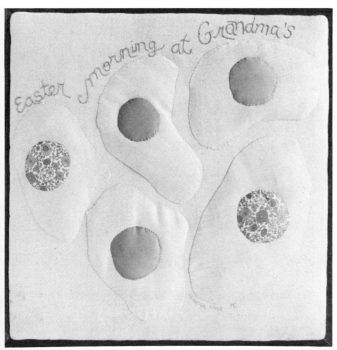

EASTER MORNING AT GRANDMA'S. Marsha Anne Isoshima. Writes the artist: "Grandma was famous for her Easter breakfasts, which is when she got the seventeen grandchildren together. The 'whites' of the fried eggs and the background are off-white linen, depending on slightly stuffed (polyester batting) relief to lift them out of the past for me; the pastel-hued yolks recall Easter eggs and Grandma's famous flower garden."

Below, left: CHRISTMAS STOCKING (detail). The image of the little girl was intended for a T-shirt, but the artist had it heat-transferred to a piece of nonwoven interfacing instead. (It would not adhere to the velveteen.) She then cut out the image and fused it to the velveteen with iron-on bonding web.

Below, right: CHRISTMAS STOCKING. Cynthia Sudholz. Laces, embroidered flowers, antique buttons, and rubber heat-transfer decal on pink cotton velveteen.

STITCHERY SAMPLER CALENDAR: JULY. Tina Fritsche. A charming interpretation of a patriotic month. The artist backed all the fabrics with iron-on interfacing to prevent fraying, then cut and glued (white glue) the parts to a piece of white cotton. She stretched the picture on a cardboard frame to steady it while she added blanket and satin stitch embellishments. *Courtesy of Gibson Greeting Cards, Inc.*

STITCHERY SAMPLER CALENDAR: JUNE. Rochelle Groonis. The artist glues or bastes cut shapes to a backing fabric, then zigzag stitches them in place using brightly colored heavy-duty threads. Detail work is added by hand. *Courtesy of Gibson Greeting Cards, Inc.*

STITCHERY SAMPLER CALENDAR: FEBRUARY. Rochelle Groonis. Note the different effect produced by the very tight (satin stitch) zigzag around the top flower and center heart, and the open zigzag stitch used around the birds and other parts of the design. *Courtesy of Gibson Greeting Cards, Inc.*

STITCHERY SAMPLER CALENDAR: DECEMBER. Rochelle Groonis. Yarn for the candy cane and stick was couched in place after the main pattern pieces were machine stitched to the backing.

THERE IS NOTHING NEW UNDER THE SUN. Becky Patterson. The banner is a summation of Ecclesiastes III, and celebrates all of life's endeavors (a time to be born, laugh, cry, love, dance, etc.). The artist places newspaper under felt when stitching by machine to prevent stretching and warping; the paper is torn off later. *Courtesty of the artist.*

CHEERS. 36 inches by 36 inches. A celebration banner by Sara Noel.

LET LITTLE CHILDREN COME TO ME. Becky Patterson. The background is of faded blue denim. Straight machine-stitching is used on lines where a soft effect is desired; zigzag stitching is used for a hard line and greater separation. *Courtesy of the artist.*

MADONNA. Sara Noel. The artist works with cut fabric pieces directly on the background, arranging and rearranging until she is satisfied. She uses machine zigzag stitch to outline the appliqué pieces, and is not afraid to leave rough edges if they add interest. *Courtesy of the artist.*

Stuffed Forms

Stuffing adds a new and interesting dimension to the treatment of fabric. Numerous varieties are available—cotton, polyester batting, loose polyester stuffing, kapok, rags, nylon stockings, feathers, foam rubber, polystyrene beads, and beans, rice, or pebbles. Since each filler will produce a different effect, it is worthwhile to get to know the special qualities of each.

In general, however, two products—polyester batting and loose polyester stuffing—will suffice for most projects. The loose fiber is good for stuffing dolls, pillows, puff patchwork, and raised appliqué, while the batting (which is polyester fiber fused into a sheet) is good for quilts and projects where it is necessary to cut a layer of stuffing to fit a particular shape. Both are lightweight, nonflammable, nonallergenic, and, unlike cotton and a number of other fillers, will maintain their fluffiness even after machine washing.

SOFT-SCULPTURE PAINTBRUSH. Jean Ray Laury. The paintbrush is intended as a housewarming gift to help friends celebrate the painting of their house.

CELEBRATION DOLL. Jean Ray Laury. Hand-stitched felt. The doll carries flowers as a birthday greeting, but these can be replaced with a heart for Valentine's Day, a basket of eggs for Easter, or a wrapped package for Christmas.

PUFF PATCHWORK WREATH. Cynthia Sudholz. The puffs are all in red print fabric; the bow is green.

Ribbon-puff ornaments, by Cynthia Sudholz. Ribbon and fabric scraps are pinned to Styrofoam balls, and polyester stuffing poked under each segment. Rickrack and lace trim are pinned in place between each joint.

BRAIDED WREATH. Stuffed tubes of fabric (three different shades of the same pattern) are braided and the ends concealed behind a machine-stitched bow.

Stuffed cat, 6 inches high, is seamed with buttonhole stitch and decorated with assorted embroidery stitches. Taiwan.

HICKETY-PICKETY, MY BLACK HEN, SHE LAYS EGGS FOR GENTLEMEN. Marsha Anne Isoshima. Done completely in black and white except for a rust-colored comb and gold beak, this elegant hen comes complete with a cameo and black satin pillow. She was inspired by the early children's nursery rhyme, which was in turn inspired by a spicy tavern song.

Chinese frog and rooster. The fabric is glue-stiffened, and in parts backed with paper.

VALENTINE PILLOWS. Ibby Pfeffer. Details are hand- and machine-embroidered.

SWEETHEART. Kathy Whitcomb. A stuffed-stocking Valentine doll. This voluptuous creature is endowed with false eyelashes and rouged cheeks; she wears a lace-trimmed nylon nightie and sleeps on a nylon jersey pillow embroidered in stem stitch. Kapok, with its beige tone and brown flecks, was chosen as the stuffing.

Coloring and Dyeing

To create a design that is totally original, you will probably want to explore the possibilities of decorating or dyeing your own fabric. Numerous coloring materials, including inks, dyes, felt pens, acrylics, and spray paints, are available for consideration. Since many of the more interesting coloring agents are designed for use on surfaces other than fabric, you may have to engage in a certain amount of experimentation to discover how best to adapt a particular product to your needs. The following guidelines may help:

1) Since synthetic materials may resist dyes, natural fibers should usually be selected. Cotton sheeting, bleached or unbleached muslin, cotton velveteen, silk, and wool are all good choices. Make sure the fabric does not have a permanent press finish, and always wash in hot soapy water to preshrink and remove sizing. (Acrylics are one exception to the general rule; they work well on polyester blends and no-iron finishes. There will be other exceptions, so experiment before unnecessarily limiting fabric choices.)
2) When applying the dye or paint, either fasten the cloth on stretcher bars or in an embroidery hoop, or stretch and pin to a flat, padded surface covered with plastic wrap or aluminum foil.
3) After they are dry, most colors benefit from being set by heat, either by ironing (five minutes at medium heat), baking (wrap in paper toweling and place in a 250° oven for five to fifteen minutes), or tumbling in a hot dryer for twenty to thirty minutes. Do not iron fabrics that have a heavy coat of acrylic or spray paint—the iron may stick to the paint.

Felt Markers

Felt markers are a boon to the textile artist. Available with fine, medium, or broad tips in a tremendous range of colors, felt pens work smoothly on fabric and are excellent whenever a great deal of control is desired.

Both water-based and waterproof felt pens can be used on fabric, although naturally the latter are more permanent. To protect work done with water-based markers, it is a good idea to spray the completed design with a water-repellent finish. Test on a scrap of fabric first, however, since a few water-based colors bleed if sprayed. In general, do not use spray finishes with permanent markers—the solvents in the spray cause most of these inks to run.

When purchasing felt markers, it is a good idea to take along a scrap of muslin or well-washed cotton sheeting for testing. Many of the waterproof markers bleed excessively on fabric, and cannot be used for controlled designs. Even when you find a brand that works well, test each marker, since there may be variations from color to color. If you are interested in washability, bring your sampler home and run it through a test wash to check on permanence. Finally, make sure that the markers you finally settle on are fresh—if felt pens have been stored incorrectly or too long, the solvent dries out, and the ink will not flow smoothly.

FELT PENS ON FABRIC

To transfer a design using a light box, tape the drawing and a piece of fabric to a sheet of glass and support the glass on the edges of a cardboard or wooden box over a light bulb.

Color in the design using water-based or waterproof felt pens. Test each marker on a scrap of cloth to make sure it won't bleed.

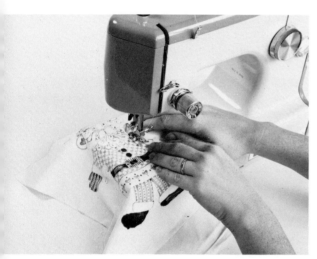

Sew the colored fabric to a piece of backing material (right sides together), then clip the seams, turn right side out, and stuff.

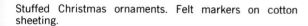

Stuffed Christmas ornaments. Felt markers on cotton sheeting.

OLD-FASHIONED VALENTINE. 8½ inches high, 7 inches wide. The figures (adapted from a colonial drawing) are drawn in permanent brown felt pen on unbleached muslin. Polyester batting cut to the shape of the figures is glued in place on the backside of the design, and supplemented by a single rectangular sheet of batting. After backing with a second piece of muslin, the design is stitched, turned right side out, and machine topstitched along the major outlines to give relief.

CHRISTMAS. Kenneth Iwai. The design was first drawn in pencil on 100 percent cotton fabric, then inked with a permanent marker and colored with drawing inks applied with a brush. Detail in the Christmas balls and sheet music was added with a technical drawing pen and India ink. Polyester stuffing and decorative stitching provide three-dimensional relief.

SANTA AND MRS. CLAUS. Sunny Aigner. The features are drawn on stretched cotton fabric with India ink and a technical drawing pen; acrylic paints, sometimes thinned to a very runny consistency, are brushed on when the ink is dry.

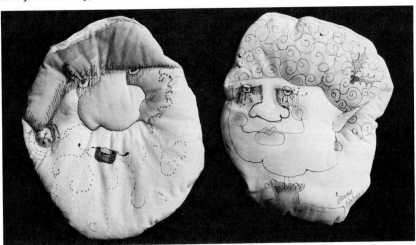

Inks

Liquid watercolors, India ink, and colored waterproof inks are liquid colors that can be brushed, sprayed, or drawn on fabric. Liquid watercolors, though they come in a beautiful range of colors, will run when wet; colored inks are more permanent. With the exception of India ink, none of these colors is particularly lightfast, so avoid exposure to bright sunlight.

India ink, if applied to smooth, closely woven fabric with either a mechanical drawing pen or metal-tipped quill pen, can produce a fine, very dark line, much stronger and more vivid than that which can be achieved with a felt pen.

Acrylics and Fabric Paints

These are pigments rather than dyes—they sit on top of the fabric rather than becoming part of it, and tend toward the opaque rather than the transparent. They are extremely versatile, and can be used for silk-screening, block printing, airbrushing, and batik, as well as for fabric painting. Generally, acrylics and fabric paints are applied as they come from the tube or jar, but they can also be thinned with water in order to be sprayed, spattered, or dribbled on for specific effects. Fixing with heat is usually required for fabric paints, but acrylics need only to air-dry. Both are considered permanent methods of coloring fabric.

Spray Paint

A speedy, permanent method to decorate fabric is to use stencils and spray enamels. The spray paint will adhere to many synthetic as well as natural fibers, and is washable as well. Always work outdoors or in a well-ventilated area (the fumes are potentially dangerous). Apply the paint lightly in short spurts to avoid soaking the fabric.

USING STENCILS AND SPRAY PAINT

Use a sharp knife to cut a design from stencil paper (available at art supply stores) or sturdy brown wrapping paper.

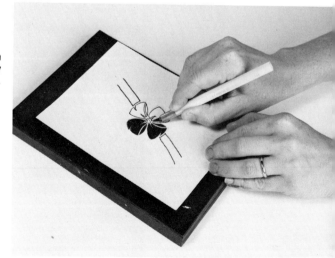

Spray the back of the design lightly with aerosol adhesive to keep it from shifting on the fabric, and attach to a sheet of newspaper or wrapping paper from which a center hole has been cut.

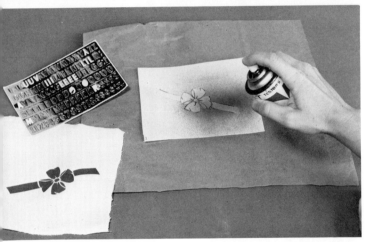

Press the stencil and backing paper face down on the fabric, and apply spray enamel in short spurts. Adhesive-backed letters and other gummed shapes can also be used as stencils.

Spray-painted Valentines. Three of the hearts are of cotton velveteen, a fabric that takes a spray-painting particularly well.

Batik

Batik is a resist technique for coloring fabric. Before a piece of material is dyed, areas not to receive the color are covered with molten wax, which repels or resists the dye. After the first dyeing, more areas are waxed; these newly waxed areas will preserve the color of the preceding dyebath. The process of waxing and dyeing is continued until the desired number of colors is built up; only then is the wax removed and the end result seen.

Although it requires a little practice to get used to the idea that in batik you add colors by blocking them out, the process is not necessarily difficult, and striking effects can be achieved with even single color dyebaths.

Batik does not have to be complicated to be effective. The pieces for this Christmas hanging, by Marge Hastert, were waxed and dyed only once. The red squares are stitched to a burlap backing and framed with green grosgrain ribbons, which extend at the bottom into tassels with bells.

Preparation

Natural fibers should be used for batik, since synthetics (along with fabrics with a no-iron finish) resist most dyes. A smooth, closely woven surface is easiest to work on, though bulky fabrics such as linen and cotton velveteen can also be dyed successfully. Make sure fabrics are preshrunk, and all starch or sizing washed out before beginning.

Once the fabric is laundered and dried, it should be stretched tight on stretcher bars, batik frames, an embroidery hoop, or even the top of a wooden or cardboard box. Elevating the fabric provides better and more even wax penetration, and less wax is required. If for some reason it is easier to work on a flat surface, place a sheet of glass or a piece of corrugated cardboard covered with aluminum foil under the fabric.

Use pencil or charcoal to transfer a design to the fabric. Most methods of wax removal will also remove these lines, but keep them light just in case traces remain.

Waxing the Fabric

Generally a combination of paraffin and beeswax is used for batik. Beeswax is pliable and adheres well to fabric; paraffin is brittle and can flake off if used alone. A fifty-fifty combination is often recommended, though the proportion of paraffin can be increased if greater crackle is desired. Preformulated mixes sold as "batik wax" are also available where batik supplies are sold.

Wax is flammable, and should never be melted directly over a heat source. Use a double boiler, a coffee tin placed in a pan of boiling water, an old electric frypan, popcorn popper, or other thermostatically controlled appliance, or (if you don't want to dirty the pan), a tin set in an electric frypan. Melt the wax until it is completely clear and liquid, but do not let it smoke. Should the wax catch on fire, smother the flames with baking soda or a cover, or use a chemical fire extinguisher. Do not use water—it will only cause the hot wax to splatter.

Wax at the proper temperature will penetrate the fabric smoothly and evenly, and the waxed portions will appear translucent. If the wax is too hot it will "sizzle" and spread when it touches the fabric; if it is too cool it will sit on the surface and look opaque. In either case it will not resist the dye properly.

Natural bristle brushes are preferred for applying the hot wax, since synthetics such as nylon may curl in the heat. The single most useful brush is the round, pointed brush used for Japanese sumi painting. It is fat enough to hold a good deal of wax (tiny watercolor brushes are useless—they run out of wax too quickly), and has a long tapered point which is perfect for fine lines and dots. Brushes that have been immersed in wax are almost impossible to clean, so they should be dedicated to batik alone.

For drawing consistently even lines, use the metal-spouted tool known as a tjanting (pronounced CHAHN-ting). Heat the tjanting in hot wax, then dip up no more than half a chamber full and carry the tool to the fabric. Hold the front part of the tool angled upward so that wax does not run out the spout, and keep a paper towel handy to catch drips. If you also hold the work surface at an angle—flattening it when you want to apply wax with the tjanting and angling it upward again at the end of a line—you will quickly learn to control the flow of wax. Do not let the tjanting sit in the wax pot for extended periods of time, or the heat may melt the solder that holds the tool together.

A recent development is the electric tjanting, a penlike tool with interchangeable spouts. Bits of wax placed in the chamber are melted and kept at "flow" temperature by the electric current, eliminating the need for a wax pot.

A small pan placed in a foil-lined electric frypan provides a good way to melt the combination of beeswax and paraffin used for batik. A candy or wax thermometer helps to keep the wax at the appropriate temperature. Turn the heat down if the wax begins to smoke, and keep a lid or baking soda handy in case of fire. Tools for applying the wax include natural bristle paintbrushes, a tjanting, and even a kistka (the tool used for waxing Ukrainian-style Easter eggs).

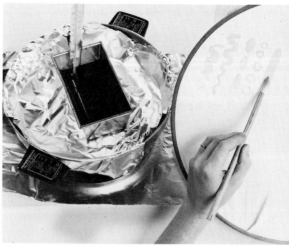

A Japanese sumi-e brush is excellent for applying wax, since it can make both broad and narrow lines. The fabric to be waxed should be stretched on a frame of some kind—here a large embroidery hoop is used.

For wax to flow smoothly from the needlelike spout of a tjanting, the tool must be kept hot. Either redip in hot wax, or reheat over an alcohol lamp. (A candle deposits soot, while an alcohol lamp burns clean—so clean that the flame is almost invisible.) Tilt the tool upward when carrying it to the fabric, and keep a paper towel handy to catch drips.

You can best control the flow of wax from a tjanting if you keep the work surface at an angle. Note that the wavy line just waxed looks translucent, meaning that the wax is at the proper temperature. If the wax is too cool when applied (as is the case for some of the other lines), it will not penetrate the fabric and resist the dye.

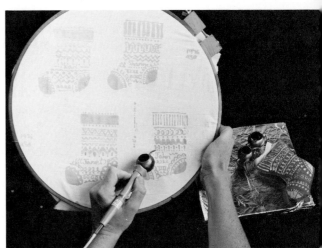

Some artists prefer to apply the wax without the aid of a hoop or frame. Stephen Blumrich, known for his skill with a tjanting, likes to hold the fabric over the palm of his hand. *Photo by Jane Dalrymple.*

A recently developed tool is the electric tjanting, a device with interchangeable spouts. Bits of wax placed in the bowl are melted by electric current; no separate wax pot is needed. The hot tool should be rested on a foil-covered tile or hot pad when not in use.

Dyes and Dyeing

The best dyes for batik are the so-called cold-water or fiber-reactive dyes. Manufactured under the trade name Procion, they are packaged and sold under different names by a number of distributors (including Dylon, Fibrec, Hi-Dye, Fabdec, Putnam, and Dyehouse). Most other dyes (including household dyes such as Rit and Tintex) are designed for use at temperatures that would melt the batik wax, and though they can be used for batik if the temperature is reduced, their brilliance and permanence will be diminished.

Fiber-reactive dyes require the use of an "assistant" (salt or urea) to make the fiber receptive to the dye. (In most household dyes, the assistant has already been added.) In addition, washing soda (sal soda) is added halfway through the process as a fixing agent. The soda, generally labeled "fixer," comes packaged with many brands of dye, but it can also be purchased separately at the supermarket.

There are several different methods of dyeing (each detailed in the accompanying chart), but in general the following directions apply:

1) Use measuring cups, tools, and a dyebath container of plastic, glass, enamel, or stainless steel, and protect the hands with rubber gloves.
2) Immerse fabric in cool water before dyeing to harden the wax and ensure even penetration of color. Use lukewarm water (to keep the wax flexible) if you want to avoid crackle.

3) Make a paste of the dye in a few teaspoons of cold water, then dissolve completely in a small amount of hot water, and add to a lukewarm dye-bath so that the resulting temperature is about 90 to 100°. Dissolve the assistant (salt or urea), and add to the dyebath.

4) Add the damp fabric. To ensure even penetration by the dye molecules, it is important to keep the fabric moving. If you worry about cracking the wax excessively, gently pour dye over the fabric. When the dyeing period is half over, lift out the fabric, add the washing soda dissolved in a bit of warm water, and return the fabric to the dyebath.

5) Dye for the recommended length of time or until the desired color is reached. (The color will be several shades lighter when it is dry.) Rinse lightly, if desired, and lay out on newspapers to dry, dabbing up any drop-lets of dye resting on the waxed portions of the cloth. Fiber-reactive dyes continue to set as they dry, so this process should never be hurried. To prolong the drying period (and intensify the bond of dye and fabric), place the wet cloth in a plastic bag for two hours before spreading out to dry.

When the fabric is fully dried, it can be rewaxed and dyed a second color. Working from light to dark, the dyeings can be repeated an indefinite number of times. Since the soda eventually eats into the wax, however, rewaxing of certain areas may be required if more than two or three immersions are planned.

After the final dyeing, rinse the fabric in cool water until the water runs clear, then remove the wax according to the instructions under Wax Removal.

Fiber-reactive dyes are designed for cool (90–100°) water dyeing; they are among the best dyes for batik. Salt and/or urea are assistants that make the fiber receptive to the dye; soda is added halfway through the dyeing process to help fix the colors. The "extra-fast" method of dyeing uses only a little water, therefore the fabric must be kept moving to ensure even dye penetration.

THREE DYEING PROCEDURES USING FIBER-REACTIVE DYES.

I. EXTRA-FAST (3-to-15-minute) METHOD

(For 1 yard fabric, or up to ½ pound.)

This method was developed by Ann Asakura-Kimura for dyeing small pieces of fabric quickly. Urea replaces salt as the assistant, with the result that the dye "take" is greatly accelerated. Relatively little water is used, meaning that the dye must be drained off and carefully poured over the fabric to ensure even saturation.

Dye: 1 tsp. (pale)
    2 tsp. (medium)
    3 tsp. (dark)
½ cup warm water

Paste dye in a few teaspoons cold water, then dissolve thoroughly in ½ cup warm water. Pour into dyebath.

2 Tbsp. urea (from chemical suppliers
    or fertilizer store)
1 cup hot water
1 cup cold water

Dissolve urea in hot water; combine with cold water; add to dyebath.
Place premoistened fabric in dyebath and gently stir or pour dye over the cloth. (This initial dyeing may take no more than 1 or 2 minutes; watch to see how the color "takes.")

1 Tbsp. washing soda
½ cup warm water

Dissolve soda in water. Lift fabric from dyebath, add soda, and replace fabric. Continue pouring on dye.
When desired shade is reached, remove fabric, place unrinsed in a plastic bag for 2 hours, then stretch flat to dry.

II. SHORT (30-minute) METHOD

(For dyeing 1 pound cloth, or 2-4 yards.)

Dye: ⅜ tsp. (pale)
    ¾ tsp. (medium)
    1½ tsp. (dark)
1 cup warm water
1¼ gallons lukewarm water
Salt: 4 Tbsp. (pale)
    9 Tbsp. (medium)
    12 Tbsp. (dark)

Paste dye in a few teaspoons cold water, then dissolve in 1 cup warm water. Place in dyebath containing 1¼ gallons lukewarm water. Add salt in proportion to the amount of dye powder.
Immerse premoistened fabric in dye. Dye for 15 minutes, gently stirring or pouring the dye over the fabric.

3 Tbsp. washing soda

Dissolve soda in small amount of warm water. Lift out fabric, add soda to dyebath, replace fabric.
Dye for 15 minutes more, stirring occasionally.
Rinse fabric quickly (optional), place in plastic bag for 2 hours (optional), spread flat on newspapers to dry.

III. LONG (1½-hour) METHOD

(For large pieces of fabric, or fabric with a very tight weave.)

Use the measurements given for short dyeing, but increase all quantities (double for 2 pounds cloth, triple for 3 pounds, etc.).

Dye the cloth for 10 minutes (stirring) *before* adding salt. Then dissolve salt in hot water, and add to the dyebath in three equal parts, with 5 minutes between each addition. Continue dyeing for 15 more minutes.

Remove fabric, add soda dissolved in warm water, and replace fabric. Dye for 30 to 60 more minutes, stirring occasionally.

Rinse (optional), place in plastic bag for 2 hours (optional), spread on a flat surface to dry.

Stephen Blumrich uses as many as twenty-four immersions to achieve the variety of colors he seeks. Here is a sample dye progression:

DYE	RESULT
1. light red	pink
2. light yellow	salmon
3. red	orange
4. yellow	light orange
5. light blue	tan
6. red	rust
7. yellow	gold
8. red	red
9. yellow	orange
10. light blue	brown
11. strong blue	blue
12. strong yellow	olive
13. black	black

Courtesy of the artist.

Crackle

Although the fine lines known as crackle are characteristic of batik, the effect is often overdone by beginners. Crackle will develop naturally in fabric which goes through multiple waxings and dyeings; if it is not minimized in the early stages, the end results will probably look muddy. The time to encourage crackle is in the final dyebath. By crushing the fabric gently between the hands, the direction and amount of veining can be rather carefully controlled. If greater crackle is desired, either increase the proportion of paraffin in the wax mixture, or chill the cloth for an hour or so before crushing and dyeing to make the wax more brittle.

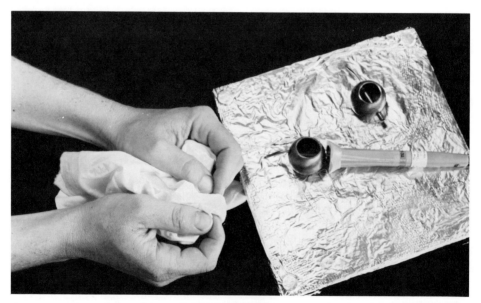

Crackle is produced by crushing the fabric to produce fine lines in the wax. To make the wax more brittle and thus increase crackle, use a higher proportion of paraffin or place the cloth in the refrigerator before crushing. Crackle is not completely random; it can be controlled if the fabric is handled carefully.

Wax Removal

Ironing is the easiest method of removing wax from batiked fabric. Stack old newspapers on the ironing surface, and sandwich the fabric between paper towels or clean (unprinted) newsprint. Use a dry iron set at medium temperature to press over the top of the sandwich, and change both top and bottom papers frequently.

Wax that remains in the fabric after ironing gives a stiffness and translucence considered desirable by many artists. The remaining wax can be removed entirely, however, by one of two methods. The first is to immerse the fabric in boiling soapy water. After a few minutes, add cold water to solidify the wax, push to one side, and lift out the fabric. Rinse in clean hot water to remove the soapy residue and any remaining traces of wax. (Do not throw wax down the drain—it will clog it.)

A second method is to soak the fabric in cleaning fluid or white gasoline. Work outside, and observe all precautions on the product label. If this approach does not appeal to you (it is smelly and somewhat hazardous), the same effect can be achieved by taking the fabric to a cooperative dry cleaner (not all will accept batiked fabric) or to a coin-operated dry-cleaning machine.

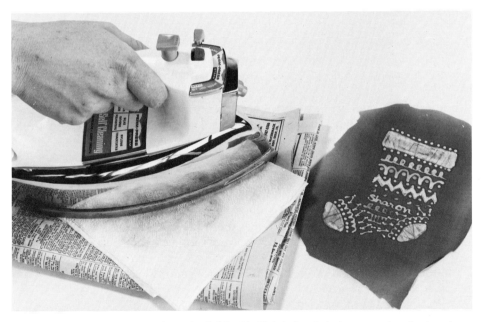

The easiest way to remove wax from the finished batik is to iron between paper towels placed on a stack of newspapers. Change the top and bottom papers frequently. The remaining wax provides body and translucence; it can be removed by boiling or immersion in cleaning fluid if desired.

Painting with Dyes

When working on small projects or when experimenting with multiple applications of color, it is often easier and faster to paint on the dye than it is to go through the long immersion process. For this technique, the dye is combined with a chemical water in which the assistant (urea) has already

Christmas ornament (detail). Santa's lines were waxed using a kistka, a small tjanting-like tool usually used for Ukrainian-style Easter eggs (see Chapter 5).

been dissolved; baking and washing soda are added just before the mixture is applied to the fabric.

One approach is to paint the whole surface of the design with the dye solution, then dry, rewax, and paint on a second color. Since drying can be speeded with the use of a hair dryer (on *low* so as not to melt the wax), a series of colors can be built up very quickly. Another method is to thicken the dye solution so that it will not run, and paint the color only on designated sections. This technique makes it possible to produce a multicolored design in just one "dyeing."

In immersion dyeing, fixation takes place during the long dyeing and the slow drying period that follows it; in direct dye application these steps are eliminated, so a separate fixation process is required. After the final application of dye, allow the fabric to air-dry, then set the colors by any of the following methods:

1) *Ironing.* Iron the fabric as for wax removal, but continue ironing until each part of the design has been subjected to at least five minutes of heat.
2) *Dry baking.* Pad the fabric with newspaper or paper towels and roll into a loose bundle, then bake in a 250° oven for five minutes.
3) *Steam baking.* Pad the fabric as for dry baking, making sure none of the fabric touches itself, and bake (275° for fifteen to thirty minutes) in an oven in which a large pan of water has been placed on a lower shelf.
4) *Steam.* Pad and wrap the fabric, then place above boiling water in a steamer. Place extra newspaper below the bundle and under the pot lid to prevent spatters or drops of condensation from contacting the material. Steam for about fifteen minutes, then unwrap the package as quickly as possible.

After the colors have been set, remove the excess wax and dye in the following manner: Rinse the fabric in cold-water baths until the water runs clear (work quickly, so that the color does not stain undyed sections of the cloth). Proceed to a hot soapy wash (followed by another cold rinse if desired), and finally speed dry (using a hair dryer, clothes dryer, or iron) to prevent any seepage of color.

O LITTLE TOWN OF BETHLEHEM. Marge Hastert. The burlap which backs the batik is hemmed at the top to allow insertion of a dowel for hanging.

CHRISTMAS TREE SKIRT. Marge Hastert. Eight wedges of fabric were waxed and dyed green, then sewn together with red grosgrain ribbon. Bits of red ribbon, yarn, and puff balls accent each snowman.

GLORIA. Stephen Blumrich. To allow color progressions impossible to achieve with only one kind of dye, the artist often combines fiber reactives with direct dyes. *Courtesy of the artist.*

THREE KINGS. Marge Hastert. The striking design in red and black was inspired by a greeting card.

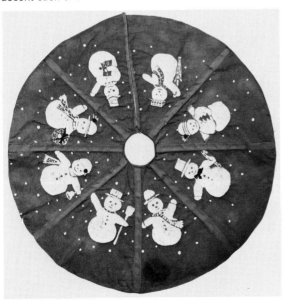

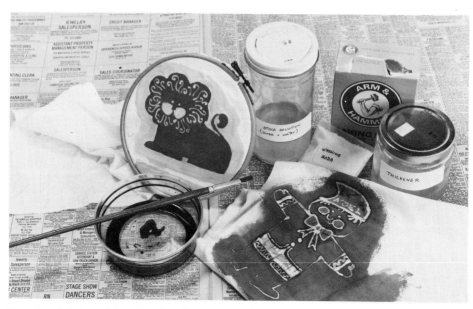

Dye which is to be painted directly onto fabric must be combined with assistants and fixers before application, and the colors must be heat-set when the work is completed. Two approaches are illustrated: at left, in imitation of immersion dyeing, the whole surface of the lion is covered with a single color; after drying and rewaxing, a second color will be applied. At right, the gingerbread man has been painted with three separate colors, each thickened so that they will not spread outside the lines where applied. Use synthetic brushes; natural bristles become too soft in the dye-chemical solutions.

After being saturated with bright pink dye, the lion was dried and rewaxed (mane, tail, and body lines), then painted in navy blue (producing purple). The dye was forced through breaks in the wax to produce crackle. Though similar to immersion dyeing in end result, this method is faster and more economical in its use of dye. Separate fixation is required to set the colors.

DIRECT APPLICATION OF FIBER-REACTIVE DYES.

(Note: Some companies package premixed combinations of chemicals for thickening dye. Follow package instructions.)

I. THIN SOLUTION
Chemical Water (1 pint):

½ tsp. Calgon (water softener; not needed in soft-water areas)

5 Tbsp. urea

1 cup hot water

1 cup cold water

Dissolve Calgon and urea in 1 cup hot water; add 1 cup cold water and and mix well.

Makes 1 pint. Stores indefinitely in a closed jar.

Per cup of Chemical Water:

Dye: ¼ tsp. (pale)
  ½-1 tsp. (medium)
  1-2 tsp. (dark)
1 tsp. baking soda

½ tsp. washing soda

Paste dye in a little chemical water, then add to measured amount of solution.

Dissolve baking soda and washing soda in a little warm water and add to dye mixture just before using. The solution will not keep long after the addition of the sodas, so plan to mix only the quantity required.

To mix less than 1 cup solution, reduce all quantities proportionately.

II. THICK SOLUTION
Stock Solution (1 pint):

1 pint chemical water (see above)

½-2 tsp. sodium alginate (depending on thickness desired; or use Keltex, Manutex RS, Halltex)

Combine and mix well (shake or mix in electric blender). Store overnight if desired to remove any remaining lumps. Keeps well in a covered jar in the refrigerator.

Per ½ Cup of Thickener Stock Solution:

Dye: ⅛ tsp. (pale)
  ¼ tsp. (medium)
  ½-1 tsp. (dark)
½ tsp. baking soda

¼ tsp. washing soda

Add dye to desired amount of thickener.

Dissolve the sodas in a little warm water and add to the mixture just before using. The sodas are necessary to activate the dye, but the mixture will begin to deteriorate after their addition, so mix only the amount required.

To mix less than ½ cup thickened solution, reduce all quantities proportionately.

HO-HO-HO, 1975. A Christmas hand puppet by Stephen Blumrich. Notice the use of dark lines to define the design. These require great control, since it is necessary to wax around rather than over the lines, leaving them open to receive a darker dye. *Courtesy of the artist.*

BATIK HEART. Linda von Geldern waxed and dyed gauzelike diapers, then patched several different-colored pieces to form the front of this heart pillow.

HEARTS. Applications of dye were painted on, and the colors heat-set with an iron.

BATIK BIRDS. Rather than immersing in dye after each application of wax, the fabric was painted with a soda-activated dye-chemical solution. After the final application of dye, the fabric was air-dried, steamed (to set the color), and washed in hot soapy water.

Glue-Stiffened Fibers

White glue is an emulsion of plastic resin in water into which fabric or thread can be dipped. As the water evaporates and the glue dries, an invisible plastic film is left behind to coat and stiffen the fibers. Fabric which has been saturated with glue solution, dried, and ironed can be cut and shaped almost like paper; the edges will not ravel. Stiffened fabric is wonderful for making gift wrap ribbon, bows for wreaths and Christmas branches, and shapes for fabric appliqué. Thread that has been stiffened will retain its shape; it is perfect for flat or three-dimensional ornaments.

Fabric will not ravel if it is stiffened with a mixture of white glue and water. Start with a mixture of ⅓ glue to ⅔ water (add more glue for greater stiffness). Immerse the fabric until saturated, then squeeze out the excess solution. Spread the fabric out and hang to dry (place newspaper underneath to catch the drips if drying indoors), then iron.

Straight scissors, pinking scissors, and scalloping shears can all be used to cut ribbons from the glue-stiffened fabric. If the design of the fabric runs in straight lines, it will be easy to cut long lengths without measuring.

Bows from glue-stiffened fabric make excellent decorations for wreaths, Christmas tree branches.

Loops of glue-stiffened ribbon are wired, then pinned to a fabric-covered Styrofoam wreath.

The finished wreath has a bow of contrasting fabric. About one square yard of stiffened fabric was required to cover the 8¾-inch wreath.

Fabrics with a nap (velvet, velveteen) cannot be stiffened with glue and water, but bows can be made with iron-on bonding fabric. One method is to fold the fabric to the center and insert bonding fabric cut to the width of the ribbon; another method is to fold the fabric so that the edges overlap, and fuse the edges only (using precut bonding tape).

Fuse the layers by covering with a damp cloth and pressing with a hot iron.

Instead of tying a real bow, which is usually too bulky, shape the fused fabric in three parts as shown. If desired, a wire can be inserted before fusing—place at the fold if fusing the whole ribbon, or between the overlapped edges if fusing only the edges.

THREAD BALLOONS

Saturate cotton embroidery thread in a half-and-half solution of glue and water, then draw the thread between the fingers and wrap around a balloon. Allow to dry in a warm place so that the balloon does not shrink before the thread dries.

When the thread is thoroughly dry, untie (or pop) and remove the balloon. If the balls do not seem sturdy enough, use heavier thread or increase the proportion of glue in the mixture.

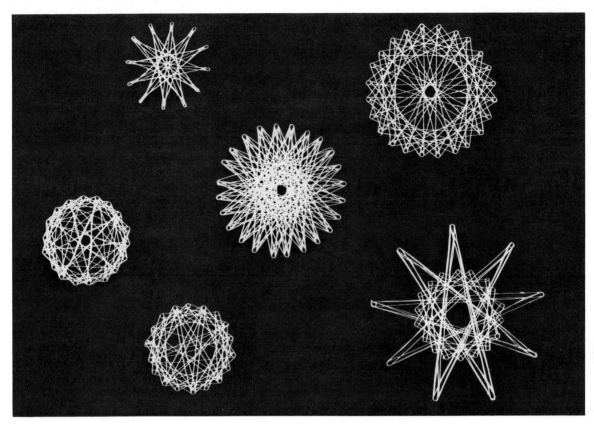

Lacy ornaments of glue-stiffened thread. String art designs are usually created around nails hammered into a board, but if the thread is stiffened the designs can be taken off the framework.

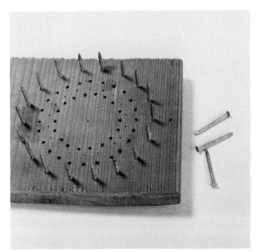

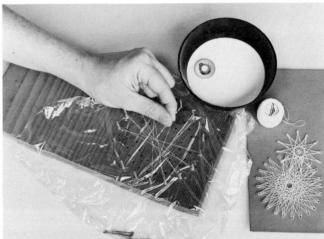

Draw several circles on a piece of scrap wood, and drill holes at equidistant points around the circle. The finished designs will differ depending on whether there is an even or odd number of points. Push nails up through the holes all around one of the circles.

Push plastic wrap down over the nails, and begin wrapping with cotton thread saturated in a mixture of white glue and water. When the thread is thoroughly dry, loosen each point and pull the nails from the back one by one.

Basic winding method. Take the thread directly across the circle, then bring it back to the nail adjacent to the first. The pattern will differ slightly depending on whether the thread is wrapped clockwise or counterclockwise around each nail.

The basic winding method is the same for odd numbered circles, but the result will always be an open or hollow-center design. (Since there is no nail directly across the circle from any other nail, there is no way to fill the center.)

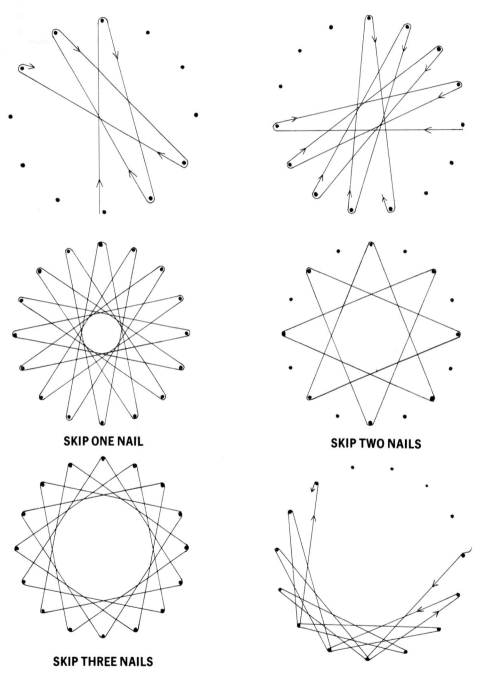

SKIP ONE NAIL   **SKIP TWO NAILS**

SKIP THREE NAILS

Variations. Instead of taking the thread directly across the circle, skip one nail (or more than one). Continue skipping a nail each time the thread is wound back and forth. The pattern will change depending on the number of nails skipped.

Edging is achieved by winding the thread a certain number of nails forward, then winding a different number of nails back. In the example illustrated, the thread moves four nails ahead and three back, all around the circle.

Yarn plaques from Mexico. To duplicate plaques such as these, cut hardboard or heavy cardboard to the desired size, and attach brightly colored yarn with white glue. Lay down the major outlines first, then fill in each section in contrasting colors.

Yarn-covered clay bird. Mexico. Similar designs could also be worked on Styrofoam balls or other three-dimensional shapes.

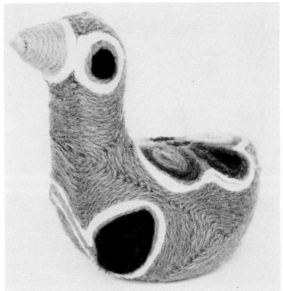

To My Sweetheart. Cynthia Sudholz. Decorative motifs such as the ones used here can be cut from greeting cards or gift wrap, or they can be ordered from companies specializing in novelty papers.

Paper

It is hard to conceive of a celebration or festival which is not in some way connected with the use of paper. Paper money is burned at traditional Chinese funerals, papier-mâché horses are carried in Indian festival processions, paper garlands festoon the streets when Japan celebrates Tanabata (Star Festival), paper piñatas bring cheer to Mexican households at Christmas, and paper headdresses light the way for paraders celebrating Saint Nicholas Day in Switzerland. Paper hearts, bunnies, flags, pumpkins, turkeys, sleighs—all are instantly recognizable as symbols of well-known holidays.

Why has paper become so intricately linked with holidays and celebrations? One reason, certainly, is that the product is inexpensive and plentiful, and thus accessible to even the poorest craftsman. Secondly, paper is enormously versatile. It can be cut and folded, shaped into geometric structures, stretched into chains, laminated into layers, twisted into string, scored, creped, curled, and crumpled. Thirdly, paper is available in such a variety of forms—thick and thin, transparent and opaque, shiny and dull, plain and decorated—that its decorative potential is virtually unlimited.

Of the hundreds of varieties of paper manufactured, some are particularly useful to the craftsman. Among these are:

Bristol board. A high-quality (often 100 percent rag) white paper available in several thicknesses (measured by the number of layers, or "ply") and two finishes—"hot pressed," or "plate" (smooth), and "cold pressed," or "kid" (slightly textured). Though fairly expensive, bristol board scores and folds beautifully, and is excellent for geometric constructions and many cut and folded ornaments.

Charcoal and pastel paper. Medium-weight papers in assorted colors with an interesting textured surface.

Color aid paper. Thin coated paper, supposedly fade-resistant, in several hundred colors. Used for package design, commercial presentations, magazine layouts, and so forth, and good for most decorative uses.

Construction paper. Inexpensive, medium-weight paper in assorted colors. Susceptible to fading.

Crepe paper. Lightweight machine-textured paper, stretchable, in a wide variety of bright colors. Good for paper flowers, party decorations, streamers, and so forth.

Flint paper. Coated, lightweight, glazed paper, white on the back, in a variety of bright colors. Often sold as gift wrap as well as in art supply stores. Displays, ornaments, Polish-style paper cutting.

Gift wrap paper. A wide assortment of thin, printed papers, including some with metallic, glossy, or flocked surfaces. Ornaments, paper folding.

Illustration board. Drawing paper mounted on a stiff backing board in a variety of finishes and weights (10-ply [$\frac{1}{16}$ inch] to 28-ply). Suitable for displays, backgrounds, and large three-dimensional projects.

Metal foil paper. Lightweight paper backed with metal foil. Numerous colors, glossy, satin, or embossed finish. Metal foils such as aluminum foil are not true papers, but often respond like metal-backed paper. Some glues will not adhere to foil.

Mylar. Plastic film (not paper) in assorted weights, available with a mirror-finish gold or silver surface. Hard to glue (use staples where possible). Good for ornaments, garlands.

Novelty papers, paper dolls, decoupage prints. Assorted designs and finishes. Cut out for decoupage, collage; back with heavier paper for use as ornaments.

Origami paper. Squares of thin, coated paper, colored and metallic. For origami (Japanese paper folding), decorations, paper cutting.

Paper straws. Coated and uncoated, cellophane or paper. Useful as a substitute for real straw in ornaments (see Chapter 3).

Paper string. Machine- or hand-twisted. Decorative Japanese strings (*mizuhiki*) are sometimes available at Oriental import shops.

Tissue paper. Brightly colored, semitransparent paper. For paper flowers, garlands, ornaments.

Typing paper. Thin, crisp white paper in assorted weights and finishes. Good for folding, pleating, lightweight ornaments.

Two-tone paper. Paper with a different color on each side. Available commercially or can be made by hand, using dry mounting tissue or spray adhesive. Excellent for ornaments, and geometrical constructions where both sides of the paper are visible.

Upson board. 4- by 8-foot panels $\frac{1}{8}$- to $\frac{3}{4}$-inch thick, in assorted colors and finishes. Good for displays, backing, and some three-dimensional ornaments.

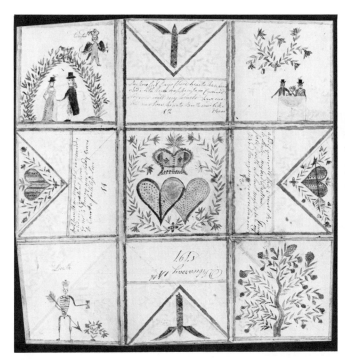

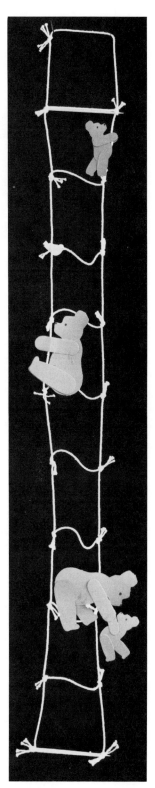

Pennsylvania Dutch puzzle purse. Handmade, 1797. A forerunner of the Valentine, folded paper puzzles were often presented as love tokens in eighteenth-and nineteenth-century America. *Courtesy of Hallmark Cards, Inc.*

Bears of construction paper climb a ladder of string. Denmark.

Each of the presents on this wreath of packages is a Styrofoam cube wrapped in colorful gift paper. Ann Swoish, Hui Hauoli Civic Club.

Paper drinking straws, clipped in segments and folded in half, are glued together to form decorative stars.

Be My Valentine. Cynthia Sudholz. Paper dolls, paper doilies, and other novelty papers are combined with ribbons and laces for an elaborate valentine.

Santa is constructed of Upson board; his beard, hat, and sleeve fringe are of heavy white paper. *Courtesy of The Upson Company.*

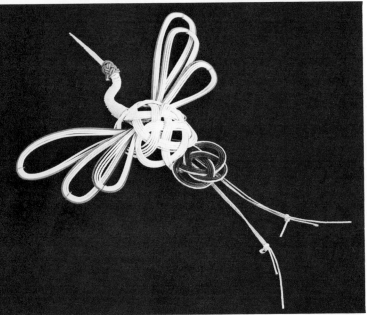

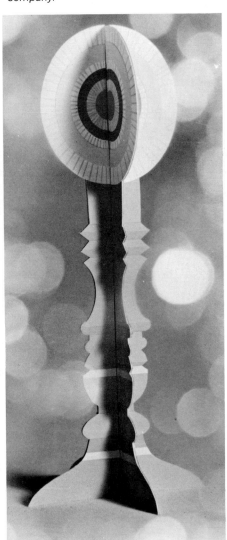

Left, top: Mizuhiki, ornamental paper strings, are used as ceremonial decorations in Japan. Here gold- and silver-colored string is shaped into a butterfly, a tortoise, and a crest of wisteria.

Center: Mizuhiki crane. The crane, which, according to legend, lives a thousand years, is a symbol of long life and good fortune.

Bottom: Tissue paper, brightly colored and inexpensive, is perfect for garlands and party decorations.

Below: Upson board is a sturdy display material that is good for large three-dimensional decorations. *Courtesy of The Upson Company.*

Tools and Techniques

For best results, always use the appropriate tools when cutting paper. Large scissors are best for general cutting, while small nail or decoupage scissors are useful for very small and intricate shapes. When it comes to cutting a straight line, scissors can never match the results produced with a stencil or mat knife guided by a metal-edged ruler. (Single-edged razor blades are fine but not as strong.) When cutting heavy board with a knife, always remember that it is better to take several passes rather than trying to cut through in a single stroke.

Paper should generally be scored before folding to make the creases even and precise. Use a stylus, a dull knife, or a ball-point pen that has run out of ink to score thin and medium-weight paper; use a light stroke with a stencil or mat knife to score heavy paper and board. Whether you crease the paper toward or away from you after scoring depends on the type of paper used and the effect desired; try each way before deciding.

Curl strips of paper by drawing the paper over a knife or scissor blade, using the thumb of the hand holding the tool to exert pressure. To put a curl in larger sheets of paper, pull firmly and smoothly over the edge of a counter or tabletop.

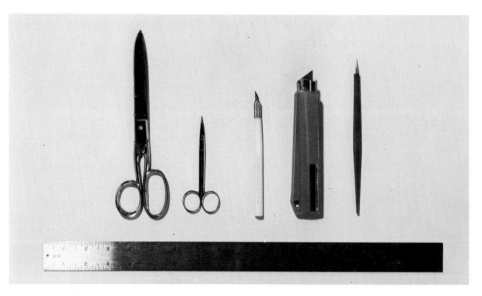

Tools for working with paper include large scissors, small curved nail scissors, stencil knife, mat knife, stylus for scoring paper, and a metal ruler (backed with rubber to prevent slipping).

Adhesives

The adhesive you choose will vary with the project. Water-based emulsion glues (white glue, polymer medium) are particularly useful with paper. Milky white and water-soluble when applied, they dry transparent and water resistant. Generally the rule is to apply these adhesives sparingly, since the moisture in the emulsions can cause paper to buckle and colors to bleed, but there are also techniques (collage, decoupage) that call for brushing polymer medium or thinned white glue all over the surface to serve as both adhesive and glaze. When it is important to create a strong bond without introducing much moisture, *thick* white glue (sold in hobby shops) is a good choice. Water-soluble mucilage and library paste can be substituted for the emulsion glues if they are handy or if children are doing the work, but the results should not be considered as strong or as permanent.

Glue sticks are a recently developed, nontoxic adhesive in lipstick form. Water-soluble but not watery, the adhesive does not cause paper to buckle, nor does it stain thin, transparent papers such as tissue. Since the glue is waxy and rather soft, however, it is hard to apply evenly over a large area, so it is best to reserve glue sticks for adhering tabs or other small parts.

Clear household cement, a vinyl-based glue that comes in a tube, is called for in certain projects requiring a fast-drying nonwatery adhesive that will not seep through thin paper. Although household cement is considered an all purpose adhesive, it has certain drawbacks (flammability, toxic fumes, and the fact that it is removable only with strong solvents such as acetone) which make it best suited for use only when its fast-drying and nonstaining qualities are particularly needed.

The disadvantage of toxic fumes and flammability also applies to rubber cement, an adhesive widely recommended for use with paper, but which tends to yellow and stain with age, making it unsuitable for anything but temporary work. Much more versatile is spray cement, an aerosol glue that can be applied in such a thin layer as to be invisible even on thin papers such as tissue. It is like rubber cement in that it does not cause paper to buckle or colors to bleed, but the bond is neater and longer lasting. Unfortunately, a completely nontoxic aerosol has yet to be created, so spray adhesive should be handled with the same precautions that apply to clear household gement and rubber cement: Always use in a well-ventilated room away from heat and flame, and avoid breathing the fumes.

Though not usually considered an adhesive, photographers' dry mounting tissue can be used to bond two layers of paper to make a single, two-sided sheet. Heat—either from a dry mounting press or from a home iron—is used to melt the thermoplastic adhesive incorporated in the dry mounting tissue and fuse the top and bottom papers into a three-layer sandwich. Tissue and other thin papers become firm enough to cut and fold like construction paper when laminated this way; heavier papers become almost like cardboard. If the added thickness if undesirable, spray cement should be used instead of dry mounting tissue to join the two sheets of paper.

Some Decorative Possibilities

Once you are familiar with the basic skills of cutting, scoring, folding, curling, and gluing, you can combine the techniques to produce an endless variety of paper shapes. What starts out as an exercise may develop into experimentation, and experimentation may lead in turn to the creation of new and interesting constructions. A number of the projects illustrated in this chapter are the outcome of just this kind of "creative play."

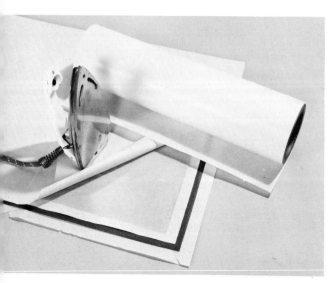

To make two-tone paper, sandwich a layer of photographer's dry mounting tissue between two different-colored sheets of paper. Cover the sandwich with newsprint or other clean paper, and iron at the recommended temperature. Here a roll of waxy tissue designed for low-temperature mounting is used; other types of dry mounting tissue may require a hotter iron.

Curlicue fish are shaped from strips of two-tone tissue paper fused with dry mounting tissue.

Aerosol glue can also be used to make two-sided paper. Lay the bottom paper face down and spray with adhesive, then carefully roll the top paper into place. Burnish to smooth out any wrinkles.

Scandinavian paper and wire ornament is 6 inches across. Four 3-inch wires and four 2½-inch wires are glued to a central star, and the spokes decorated on both sides with additional paper stars. Note that the stars are graduated in size, so that the smallest can be cut from the center of the next size star, and so on.

Paper strip stars. Each consists of two five-point stars laid one on top of the other. The smallest of the stars was made from strips of 11¼-inch, 12½-inch, and 13¾-inch paper. Each strip was folded into fifths, and glued to the others at the folds.

Take three or more strips of quilling paper, 1-ply bristol board, or other paper, and cut so that each strip is slightly longer than the next. Fold the strips in thirds, fourths, or fifths, and glue together at each fold. Bring the ends together with the points on the outside to produce a starlike shape, or join the ends with the points on the inside for a curved flowerlike shape.

If the strips are divided into thirds and joined so that the points are on the inside, the figure will look like this.

Three-dimensional hearts are often found on the Danish Christmas tree. These examples, done in the Danish style, are cut from sheets of glazed and polka-dotted wrapping paper joined back to back with spray adhesive.

Cut four or more heart-shaped pattern pieces, crease each down the center, and glue together at the crease. Complete half the ornament at a time, then insert leaves and a string for hanging when joining the two halves.

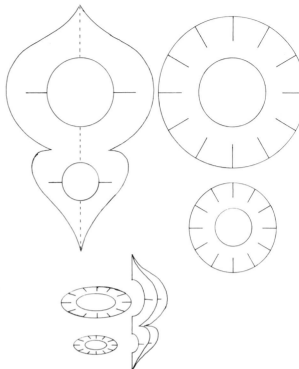

Hanging ornaments of folded two-ply bristol board. The folded sections are inserted into notched rings, which hold them in place without glue.

Cut and notch six teardrop shapes and two circles as indicated. Fold each teardrop shape in half and insert into the notches on the upper and lower circles, continuing until all six segments are in place. The sizes and shapes of the ornaments can be changed provided that the inner and outer diameters of the circles are made equal to the inner and outer diameters of the pattern piece at the point where the two are to be joined.

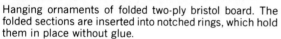

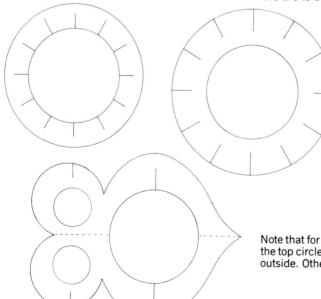

Note that for this ornament *(lower left in photograph)* the top circle is notched on the inside rather than the outside. Otherwise, construction is the same.

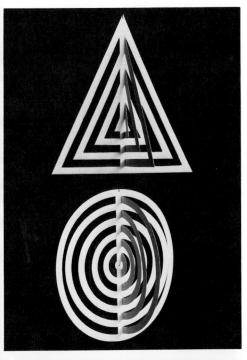

Only cutting and folding are needed to turn flat triangles and circles into three-dimensional shapes.

Cut on the solid lines and fold on the dotted lines, bringing every other strip on the right side forward, and folding the equivalent strip on the left side to the back.

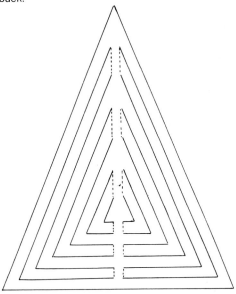

Three ornaments of two-tone tissue paper. The ornaments are incised as for the previous circle and triangle, but they are folded and glued in a different manner.

Cut along the solid lines, then lay the figure flat on the table. Pick up the two corners marked A between the thumb and forefingers of the right and left hand, roll toward the center so that the top of the paper faces down, overlap, and glue. Bring alternate strips to the front and glue in the same way, then reverse and bring the remaining strips to the back.

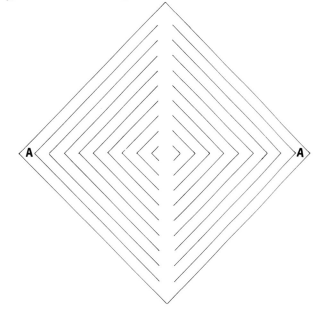

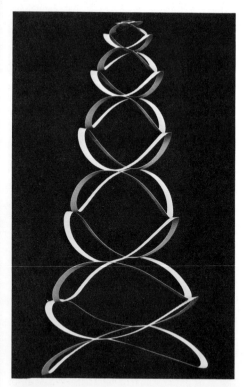

An expanded circle, hung from the center, falls with grace and symmetry. Two-tone paper particularly suits this design. Note how easy it is to give volume to a flat piece of paper.

Cut on all the solid lines, then lift from the center.

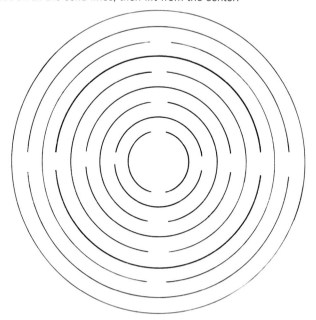

Porcupine ball. An ornament of Polish origin. Circles of white tissue paper are divided into segments, and each segment rolled into a cone. The pieces are then tied so that they open out into a ball.

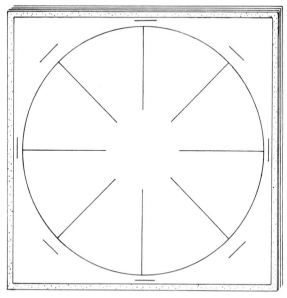

Make a paper pattern consisting of a circle divided into eighths, with the eight incisions reaching about two-thirds of the way toward the center. Staple the pattern to a stack of tissue or other thin paper, and cut out a number of identical forms.

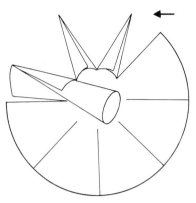

Wrap each segment around a paper cone or sharpened pencil, adding a dab of glue (white glue or glue stick) to secure. The number of pattern pieces required depends on the thickness of the paper and the size of the ball, and can vary from about eight to twenty. Use about twelve for a small tissue paper ball, eighteen or more for a large one.

To assemble, pass a needle and thread through the center of half of the star-shaped pieces, then thread on a small cardboard circle, and finish with the remaining star shapes. Bring both ends of the thread together and tie tightly (the cardboard circle will prevent overtightening). The points will spread naturally into a ball.

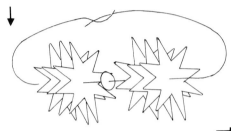

Foil porcupine balls. The upper ball (consisting of eight 2-inch-diameter circles) is of metal tooling foil; the lower ball (requiring eleven 3-inch diameter circles) is of heavy-duty aluminum foil. The points are wound tightly around a sharpened pencil; they retain their shape without glue.

When using foil, cut the pattern pieces individually rather than in a stack. Tooling foil (see Chapter 9) is not flexible enough to gather into a ball when tied with thread, so fasten with wire. Thread the star-shaped pieces onto a piece of wire bent into a U, then pull up on the ends of the wire and twist to secure the ball.

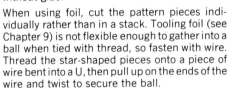

Cone balls in graduated sizes. A different set of colors is used for each of the tissue paper balls.

Fold circles of thin paper into quarters, and make curved cuts partway in from each side. Open and cut along the creases as indicated, then wrap each segment around a paper cone and glue. String about twenty of these pieces together and tie as for porcupine balls.

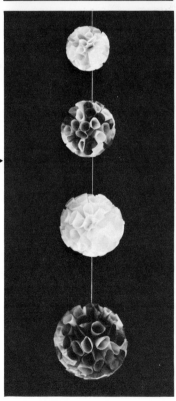

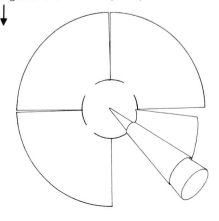

MANY INTERESTING DESIGNS CAN BE CONSTRUCTED WITH THESE AND OTHER GEOMETRIC SOLIDS AS A BASE.

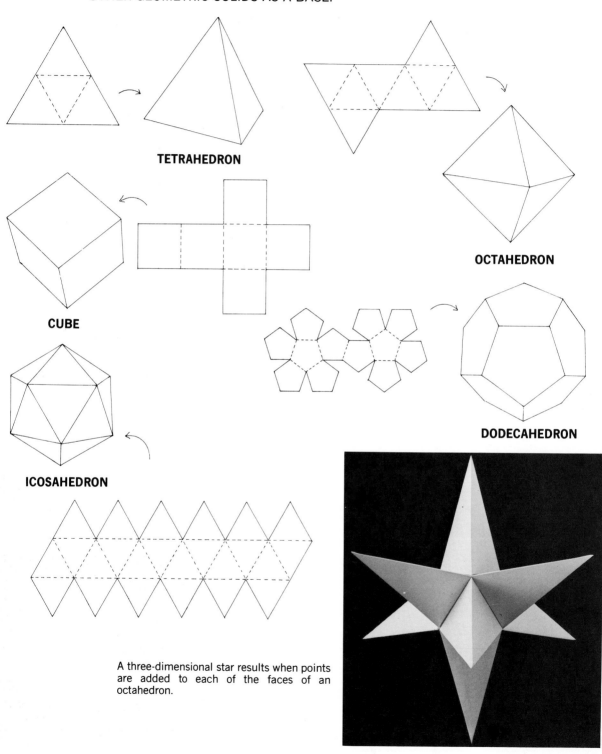

TETRAHEDRON

OCTAHEDRON

CUBE

DODECAHEDRON

ICOSAHEDRON

A three-dimensional star results when points are added to each of the faces of an octahedron.

Geometric Solids

Geometric solids not only have an interest and beauty of their own, they also provide the structure on which many more elaborate ornaments can be built. Five basic solids—tetrahedron, cube, octahedron, dodecahedron, and icosahedron—provide a good starting point, but whole books are available for those who might want to explore more complex models. Even if you limit yourself to the basic solids, you will find that great variety can be introduced by such techniques as leaving the faces open (see, for example, the geometric models of straw in Chapter 3), stellating the faces (i.e., adding a star point to each flat surface), or replacing the flat faces with assorted three-dimensional forms.

Most geometric models are best constructed of firm paper such as two-ply bristol board, but assorted lightweight colored or foil papers can be substituted if they are properly backed. (Use dry mounting tissue or spray cement to attach the lightweight paper to a backing paper.) Always measure, score, and fold carefully, since the appearance of many geometric models is dependent on the parts fitting together with precision.

If the models are made on a large enough scale, they can serve as lamps or lighted decorations. Since the details of construction may show when the shape is lit, neatness is of primary concern. Fire is always a threat when heat is generated, so choose the lowest watt bulb which still produces the desired effect, and make sure that it does not directly touch any of the paper surfaces.

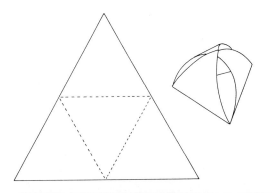

CONSTRUCTIONS BASED ON A TRIANGLE

Draw an equilateral triangle, mark the midpoint of each side, and connect these points to inscribe a second triangle inside the first. Score and fold upward on the dotted lines, and curl the three corners from the dotted line to the tip by drawing over a knife blade. Glue the three tips together in the center.

Combine the units (glue along the bottom edges) to produce an assortment of decorative shapes. The base for each ornament is (left to right): triangle (two units), tetrahedron (four), triangular dipyramid (six), octahedron (eight), and icosahedron (twenty). Using two-tone paper will make particularly attractive ornaments.

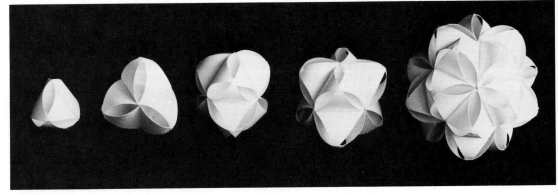

PYRAMIDS FROM CIRCLES

Inscribe a square in a circle as indicated and score along the dotted and dash lines. Fold away from you on the dash lines, towards you on the dotted lines. Trim the shaded area, and cut along one side of the flap to center, then glue the flap under the adjacent triangle to make a pyramid.

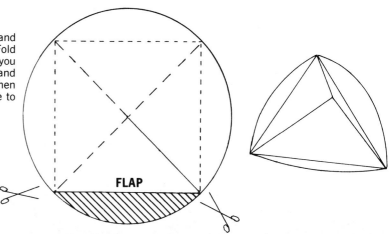

Combine the pyramids with the curved flaps to the outside, or push the flaps to the underside as in the ornament at far left. These decorations are made from metallic gold paper backed with thin card.

Both these decorations are based on an icosahedron, and both are made from the same size unit, but the pyramids are turned outward on the left-hand ornament and inward on the right. Single-ply bristol board.

MORAVIAN STAR

The Moravian Star originated in Germany around 1850, and spread to Moravian communities around the world. Also known as the Advent Star, it is traditionally hung the first Sunday in Advent. The geometric solid on which the star is based is known by the tongue-twister name of rhombicuboctahedron.

The star is composed of eighteen four-sided and eight triangular units. Paper cones are glued to cardboard bases, and the bases joined with paper fasteners.

UNCREASED CONES WITH CARDBOARD SUPPORTS

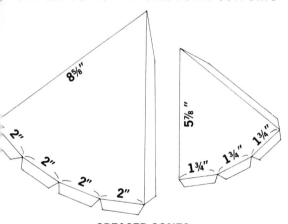

Make uncreased paper cones (shelf paper or typing paper is good) to fit the inside dimensions of the cardboard supports. In the example shown, the square cones are 8⅝ inches in length, the triangular cones 5⅞ inches. Allow extra for tabs at the bottom. If the cardboard supports are not used, construct *creased* cones of firmer paper (drawing paper or single-ply bristol board), making the base of the three-sided cones equal to that of the four-sided cones. Join the points by gluing the bottom tabs together on the inside of the figure.

CREASED CONES

Place the cones in the arrangement indicated. If cardboard frames are used, lay the frames on top of one another in the same direction and attach with paper fasteners. Draw the grid into a circle, joining X and X', then join the triangles to the adjacent squares so that the star assumes a closed shape. Attach square cones to the top and bottom openings, or leave one of the squares open and insert a low-wattage electric light bulb.

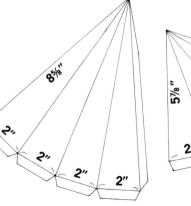

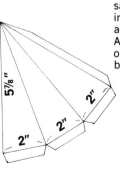

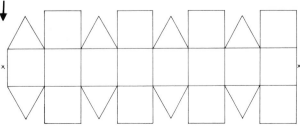

Lighted Danish Star. Ingenious design allows the three-dimensional star to fold flat for storage.

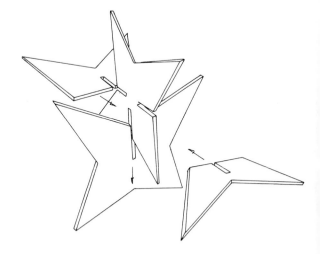

Hanging ornaments of Upson display board. *Courtesy of The Upson Company.*

Construction of a three-dimensional star. *Courtesy of The Upson Company.*

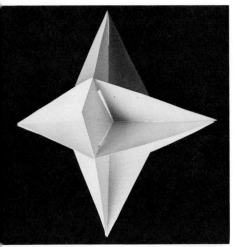

Three-dimensional star from two-ply bristol board.

Cut four diamonds and notch as indicated. Fit diamond 1 inside 2, keeping both shapes upright, and adjusting so that they are at right angles. Lay diamond 3 horizontally on top and bring the X in the center down over the points of diamonds 1 and 2. Slide the two segments of diamond 4 over the points of diamond 3, and the figure will be complete. Use spots of glue at strategic points to stabilize the shape.

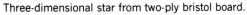
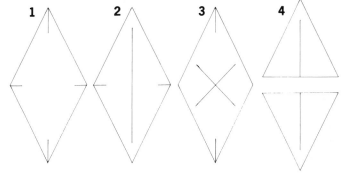

Hollow sphere results when four circles are combined.

Cut and notch the circles as indicated. Fit 2 inside 1, then fit 3 inside 1 and 2. Finally, adjust 4 inside the shape formed by 1, 2, and 3.

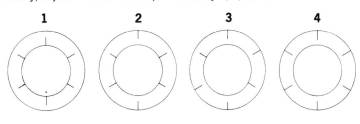

Hollow star. Four 6-pointed flat stars are joined to make the three-dimensional shape.

Cut and notch as indicated, then assemble as for the hollow spheres (2 inside 1, 3 inside and 2, 4 inside 1,2, and 3).

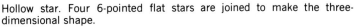
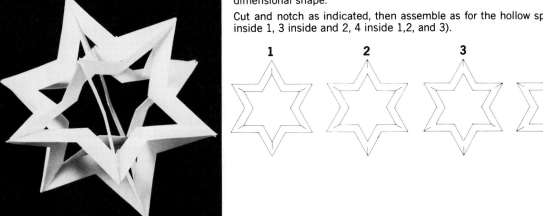

Weaving

Strips of paper can be woven into a number of flat and three-dimensional designs. One particularly interesting ornament is the red and white heart so often seen on Danish Christmas trees—if woven correctly, the heart opens into a miniature basket to hold candies or other treats. More complex is the Scandinavian star, which combines folding and curling with over-and-under weaving to produce a beautiful three-dimensional ornament. Inspiration for other woven paper projects can come from baskets, woven straw ornaments, and the assortment of plaits used in weaving palm fronds and other natural materials.

Woven Valentine. American, handmade. 1850–1880. *Courtesy of Hallmark Cards, Inc.*

Danish Christmas hearts, woven from red and white glazed paper, open into miniature baskets.

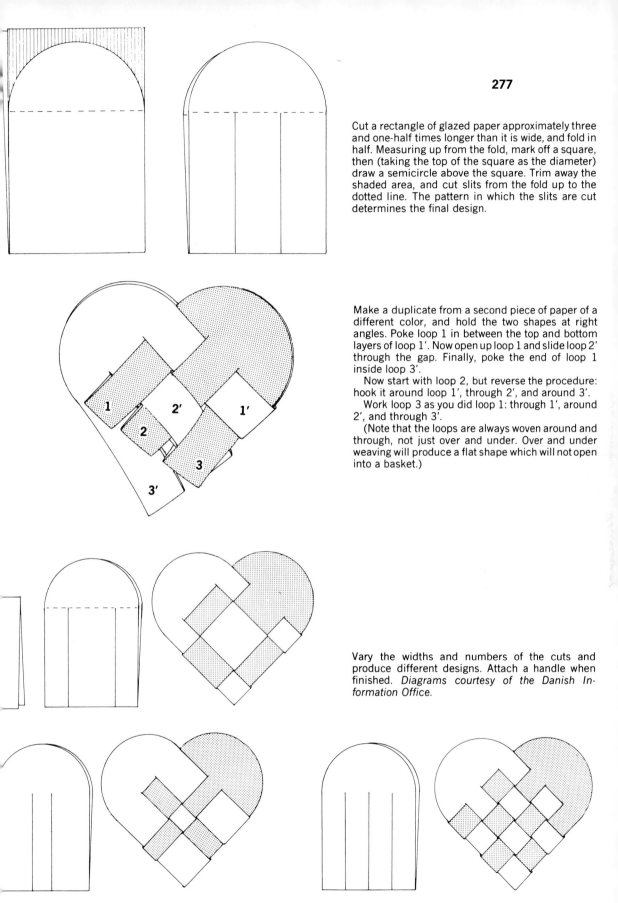

Cut a rectangle of glazed paper approximately three and one-half times longer than it is wide, and fold in half. Measuring up from the fold, mark off a square, then (taking the top of the square as the diameter) draw a semicircle above the square. Trim away the shaded area, and cut slits from the fold up to the dotted line. The pattern in which the slits are cut determines the final design.

Make a duplicate from a second piece of paper of a different color, and hold the two shapes at right angles. Poke loop 1 in between the top and bottom layers of loop 1'. Now open up loop 1 and slide loop 2' through the gap. Finally, poke the end of loop 1 inside loop 3'.

Now start with loop 2, but reverse the procedure: hook it around loop 1', through 2', and around 3'.

Work loop 3 as you did loop 1: through 1', around 2', and through 3'.

(Note that the loops are always woven around and through, not just over and under. Over and under weaving will produce a flat shape which will not open into a basket.)

Vary the widths and numbers of the cuts and produce different designs. Attach a handle when finished. *Diagrams courtesy of the Danish Information Office.*

Scandinavian woven paper star.

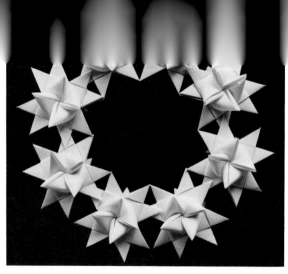

Wreath of woven stars glued at the points.

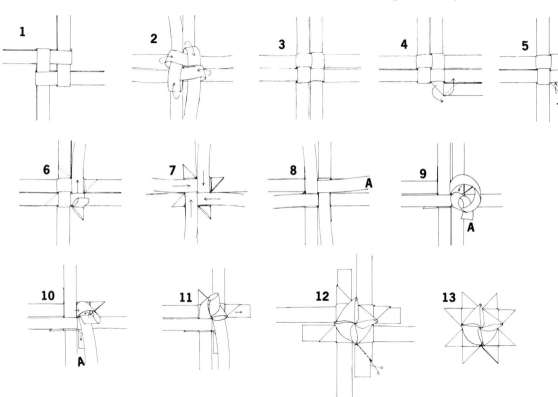

Choose a medium-weight paper (such as single-ply bristol board) and cut four long strips. Weave the strips as follows:

1) Fold the four long strips in half; interlock in a basket weave.

2) Lift the four top strips and bring back toward the center, interlocking in a second basket weave.

3) Pull tight.

4) Make a point by folding the lower right-hand strip backward and to the right, then upward and toward the front.

5) Fold the point in half from right to left, then slip the end of the strip under the lower right-hand loop of the basket-weave square.

6) Pull tight. Repeat with the three remaining right-hand strips so that all are formed into points.

7) Lift all four of the top strings up toward the center and fold down in the opposite direction.

8) The figure will look like this. To start weaving the center points, grasp the end of strip A in the right hand.

9) Loop strip A as diagrammed, inserting the end of the strip (backside up) into the gap indicated by the arrow. Push the strip through the gap until the bottom comes out through the lower right-hand point.

10) Pull gently on strip A with the right hand, at the same time holding the left thumb at the arrow to help guide the curl.

11) Continue pulling until a sharp standing point is formed. Repeat with the three remaining top strips.

12) The top side of the figure is now finished. Trim off the four strips where they extend beyond the points. Reverse the figure, and repeat steps 4 through 12 on the back side.

13) The completed star.

Pleated Paper

Pleating adds strength and dimension to flat paper. To make accordion pleats quickly and neatly, start by measuring and creasing two pieces of graph or construction-weight paper in the appropriate intervals. Place the paper to be pleated in between the creased pattern papers, and refold all the layers at once. It is a good idea to crease several sets of pattern papers in different intervals and keep them on hand, since they can be reused indefinitely.

Heavier papers and thin card should generally be scored before pleating. To mark lines for scoring, lay a ruler or piece of graph paper along the upper edge of the paper to be scored, and use a pencil (or compass point) to make dots (or poke small holes) at the desired intervals. Repeat along the bottom of the paper, then connect the upper and lower markings with a score line made by drawing a stylus or stencil knife down along the length of a metal-edged ruler.

Dove with pleated wings. The body is of two-ply bristol board.

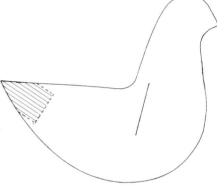

To pleat paper quickly and neatly, use two sheets of stiff paper, measured and creased into pleats of the appropriate size. (Or use graph paper, which can be folded along the lines without measuring.) Place the paper to be pleated between the two pattern layers, and refold all the layers together.

Insert the pleated wings through the slit in the body, and glue the pleated tail at the end.

The peacock is constructed like the dove, but the wings and tail are inserted in horizontal slits in the body and the edges glued together at the top so that the pleated paper opens out in an arc.

Pleated snowflakes. Staple a strip of pleated paper across the center, and cut incisions in the pleats along either side. Open the pleats out and glue the edges to make a full circle.

Below, left: Stars from pleated typing paper.

Below: Pleat the typing paper, staple in the center, and cut away the shaded areas. Open out the pleats and glue the edges to make a circle.

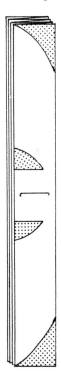

Paper star from Germany. A beautiful example of pleating and folding.

Copy the diagram onto a piece of paper, then lay the pattern onto firm paper (such as library notecards or two-ply bristol board). Using a pin or the sharp tip of a compass, poke holes through the pattern at all the dots and all the points marked X and X'.

Remove the pattern, and score along the lines connecting X to X' (indicated by dashes). Cut around the outside of the pattern, and crease all score lines away from you.

With scissors, cut from points X and X' to the dots, removing the shaded areas. The points will be sturdier if the tips are left blunt rather than sharply pointed.

Accordion-pleat the figure, using the creases already scored from point to point, but adding folds in the opposite directions from dot to dot. Turn the shape over.

Score diagonal lines from dot to dot (indicated by the dotted lines), and crease these lines firmly away from you. Draw the tab around and glue in place at the spot marked TAB. The result will be a circle, with the diagonal lines toward the center and all points radiating outward.

Cut the center strip exactly as indicated, then curl slightly by drawing over a knife. Accordion-pleat, then glue the pleats together at the base. When the glue is dry, open out the folds into a flower shape, and press into place in the center of the star, rounding out each pleat so that they will all fit.

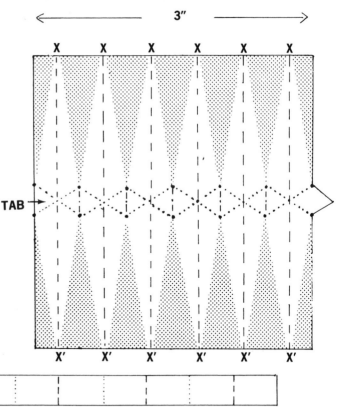

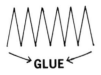

GLUE

Pyramid-fold stars from gold wrapping paper. A long strip of paper is pleated and folded, and the ends brought together to make a star.

Pyramid-fold stars in white bristol board. Rounded openings are made between each point by inserting a pencil in the gap. The star at left has been turned to show the back side.

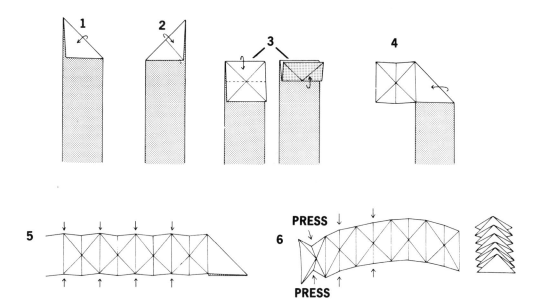

Pyramid-fold stars:
1) Starting with a long strip of paper, fold the top down to the left as indicated. Open.
2) Fold the top down and to the right. Open.
3) Fold the top down to make a square, then fold the end of the strip up to meet the fold. Open.
4) Using the crease that marks the square as the starting point, repeat steps 1 to 3 until a second square is folded.
5) Continue until a number of squares have been creased. Now reverse the crease lines that separate each square, folding the paper toward rather than away from you.
6) By pressing in at the points indicated, the square will automatically shape itself into a pyramid. Fold the whole strip in the same way.
   To make a star, fold a long strip pyramid-style, creasing one more pyramid than the number of points desired. Draw the strip into a circle, overlap the ends, and glue at the center. Hold the shape in place with pins until the glue dries.

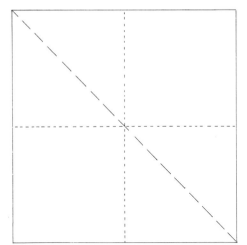

STARS FROM A FOLDED SQUARE

To make a star point from a square piece of paper, crease along the lines shown. First fold the paper away from you along the diagonal, then open. Crease the paper toward you along the horizontal and vertical lines, opening after each fold. Bring all four corners up and in toward the center and crease.

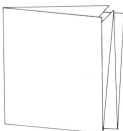

Glue the flat faces of the folded squares together to form a star.

Bright stars of two-tone paper (made by joining squares of origami paper back to back with spray cement). Press down on the center of the stars, and you will get shapes like the two stars at right.

Garlands and Honeycomb Decorations

Garlands and honeycombs are expanded paper decorations that rely for their effect on a special method of gluing. Paper is stacked, glued at alternate points on each layer, and cut to shape. If the adhesive is applied in parallel lines, the figure will open into a honeycomb; other gluing patterns will produce instead a long chain or garland.

In making either garlands or honeycomb designs, the proper adhesive is important. Ordinary white glue is suitable if it is applied very sparingly and not allowed to penetrate more than one layer. Clear household cement is good for thin paper such as tissue, though even this fast-drying adhesive can seep through more than one layer if too much is applied or if a particularly liquid brand is chosen. (Some brands are excessively runny when fresh, but will become stiffer if the tube is allowed to age.) A glue stick is effective for honeycomb ornaments, since it does not penetrate even the thinnest paper, but it is hard to apply in a thin line unless one of the illustrated techniques is used. Staples may be substituted for glue in some cases, especially if the garland or honeycomb decoration is being made from firm paper.

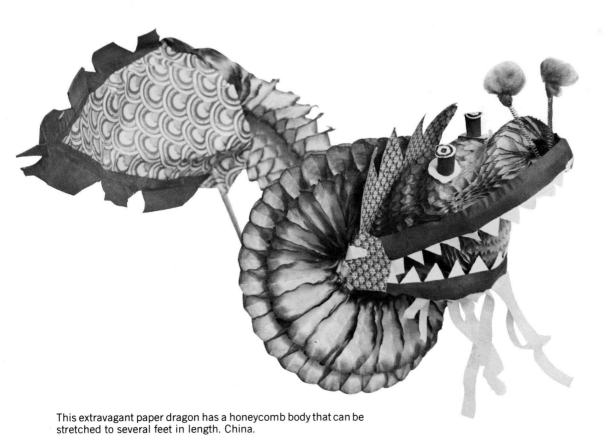

This extravagant paper dragon has a honeycomb body that can be stretched to several feet in length. China.

Ingenious honeycomb toys from China. The designs change shape depending on the way the ornament is opened.

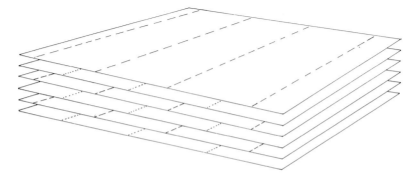

Diagram showing how alternate layers of paper are glued to create a honeycomb effect. The closer together the glue lines are, the smaller will be the cells in the opened honeycomb, and the more layers of paper will be required to create a full circle.

Accordion-pleat the paper to establish easily visible lines for gluing. Place a sheet of measured and scored paper on a stack of tissue paper, then fold up all the layers together. Glue one sheet at a time, even layers along the even-numbered folds, odd layers along the odd-numbered folds.

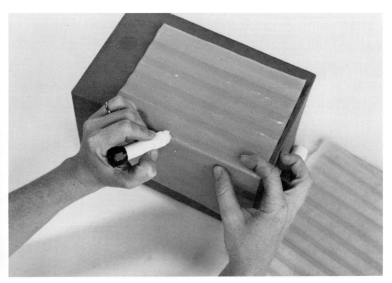

One way to apply a fine line of adhesive using a glue stick is to place the fold being glued over the edge of a box.

Another method is to hold a card under the fold being glued. Clear household cement can also be used instead of a glue stick, but do not apply too much or it may seep through more than one layer.

Cutting paper flowers from a stack of honeycomb tissue. Reinforce front and back with cardboard, then glue along the center seam and secure with paper tabs.

The opened honeycomb flowers. These were cut from a stack of forty layers.

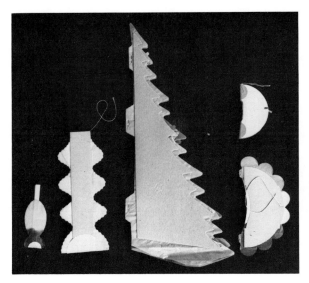

Assorted methods for backing honeycomb ornaments.

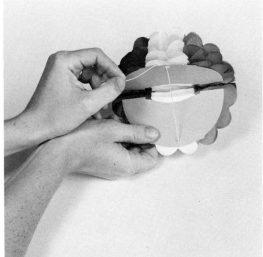

An ingenious method for hanging a honeycomb ball. The string is hooked onto the cardboard backing on one side, then through a hole in the backing on the other side. When hung, the ornament will be kept open by its own weight.

Honeycomb ball, 8-inch diameter, from Denmark. Note that the glue lines are fairly far apart and the cells rather large, meaning that fewer layers are required for a fully opened ornament.

Christmas tree. The glue lines are closer together than in the preceding ball, therefore many more layers are required.

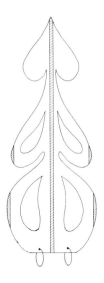

Fold-open star. 11-inch diameter. The ornament folds closed for storage.

Cut twenty-six pattern pieces from typing-weight paper. Stack the pieces, gluing the first to the second at the edges where indicated, then glue the second to the third piece along the center. Continue stacking and gluing, alternating between the edges and center. When all the pieces are assembled, run two wires shaped into rings through the center bottom of the stack and reinforce the top and bottom pattern pieces with a narrow strip of cardboard. The rings and the cardboard provide stability when the design is opened.

GARLANDS FROM CREASED SQUARES

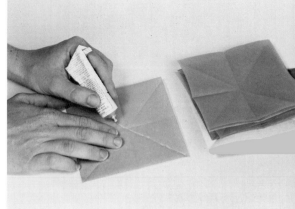

Many kinds of garlands can be made from the basic shape produced by this method. Start by creasing tissue squares to mark the glue lines. Fold a stack of squares in half horizontally and vertically, then make creases along both diagonals.

Starting with a single square of tissue, apply clear household cement along the diagonal creases forming an X.

Immediately put a second square of tissue on the first and press in place.

On the second square of tissue apply glue in a "plus" pattern along the horizontal and vertical lines. Continue building up layers, gluing alternately in an X and a "plus" pattern. Stop when twelve to eighteen sheets have been glued.

A number of different shapes can be cut from the stack of glued squares. Start a cut by folding the stack in half and making an incision with the scissors, then open and continue cutting the design. Glue and cut several stacks of paper (each twelve to eighteen layers), then join the stacks to make a long chain.

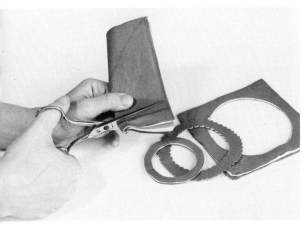

Three different styles, all cut from the same stack of squares.

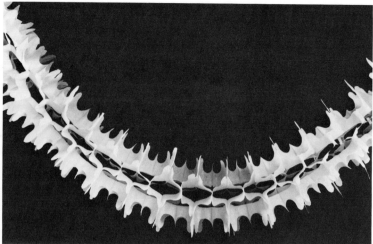

Changing the way the outside of the square is cut produces still another style of garland.

Diagram for the preceding garland. Other designs could also be cut from the inner circle.

LARGE SQUARE GARLAND

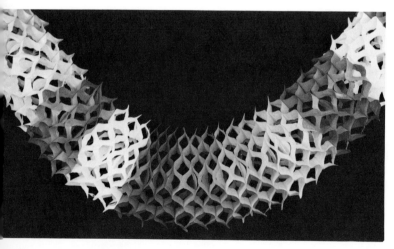

Square tissue paper garland in six colors.

More intricate than the previous garlands, this chain is glued at eight points on every layer. (X's mark the even layers, O's mark the odd layers.)

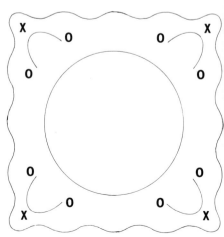

EXPANDING CIRCLE GARLAND

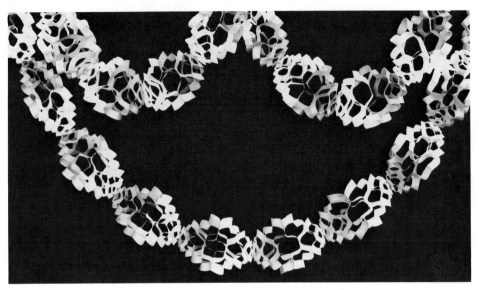

A garland from expanding circles. Two sheets of tissue paper will make a chain many feet in length.

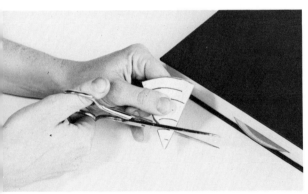

Fold several sheets of tissue paper into eighths and make cuts in from the fold along either side. Open the circles, and press in a book (or iron) to flatten.

Pattern for cutting circles folded into eighths. The shaded areas indicate the points where glue will be applied.

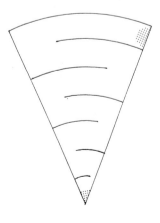

Glue the first two circles together at four points along the outer edge (see diagram), then glue the next circle at the center only. Continue adding circles, gluing alternately at the edges and the center, until a chain of the desired length is formed.

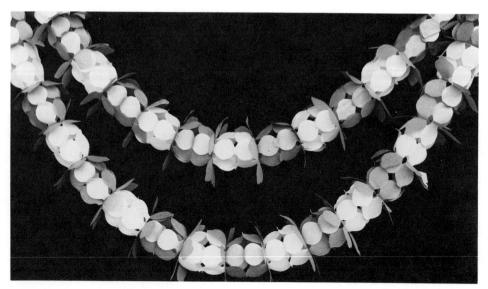

Leaf and petal garland. The pink flowers and green leaves are cut from the same pattern.

Pattern for a leaf and petal garland. Glue all flower petals together at the tips and insert a leaf, glued at the center only, between each flower.

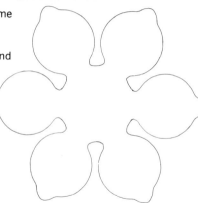

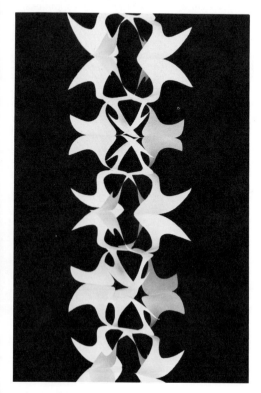

Whirling circle garland. This is best made in typing-weight paper; staples are more convenient than glue.

For a whirling circle garland, glue or staple the first circle to the second circle at the four points marked A. Attach the second to the third circle at the four points marked B. Continue adding circles, fastening alternately at A or B.

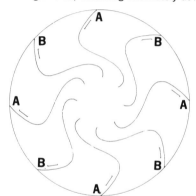

Cross center garland. Two sheets of tissue paper will produce a garland seven feet long. Variations are produced by changing the shape of the petals.

Pattern for cross center garland. Cut along the solid lines. Join the pattern pieces in pairs, gluing (white glue or clear cement) at the four points marked X. Then glue the pairs together at the center.
   Place a small circle of cardboard under the top and bottom crosses, and staple a loop of thread in place, as indicated, in order to have a convenient method of opening and closing the chain.

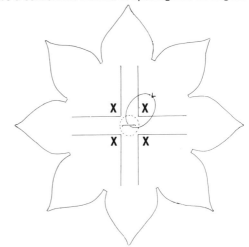

Four-finger garland. Denmark. Each of the fingers is dipped in a different color dye, to produce a four-colored chain.

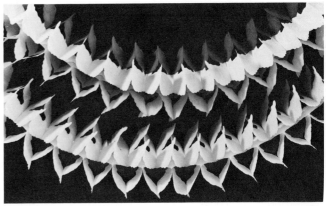

Pattern for four-finger garland. Glue layer one to layer two at the three areas marked A, then glue layer two to layer three at the points marked B. Continue adding layers, gluing alternately at A and B, until the chain is of the desired length.

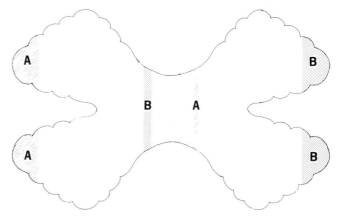

Paper Flowers

Paper flowers are colorful, cheerful, and make excellent table or room decorations for parties or other special occasions. For the most dramatic impact, use bright colors and choose simple shapes so that a large quantity can be made easily. Don't try to imitate nature; concentrate instead on color, form, and texture to produce fantasy flowers that are a frank exaggeration of the real thing.

The examples shown here have been chosen because they are among the easiest and most decorative of the paper flowers, and because they illustrate certain streamlined methods which can be employed. (Using staples instead of spool wire to secure the base of a flower, for instance, will greatly speed the flower-making operation.) If you become familiar with these techniques, they may prove helpful when it comes to creating your own designs.

Fold-open flowers. Large and showy, these flowers are perfect as party decorations. Since they fold flat, they can be transported easily.

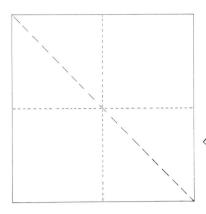

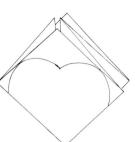

Stack five or six squares of tissue paper, and crease as diagrammed. Crease the paper away from you on the diagonal, then open. Crease the paper toward you on the horizontal and vertical lines, opening after each fold.

Bring the corners in toward the center to form a square. Press flat.

Fold the square in half and cut the top in a semicircle (or vary by cutting the edge in a fringe, using pinking scissors, etc.). Make a crook in the end of a length of floral wire, and staple to the base of the flower. This will keep the wire from pulling out.

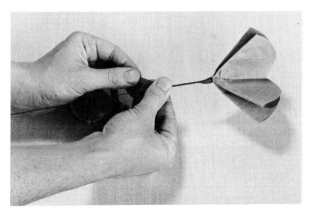

Wrap the base of the flower with floral tape, and continue down the stem. If green wire is used, it is not necessary to wrap the stem completely.

Fold back all the tissue layers, then fluff out the flower by pulling the layers, one by one, up toward the center. To store the roses, refold so that they lie flat.

Yardstick roses. The crepe paper effect comes from gathering tissue paper over a ruler.

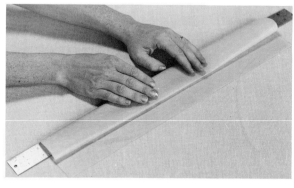

Lay a yardstick or ruler along the long side of a 10-by-20-inch piece of tissue paper (the size can be varied). Fold down ruler and paper, wrapping the ruler *very loosely*, and leaving an inch or two unwrapped at the bottom.

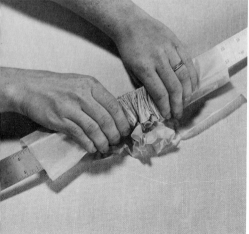

←—— Using both hands, push the tissue paper in toward the center. When the whole length is crushed, slide out the ruler.

Hold the strip so that the "tail" or margin is on the outside, and wind up the flower from one end. Wind tightly at first, more loosely toward the end. Staple a length of floral wire to the base of the flower, then wrap the stem with floral tape.

Roll-up roses. Take a long strip of tissue paper and fold in half lengthwise *without* creasing. Make a crook in the end of a length of floral wire and staple to one end of the folded strip. Roll up the rose, winding tightly at first, loosely toward the end. Gather at the base, staple to secure, and wind with floral tape.

Paper Cutting

The technique of cutting shapes out of paper to produce a meaningful design has been practiced for many years. The tradition is oldest in China, where paper was invented and first widely used. One of the earliest surviving Chinese examples, a cutout of a shrine with monkeys, unicorns, and phoenixes, dates back over a thousand years.

As the use of paper spread to Europe, so too did the interest in paper cutting as a decorative art. As early as the seventeenth century, elaborate scenes featuring people and animals were being cut in Germany and Switzerland. By the 1800s, Swiss paper cuts were common on birth certificates, love tokens, and New Year's greeting. In the nineteenth century, when paper became commonly available in the rural areas of Poland, peasants began using their sheep-shearing scissors to cut designs for decorating the walls and ceiling beams of their farmhouses. By embellishing the typical monochrome designs with bits of brightly colored paper, they developed a new tradition of cutting, one that is carried on in the multicolored designs popular in Poland today.

Mexican cut tissue paper: birds, flowers, and a greeting.

Methods of Paper Cutting

In most types of paper cutting, more than one layer is cut at a time. The Chinese approach is to make duplicate copies of a single design by stacking and cutting a number of layers together. Though scissors can be used, one traditional technique is to lay the papers on a slab of wax and cut through all the layers with a knife. The wax provides an excellent cutting surface, keeps the papers from slipping, and can be remelted whenever the surface becomes excessively marred with cuts.

An alternative method for keeping layers of paper from slipping when making duplicate copies of a single design is to use staples around the edge of the area to be cut out. When cutting thin paper such as tissue, it is also helpful to sandwich the layers between pieces of typing-weight paper for added stability.

Folding a piece of paper before cutting is a technique popular in many paper-cutting traditions. The simplest approach is to fold the paper in half; the result will be a symmetrical pattern repeated on either side of the central axis. If the paper is thin enough, it can be folded into smaller segments, anywhere from quarters to sixteenths or even twentieths. Four-, eight-, and sixteen-part designs can easily be folded without measuring, but designs in multiples of three or five may require the use of a paper scale to aid accurate dividing. If it is necessary to secure the folded layers while cutting, staple around the perimeter of the design and through those areas to be cut out.

When a multifold design is cut and unfolded, it will need flattening. Use an iron set at low heat, or press between the pages of a book.

To cut duplicate copies, staple together a stack of paper with the design on top. The more staples that are used the less chance of the paper slipping.

Cut through all the layers at once, using nail scissors for curves and intricate cuts. About a dozen sheets of tissue can be cut at one time; fewer of heavier paper.

Chinese paper cuts are generally cut in layers, so that a number of identical shapes are produced at once. Scissors may be used, or the papers may be pinned to a sheet of hardened wax and cut with a sharp knife.

Intricate Chinese paper cuttings are tinted in delicate pastel hues. Many of the images symbolize fortune and good wishes.

Mexican tissue paper cutting depicting the Crucifixion. Although the design is not perfectly symmetrical, much of the pattern was cut with the paper folded in half.

Hans Christian Andersen, the famous story-teller, was also known for his paper cuttings. This particular design was created in homage to Andersen's friend and, in later years, his nurse. *Courtesy of the Danish Information Office.*

It is easy to fold a square of paper in two, four, or eight parts, but more difficult to make a five- or six-part fold. Cut a scale out of stiff paper or card and use as illustrated to mark the folding line. The 120° angle is for dividing a figure into three, six, or twelve parts; the 108° angle for five, ten, and twenty parts.

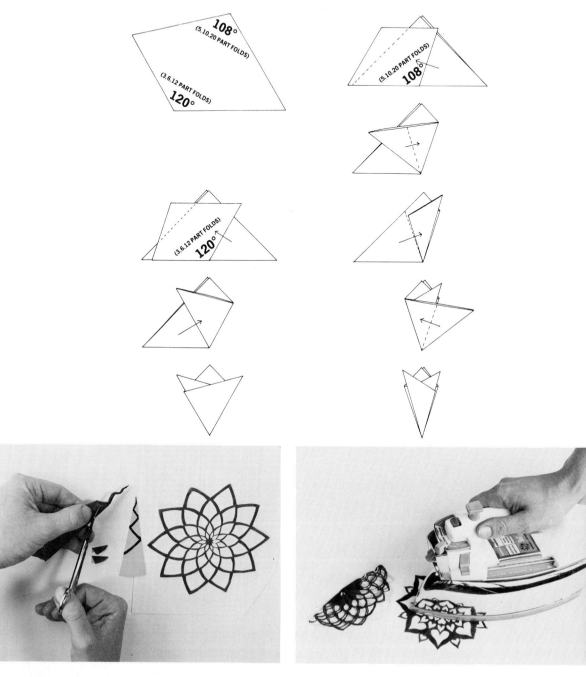

Fold a piece of tissue or other thin paper into fifths using the cardboard scale, then crease again to make a ten-part fold (actually twenty-part, since the paper is folded in half to begin with). Cut in from the folded edges to produce a design.

To flatten the unfolded paper, press with a warm iron or store between the pages of a book.

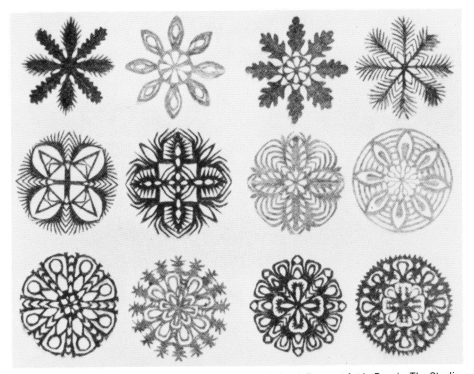

Early twentieth-century cut paper designs from Siedlce, Poland. *Peasant Art in Russia,* The Studio Ltd., 1912.

In Küssnacht am Rigi in central Switzerland, a parade of *Klausjagen,* or Saint Nicholas figures, takes place on December 6. Impressive candle-lit headdresses, fashioned from intricately cut paper, are worn by the marchers. *Courtesy of the Swiss National Tourist Office.*

A detail from one of the headdresses (known at *Iffelträger*) shows the intricate cutting involved. *Courtesy of the Swiss National Tourist Office.*

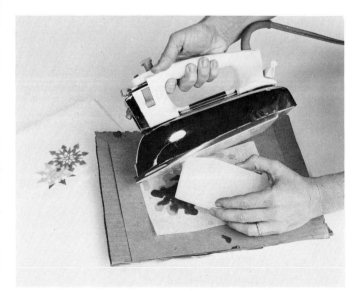

WAX MEDALLIONS

Thin paper cuts can be embedded between layers of tissue paper to produce wax medallions. Place a piece of white or colored tissue paper on a flat piece of cardboard, and melt some paraffin onto the tissue. (The wax will not hurt the iron.) Add a paper cutout, then another piece of plain tissue, and melt on more wax. Continue building up layers until at least two cutouts and three plain sheets of paper are incorporated in the sandwich.

An alternative method is to sprinkle grated wax between each layer, and wait until the final step to melt the wax.

Fuse all layers by pressing with a warm iron. While the wax is still flexible, peel the layers from the cardboard and place on a smooth surface to harden. Then trim, and pierce with a needle and thread for hanging.

Hang wax medallions so that the light comes from behind to illuminate the translucent disks.

Brightly colored glazed paper is most commonly used for Polish paper cuts. Note how the design is built up with colorful overlays.

An elaborate cutting from the Lowicz region of Poland. Symmetrical designs based on a single fold are typical of Polish paper cutting, though multifold designs are also encountered.

A radial-fold design. The pattern is cut from a single sheet of paper folded into sixteenths, then the opened design is embellished with colorful cutouts.

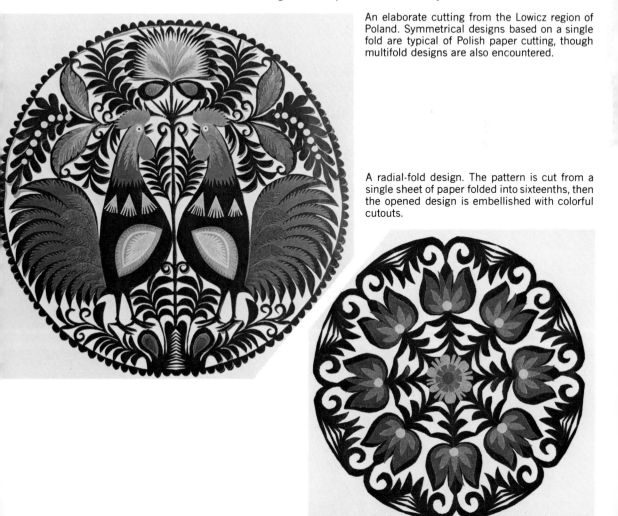

Three ornaments of embossed and colored tin. Mexico

Metal and Glass

Metal Tooling

Mexican folk artists of the Oaxaca region are known for the variety of ornaments, sconces, boxes, and wall decorations they create from brilliantly colored embossed tin. Although tin (actually tinplate—rolled steel with a thin coating of tin) is sturdy and shiny, it is difficult to work without special tools, and it rusts fairly easily. Much easier to work are the tooling foils and sheet metals of copper, aluminum, and brass sold by craft suppliers and some hardware stores. These metals can be cut with scissors and embossed with a variety of easily available implements.

Metals are measured in thicknesses, or gauges: the higher the gauge, the thinner the metal. Copper and brass are commonly sold in 12-inch-wide 36-gauge rolls. Aluminum, which is considerably less expensive than either copper or brass, is sold in 36- (.005-inch) and 38-gauge (.004-inch) rolls in both natural (silver) and colors (gold, copper, red, blue, green); thicker gauges can be purchased in the form of aluminum flashing at hardware stores. For small ornaments, aluminum cut from the unembossed portions of TV dinner trays and foil baking pans substitutes nicely for 36- or 38-gauge foil.

Base metal is another product that can be used for tooling. Available in 25-inch-wide rolls in silver, gold, and colors, it is somewhat stiffer than the tooling foils. Base metal is especially good for three-dimensional ornaments that combine bent lines and flat or embossed planes (such as the raised stars illustrated).

Embossing

Work on a surface which is firm but has a little give: a stack of newspaper, a sheet of heavy cardboard, a hard rubber mat, or a piece of thick felt. Lay a design on top of the metal, and go over the major outlines with a pencil, ball point pen, metal stylus, pointed clay-modeling tool, or the sharp end of a manicure stick. Once the pattern is traced, remove the drawing and use any of the same tools to reinforce the lines.

To make raised areas in the design, turn the metal over and work on the back, using a pointed instrument for lines and a flat or rounded tool (flat end of a manicure stick, rounded modeling tool, etc.) for broader areas. Continue working the metal on front and back until the embossed and recessed areas are shaped as planned. Finally, cut out the design. (The metal is harder to work if it is cut out before embossing.

Coloring

The best materials for coloring the metal are permanent felt pens and transparent glass stains. The felt markers, available in both broad- and fine-tipped versions, are easy to apply and excellent for detail, but not quite so vivid as the glass stains, which have greater body. The stains come with their own thinner and solvent, and, like most lacquer-based paints, should be used in a well-ventilated area.

Embossed metal can be antiqued as well as colored. Liver of sulfur dissolved in water is traditionally used to oxidize copper (or brass) and turn it black. The chemical solution (from the pharmacy or craft supply house) is brushed or sponged onto the embossed surface and allowed to dry for about twenty minutes, after which the metal is rubbed with steel wool to remove some of the discoloration. The completed design must be varnished or lacquered to prevent further oxidation.

Aluminum will not respond to chemicals in the same fashion as copper and brass, but an antique effect can be achieved if the metal is coated with flat black enamel paint—either spray or brush-on—and the excess rubbed away before the paint is fully dry. India ink can be substituted for paint if the aluminum is first rubbed with steel wool so that it will not repel the ink.

Tin bird. Mexico. The wings and body are tooled separately, then soldered together.

Mexican Santa is of embossed tin colored with transparent lacquers. Such metalwork is typical of the Oaxaca region of Mexico.

Candelabrum of embossed tin. Some of the designs are punched as well as embossed.

Our Lady of Guadeloupe. Mexico. Case and stand are of embossed tin; foil flowers decorate the interior.

Base metal stars. Lines radiating from the center to the points are drawn on the back of the metal, lines between the points are drawn on the front. Careful bending along the lines turns the flat metal into a three-dimensional shape.

EMBOSSED FOIL ORNAMENTS

Place metal tooling foil on a stack of newspapers, and trace a design with a pointed instrument. Tools illustrated include pencil, round-tipped modeling tool, orange stick, and metal stylus.

Turn the design over, and mark some of the lines on the back to produce raised areas. Continue working the metal on front and back, using both pointed and rounded tools.

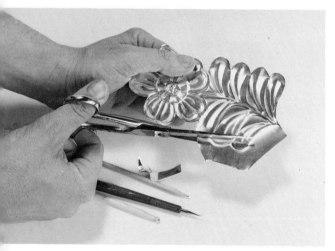

When embossing is complete, cut out the design with an old pair of household scissors.

Use either transparent glass stain or permanent felt pens to color the metal. Glass stains have the consistency of nail polish, and are somewhat more radiant than felt pens.

Christmas ornaments. Aluminum tooling foil (36-gauge) embossed and colored with glass stains and felt markers.

Ornaments of aluminum tooling foil. Note the variety of impressions that can be made with an orange stick.

Embossed stars.

Angel, 3 inches high, has a body and wings of gold base metal. The head is a small gold Christmas ball.

Pierced Metal Lanterns

With the aid of an ice pick, a hammer, and a few other simple tools, ordinary tin cans can be turned into glowing lanterns. If the proper size can is not available, sheet aluminum (aluminum flashing) can easily be substituted and the lantern fashioned in any size desired.

Metal cans are not difficult to puncture, but the surface is likely to buckle and dent if the can is not supported from the inside during the piercing operation. There are two possible solutions: to fill the cans with melted wax, and allow the wax to harden, or to fill the cans with water and freeze until solid. Since a large quantity of wax is required, and since it is rather messy to melt away the wax when the design is complete, freezing water in the cans is usually the more practical approach.

It is best to leave the top on the can for added support, so try to empty the contents without completely removing the lid. Fill the can one-half to two-thirds full of water, then place in the freezer for a day or so, adding more water when the first is frozen solid. Water expands as it freezes, and the seams of the can are likely to burst if the water is not frozen in stages. When the ice is solid, wrap the can with a piece of paper on which the design has been drawn, and lay on a folded absorbent cloth.

The design can be punched using a number of tools, including awl, ice pick, nail, or electric drill (for round holes); chisel (for thin rectangles); or wood carving tools (for crescents, chevrons, and other shapes). Often it helps to go over the design with a center punch (a spring-loaded pointed tool that will make a small dimple in the metal) before beginning the piercing operation. An electric drill will produce very uniform holes, whereas the opening made by most other tools will vary depending on how deeply the tool is punched. Use a light touch with aluminum cans; they are soft and it is easy to make the holes too big.

As work progresses, the ice will begin to melt, so it may be necessary to return the can to the freezer from time to time. The paper pattern will also begin to disintegrate, though it usually survives one punching operation, but it is a good idea to have a copy on hand if the design will have to be repeated.

When the punching is complete, take the top off the can and discard the ice. Use a votive candle in a small glass container or a regular candle secured in floral clay to light the lantern.

To punch sheet metal, lay the metal on a thick stack of newspaper, and pierce as for cans. (To use a drill, clamp the metal between two pieces of hardboard paneling and drill through all the layers at once.) As the design progresses, the metal will begin to curl upward, so plan to use the punched side as the inside of the lantern to take advantage of the natural curve. To keep the metal from warping when holes are pierced near the top and bottom edges, leave an unpunched margin of several inches, and cut off the excess only when the piercing is complete.

To finish the lantern, draw the metal into a cylinder and punch a line of holes where the ends overlap. Rivet the holes or fasten with cotter pins to secure.

Cone shaped lantern caps can be cut from sheet metal or punched on metal funnels. If using the sheet metal, make a paper pattern for the cone, allowing an excess margin at the bottom so that the lower edge does not warp in pounding. Metal funnels are best placed on their side on a scrap piece of wood and the design punched from the inside out. Cut off the top with tin snips if desired.

Attach the lantern cap (and a circular base, if necessary) with wire loops or epoxy glue. Purchased metal funnels often fit securely over a can or cylinder without wiring or gluing. Note that lanterns with closed tops will retain a good bit of heat, so place votive candles inside (ordinary candles may "wilt") and use the lights only in places where they will not constitute a fire hazard.

PIERCED LANTERNS

Fill a can with water, then place in the freezer to harden. Tape a design in place, and hammer holes along the pattern using an awl, ice pick, or nail. The deeper the tool penetrates, the larger the hole will be.

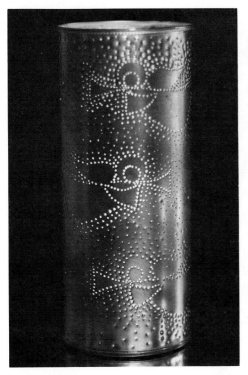

Completed lantern is lit by a candle held upright with floral clay.

Wood chisels in assorted sizes can be used to punch rectangular openings.

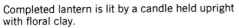

Pierced candle holders. Both tin and aluminum cans can be used, but since aluminum is softer, it requires a gentle touch.

Albert Lees, in the role of the nineteenth-century tinsmith, piercing tin panels for a lantern. *Courtesy of Old Sturbridge Village, Sturbridge, Massachusetts.*

Pierced tin "Paul Revere" lantern, common in New England in the early nineteenth century. Index of American Design. *Courtesy of the National Gallery of Art, Washington.*

To pierce sheet aluminum, lay the metal on a wooden board or a thick stack of newspapers and punch with an awl, chisel, or wood-carving tools. Leave a margin of several inches at the edges to prevent warping (the margin can be trimmed when the piercing is complete).

Covered lantern from aluminum flashing. When the piercing is finished, the base is shaped into a cylinder and the top into a cone.

Wood carving tools can be used for chevrons, scallops, and other interesting cuts. Inexpensive hobby sets are often available at hardware stores.

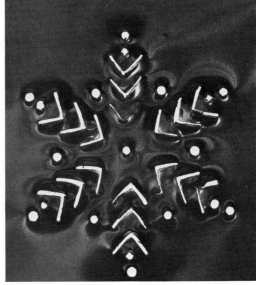

Metal Stars

If metal is cut in thin strips, it curls naturally—down from the snips if the cut is on the right, and up from the snips if the cut is on the left. This characteristic can be put to good use when making stars and other decorative shapes from aluminum flashing or tin-can lids. The flashing requires only a sturdy pair of kitchen shears for cutting, while the tin cans generally call for metal cutting snips.

Many variations on the star shape are possible, so it is worthwhile experimenting. Allow the metal to curl naturally, or direct the curl either with the fingers or (for tight coils) needle-nose pliers. Cutting the strips thinner or wider will also vary the effect. For elaborate ornaments, stack two or more curled stars and glue (using clear cement or epoxy) at the center.

Curled stars of aluminum flashing. The metal curls naturally as it is cut; no special shaping is needed.

 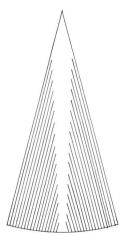

Wedge-shaped pieces of aluminum flashing become Christmas trees when cut and curled.

Christmas tree pattern. Ordinary kitchen shears will cut aluminum flashing, but metal snips should be used for tin-can lids.

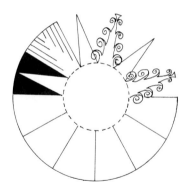  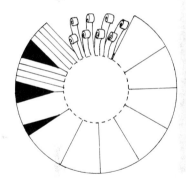

Some patterns to experiment with when making metal stars.

Ornament of cut and twisted metal. West Germany.

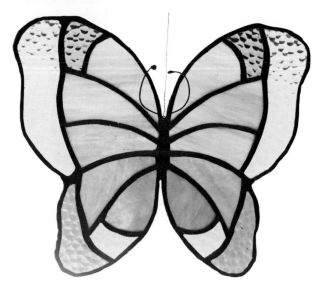

Lead Glass Butterfly. Jeri Johnston. Note how the design has been planned to incorporate gentle curves and to avoid deep inward cuts.

Stained Glass

Stained glass is an ancient craft which is today enjoying a revival. A few specialized tools are required, but they are neither costly nor difficult to use. Simple ornaments and leaded panels are within the scope of the beginner; with practice, projects of any size and complexity can be undertaken.

Cutting the Pattern

In any stained-glass project, the pieces of glass must fit together exactly; therefore a pattern is required. Start with a simple design, one incorporating straight lines and gentle curves, and make two full-scale copies on heavy paper. The original and one copy will serve as work surfaces on which the pieces are assembled; the second copy will be cut up to use as pattern pieces for scoring the glass. Number each segment on all copies of the sketch in order to save time when assembling the cut glass for leading.

Professionals generally use special pattern shears which remove $\frac{1}{16}$ inch of paper (the width of the lead came) when they cut apart the design. A mat knife with two blades inserted $\frac{1}{16}$ inch apart makes a good substitute—use strips of cardboard to space the blades. A third approach is to draw over the pattern lines with a felt marker $\frac{1}{16}$ inch wide, then use ordinary scissors to cut around the lines, discarding the $\frac{1}{16}$-inch strip.

Leading and copper foiling are the two primary methods used to join pieces of stained glass. At left are segments of U-channel and H-channel lead came, along with a reinforcing bar used on large panels. At right is a roll of adhesive-backed copper foil tape, a soldering iron, and a coil of solder.

Tools used for leaded stained glass include (top) double-bladed utility knife (with blades held 1/16 inch apart with pieces of cardboard), pattern shears, small jar of lubricant, two glass cutters (one a modified, rubber-tipped version), sharpening stone, glass pliers; (bottom) lead knife for cutting came, strip of U channel lead came, wooden lathikin, horseshoe nails, flux (oleic acid) and brush for applying, 50/50 (50 percent tin, 50 percent lead) solid core ⅛-inch solder wire, 100-watt soldering iron with chisel tip, window glazing compound, jar containing whiting (calcium carbonate or powdered chalk).

Three copies of the pattern are drawn on heavy paper. One copy is cut apart with pattern shears, double-bladed knife, or scissors. Another copy is used to organize the cut pieces of glass, and the third becomes the work surface for leading. All segments are numbered and color-coded so that reassembly is easy.

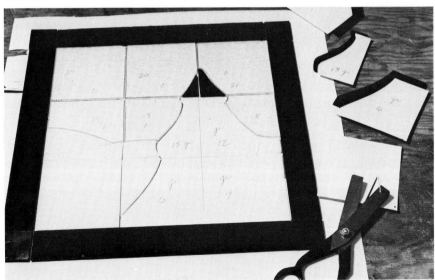

Cutting the Glass

Cutting the glass is probably the only difficult part of the project, so this is the skill tht beginners are most advised to practice. Actually, the glass is not "cut" at all, but scored (scratched) with a tool equipped with a tiny sharpened metal wheel on one end. Immediately after scoring, pressure is applied and the glass fractured along the score line. If the glass is not broken immediately after scoring, a clean break may be impossible to achieve.

To begin, lay the glass smooth side up on a firm, level surface. Dip the cutter in a lubricant (kerosene or a mixture of kerosene and light oil) and wipe off the excess with a rag. Do this before each cut. Hold the cutter perpendicular to the glass, and move it either toward or away from you with firm, even pressure (enough pressure to produce a gritting, rasping sound). Always start a cut about ⅛ inch in from one edge of the glass and score continuously across to and off the other edge. Do not lift the cutter, do not back up, and do not retrace a score line.

A metal ruler is helpful as a guide for cutting straight lines, but make sure it is rubber-backed or held in place with floral clay so that it does not slip. Curved lines are most easily scored by drawing the cutter along the edge of the paper pattern.

As soon as the glass has been scored it must be broken. The easiest method is to grasp the glass with one hand on each side of the score line. Bend down and out, and the glass should snap. To encourage the glass to break, the glass can be tapped on the underside of the score line with the ball end of the cutter until a small fracture appears. Start by giving a tap ½ inch in from one end, then grasp the glass as described previously and exert pressure on the two sides of the fracture. If the glass is still stubborn, or if working on a deep inward curve, tap all along the underside of the score. Hold the glass over the table while fracturing in case it should suddenly fall into two pieces. Be prepared for the fact that the break may be more ragged than one produced without tapping.

Pieces which are too small or narrow to be held in both hands can be broken off using ordinary or glass pliers. Place the pliers on the narrow section of glass, approximately one-half inch in from the end of the score and almost up to the score line. Grab the larger section of glass between thumb and fist, and snap down and out.

Once the glass is cut and any protrusions grozed (or chipped) away, arrange the glass on the first copy of the pattern in preparation for leading. Place the original of the design on a piece of plywood or other surface into which nails can be driven.

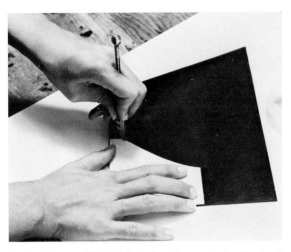

Stained-glass artist Jeri Johnston demonstrates the traditional grip for cutting glass. The glass is placed smooth side up, and the cutter dipped in lubricant (kerosene and oil) before beginning. She starts the cut ⅛ inch in from the edge of the glass and pushes the cutter smoothly away from her, following the contours of the paper pattern for the first part of the cut, and extending the score line to the other side of the glass.

Jeri Johnston does most of her work with a modified glass cutter. She cuts away part of a wooden-handled cutter, then caps the handle with a rubber chair leg cover. This way she can get her shoulder directly over the cutter to exert sufficient pressure while still keeping the tool vertical.

Once a cut is begun, it must be continued to the other side of the glass, even if this means cutting beyond the pattern piece. When the far side of the glass is reached, relax pressure slightly so the cutter does not chip the edge of the glass.

With the ball end of the cutter, lightly tap the underside of the score line ½ inch in from the edge to produce a small fracture. (Curved or difficult shapes may need to be tapped the whole length of the score line.) Hold the glass over the table in case it should suddenly separate into two pieces.

Grasp the glass on either side of the score line and exert pressure downward and out. If the glass is handled firmly, gloves are not necessary.

A smooth break. Note that pressure exerted at only one end of the score line is sufficient to separate the whole length of glass. If the break is ragged, pliers can be used to chip off (groze) the unwanted projections.

Smooth the rough edges of the glass with a sharpening stone. Move the stone parallel to the glass, never perpendicular to it.

Leading

Lead came is the material used to hold the pieces of glass together. It is available in a number of widths and two different designs: H channel, which goes between the pieces of glass, and U channel, which frames the outside. Before being used, came must be stretched. Either put one end in a vise, or have a helper pull on the other end until the lead is straight and firm, without any slack. A 6- or 7-foot length should lengthen from 3 to 6 inches. If the came needs further widening or straightening, it can be shaped with wooden modeling tools or a lathikin.

Start the leading in the corner of a rectangular panel, or on one edge of an irregularly shaped design. Fit the first piece of glass into the prepared U-shaped leading, and press into place using the lathikin or a spare scrap of wood. Use flat-sided horseshoe nails or lath nails to hold this and each succeeding addition in place. Work from the corner outward, joining all interior pieces with H-channel lead, and finally completing the border in U channel. Make sure that each piece of came is cut about $\frac{1}{16}$ inch shorter than the glass it is to bind; this will ensure that the lead is butt jointed and the ends do not overlap.

When all the pieces are cut, place the unused copy of the design on a wood surface, and begin leading from an outside corner. Use lead came that has been stretched to its full length. Cut the came slightly shorter than the piece of glass it is to frame so as not to overlap the adjacent came at the joint. When cutting lead came, place on a hard surface and use a rocking motion with the knife blade.

Fit the glass carefully into the lead came (it may be necessary to widen the channel slightly), then hammer in lath or horseshoe nails to hold the pieces in place. Remove the nails when the next piece of glass is added.

To make sure the glass is firmly embedded in the lead channel, tap with the wooden lathikin (or a scrap of wood) against the glass. Notice how a piece of scrap came is used between a nail and the raw edge of the glass; this is insurance against chipping the glass.

Soldering

When the design is completely leaded, all joints must be soldered. For this use an 80- to 100-watt soldering iron. If the soldering iron has never been used, it must be tinned as follows: clean the tip of all traces of oxidation and soil, heat, brush with liquid soldering flux (oleic acid), and melt on a thin coating of 60/40 or 50/50 ⅛-inch solid core solder. (The numbers represent the percentage of tin and lead respectively.) The flux and solder are the same that are used on each leaded joint. Without the flux, the melted solder would roll off in balls.

Clean all joints with a wire brush or sandpaper and apply flux before soldering. Hold the tip of the heated iron close to the joint to be soldered, and touch the end of the solder wire to the tip of the iron. Use the minimum amount of solder, and hold the iron lightly on the joint so that the solder puddles and flows into the crevices. Do not leave the soldering iron in place for more than a second, however, or the lead may also begin to melt. To learn the characteristics of solder and the soldering iron, it is a good idea to practice on a scrap of came before starting on the finished piece. If the solder bubbles up, the iron is too hot and should be unplugged (or turned down, if it has a built-in rheostat or is hooked up to a dimmer switch). If the solder mounds up rather than forming a flat puddle when the iron is lifted away, the tip is too cool (or the joint not fluxed). Always work in a well-ventilated area when soldering.

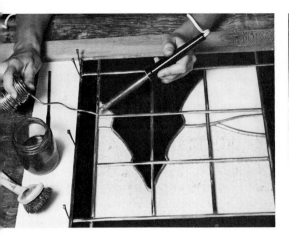

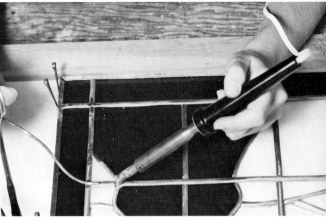

Scrub all joints with a wire brush and apply flux before soldering. Hold the heated end of the soldering iron just above the joint, and touch with the tip of the solder wire. Heat and gravity will make the melted solder flow into the joint.

When a puddle of solder has been melted, draw the soldering iron lightly over the joint to spread and smooth the solder. Solder all of one side; then carefully turn the panel and solder all remaining joints.

Finishing

After the design has been soldered on both sides, gray window glazing compound is forced under the came to strengthen the panel and eliminate any "play"; the excess is scraped away with a nail or pointed stick. To clean the panel of remaining putty and flux, sprinkle with whiting (calcium carbonate, also known as powdered chalk) and scrub with a stiff brush. Remove the excess with a damp cloth or sponge. Repeat on the other side of the piece, then allow to dry flat for twenty-four hours before hanging.

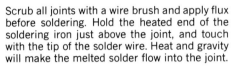

Push window glazing compound under the came to strengthen the structure and ensure a tight fit. Remove excess putty by running a nail or pointed wooden stick along all the leads.

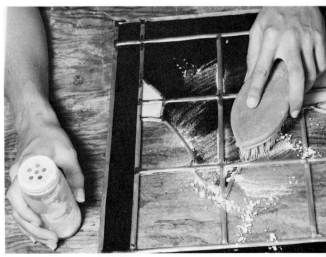

To clean the panel of remaining glazing compound and flux, sprinkle with whiting and scrub with a stiff brush. Wipe away the remainder with a cloth or damp sponge. Repeat the puttying and scrubbing procedure on the reverse of the panel, then allow to dry flat for 24 hours.

Copper Foil Method

Copper foiling is a method of joining pieces of glass with solder instead of lead came. Since solder will not stick to bare glass, the glass must first be edged with copper tape to provide a surface that the solder can grip. Copper foiling is a technique especially suited to ornaments or designs incorporating small pieces of glass which might be overpowered if surrounded by lead came.

Begin by cutting the glass according to the directions for leaded stained glass, allowing for a $\frac{1}{16}$-inch margin between the pieces. Using either $\frac{1}{4}$-inch or $\frac{3}{16}$-inch adhesive-backed copper foil tape, carefully wrap all around the edges of each piece of glass, allowing a $\frac{1}{4}$-inch overlap at the ends. It is important that the glass be clean for the tape to stick (use alcohol or acetone to remove grease), and that the tape be centered on the edges of the glass so that an equal amount extends on either side. When the tape is in place, fold the foil edges tightly over the glass, pressing or burnishing with an orange stick.

Lay the foiled pieces in place on top of the pattern, then brush with flux and spot solder at several points to hold the pieces together. Next brush flux on all the exposed copper foil and apply enough solder to completely cover the tape. Draw the tip of the soldering iron along the copper tape, spreading the solder, but do not let the iron rest at any point for more than an instant. When the front is soldered, allow the piece to cool, then turn and repeat on the back. If solder collects on the outside of the piece, smooth by running the iron around the outside edge, allowing the excess to melt and drip off onto newspapers. The fumes produced when soldering are potentially harmful, so always work in a well-ventilated area.

WHITE CHRISTMAS. Jeri Johnston.

PARTRIDGE IN A PEAR TREE. Leaded glass ornament by Jeri Johnston.

BIRD OF PARADISE. Marty Wilson.

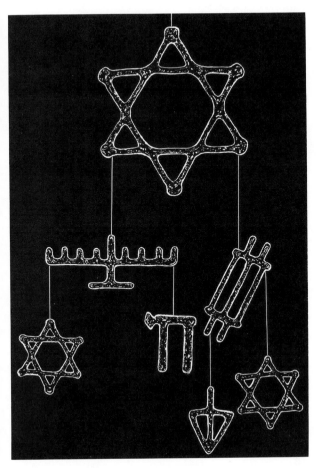

BUTTERFLY ORNAMENT. Jeri Johnston and Marty Wilson. The pieces of glass are edged in copper foil tape, then soldered rather than leaded together.

CHANUKAH. Carl H. Betz. The artist fuses pieces of cut window glass into the elements for a mobile, which is hung with nylon thread.

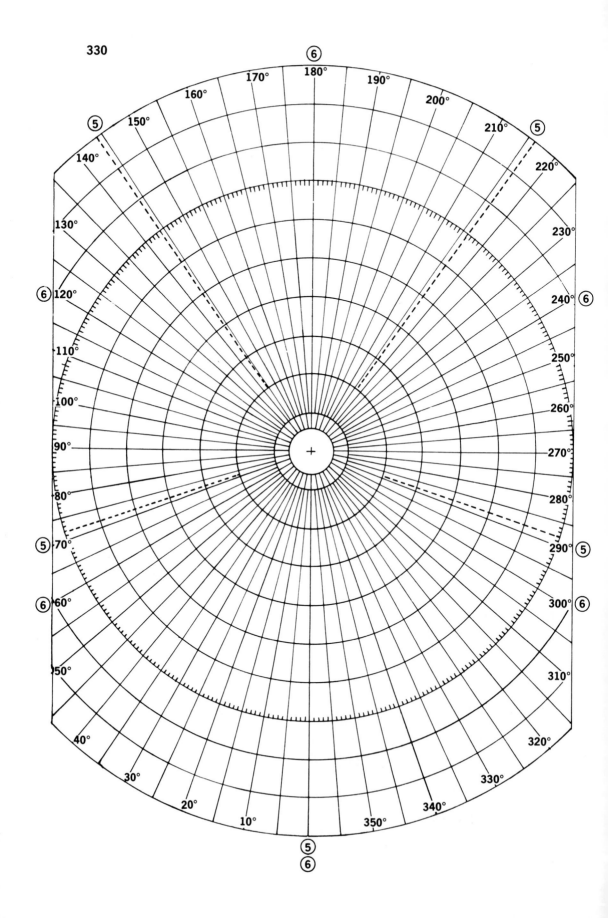

Appendix

The 360° circle is divided into units of 5°.

Circled numbers 5 and 6 indicate the points that divide the circle into five and six parts.

Selected Reading

Bread Dough Artistry. Rosemead, California: Hazel Pearson Handicrafts, 1968.

CUNDY, H. MARTYN, and A. P. ROLLETT. *Mathematical Models.* 2nd ed. Oxford: Oxford University Press, 1961.

Dough-It-Yourself Handbook, The. Chicago: Morton Salt Company, 1975.

FACKLAM, MARGERY, and PATRICIA PHIBBS. *Corn-Husk Crafts.* New York: Sterling Publishing Company, 1973.

HASLEIN, INGE, and RITA FRISCHMANN. *Curling, Quilling and Coiling.* New York: Sterling Publishing Company, 1973.

JOHNSON, PAULINE. *Creating with Paper.* Seattle: University of Washington Press, 1958.

KREISCHER, LOIS. *Symmography.* New York: Crown Publishers, 1971.

LALIBERTE, NORMAN, and MAUREEN JONES. *Wooden Images.* New York: Reinhold Publishing Corporation, 1966.

LAURY, JEAN RAY. *Appliqué Stitchery.* New York: Van Nostrand Reinhold Company, 1966.

———. *Wood Appliqué.* New York: Van Nostrand Reinhold Company, 1976.

LUCIOW, JOHANNA, ANN KMIT, and LORETTA LUCIOW. *Eggs Beautiful: How to Make Ukrainian Easter Eggs.* Minneapolis, Minnesota: Ukrainian Gift Shop, n.d.

MEILACH, DONA. *Contemporary Batik and Tie-Dye.* New York: Crown Publishers, 1973.

333

MERGELER, KAREN. *Too Good To Eat.* Santa Ana, California: Folk Art Publications, 1972.

MILES, BEBE. *Designing with Natural Materials.* New York: Van Nostrand Reinhold, 1975.

MUSEUM of CONTEMPORARY CRAFTS. *Cookies and Breads: The Baker's Art.* New York, Reinhold Publishing Corporation, 1967.

NEWMAN, THELMA R. *Quilting, Patchwork, Appliqué, and Trapunto.* New York: Crown Publishers, 1974.

NEWMAN, THELMA R., JAY HARTLEY NEWMAN, and LEE SCOTT NEWMAN. *Paper as Art and Craft.* New York: Crown Publishers, 1973.

NEWSOME, ARDEN J. *Egg Decorating: Plain and Fancy.* New York: Crown Publishers, 1973.

NICKELL, MOLLI. *This Is Baker's Clay.* New York: Drake Publishers, n.d.

PETTIT, FLORENCE H. *How to Make Whirligigs and Whimmy Diddles and Other American Folkcraft Objects.* New York: Crowell, 1972.

ROTHENBERG, POLLY. *Creative Stained Glass.* New York: Crown Publishers 1973.

SANDFORD, LETTICE. *Straw Work and Corn Dollies.* New York: The Viking Press, 1974.

SANDFORD, LETTICE, and PHILLA DAVIS. *Decorative Straw Work.* London: B.T. Batsford Ltd., 1964.

SARGENT, LUCY. *Tincraft.* New York: Simon and Schuster, 1972.

————. *Tincraft for Christmas.* New York: William Morrow & Company, 1969.

SOMMER, ELYSE, and MIKE SOMMER. *A New Look at Felt.* New York: Crown Publishers, 1975.

STEPHAN, BARBARA B. *Creating with Tissue Paper.* New York: Crown Publishers, 1973.

Straw Harvest. Rosemead, California: Hazel Pearson Handicrafts, 1974.

TANGERMAN, E. J. *The Modern Book of Whittling and Woodcarving.* New York: McGraw-Hill, 1973.

VAN RENSSELAER, ELEANOR. *Decorating with Pods and Cones.* Princeton, New Jersey: Van Nostrand, 1957.

VERCOE, BERNICE, and DOROTHY EVANS. *Cake Decorating.* Dee Why West (Australia): Paul Hamlyn Ltd., 1973.

WALLACE, EVELYN. *Cake Decorating and Sugarcraft.* New York: Arco Publishing Company, 1975.

Wilton Cake and Food Decorating Yearbook. Chicago: Wilton Enterprises. Yearly.

List of Suppliers

American Handicrafts
Tandy Corporation
1001 Foch Street
Fort Worth, Texas 76107

General hobby supplies, including paints, sprays, glazes, adhesives, quilling paper.

S. A. Bendheim Company, Inc.
122 Hudson Street
New York, New York 10013

Stained glass supplies.

The Borden Chemical Company
350 Madison Avenue
New York, New York 10017

White glue, school glue, clear acrylic spray, several types of spray adhesive.

Brandon Memorabilia
13 E. 53d Street
New York, New York 10022

Decoupage prints, novelty papers.

Art Brown and Bros., Inc.
2 W. 46th Street
New York, New York 10036

General art supplies, including paints, papers, glass stain, batik supplies.

Brown Seed Company
P.O. Box 1792
Vancouver, Washington 98663

Pinecones, dried materials.

CCM—Arts and Crafts, Inc.
9520 Baltimore Avenue
College Park, Maryland 20740

General art and hobby supplies. *Craftstraws* (unsized white paper straws).

Connoisseur Studio, Inc.
Louisville, Kentucky 40207

Protect-It (clear acrylic varnish), decoupage supplies.

Albert Constantine and Son, Inc. 2050 Eastchester Road Bronx, New York 10461	Wood veneer, veneer edging, thin plywood, basswood.
Craftsman Wood Service Company 2727 South Mary Street Chicago, Illinois 60608	Wood veneer, veneer edging, thin plywood, basswood.
Dap, Incorporated 5300 Huberville Road Dayton, Ohio 45431	Vinyl spackling paste, glazing compound.
Dennison Party Bazaar 390 Fifth Avenue New York, New York 10018	Base metal foil, velour paper, novelty papers.
Dharma Trading Company 1952 University Avenue Berkeley, California 94701	Batik supplies.
Dremel Manufacturing Company Racine, Wisconsin 53406	Table model jigsaw.
E. I. du Pont de Nemours & Company, Inc. Wilmington, Delaware 19898	*Duco Cement* (clear household cement).
Fibrec 2795 16th Street San Francisco, California 94103	Batik supplies.
Finn-Matkos, Inc. 241–24 Hamilton Avenue Stamford, Connecticut 06902	Finnish wood shaving strips, curls, ornament kits.
Flax Artist's Materials 250 Sutter Street San Francisco, California 94108	General art supplies.
Bruce J. Forman Company P.O. Box 901-B Venice, California 90291	Electric tjanting.
Gail's Decorative Arts Studio P.O. Box 696 Olympia Height Station Miami, Florida 33165	Egg-decorating supplies, decoupage.
Handicraft Originals 1702 Cornwallis Parkway Cape Coral, Florida 33904	Goose, turkey, quail, duck eggs.
Homecraft Box 331 Wadena, Minnesota 56482	United States-manufactured wood curls.

House of Rachel P.O. Box 38406 Dallas, Texas 74238	Goose, turkey, ostrich, rhea eggs.
R. B. Howell Company 630 N.W. 10th Avenue Portland, Oregon 97209	Finnish wood shaving strips.
Janovic Plaza 1292 First Avenue New York, New York 10021	Mylar.
Junior's Plant Shop Glen Street Rowley, Massachusetts 01969	Pinecones, dried materials.
LeeWards 1200 St. Charles Street Elgin, Illinois 60120	General hobby supplies, including cornhusks, wreath frames, wooden doll shapes, quilling paper, paints, glazes.
LeJeune, Inc. 1060 W. Evelyn Avenue Sunnyvale, California 94086	Batik supplies.
Maid of Scandinavia 3244 Raleigh Avenue Minneapolis, Minnesota 55416	Cake-decorating and baking supplies, including sugar molds, summer coating, meringue powder, gum tragacanth, gum arabic, clay gun, miniature cutters; rye straw.
Natcol Crafts, Inc. P.O. Box 299 Redlands, California 92373	Dough art tools, plastic cutters.
O-P Craft Company, Inc. 425 Warren Street Sandusky, Ohio 44870	Wooden boxes, turned wood shapes.
C. S. Osborne and Company Harrison, New Jersey 07029	Leather punches.
Hazel Pearson Handicrafts 4128 Temple City Boulevard Rosemead, California 91770	General hobby supplies, clay gun, miniature cutters, cornhusks, thick white glue.
Permanent Pigments, Inc. 2700 Highland Avenue Cincinnati, Ohio 45212	*Liquitex* acrylic paints, polymer medium, gesso.
The Pine Cone Shop Route 2 Park Rapids, Minnesota 56470	Pinecones, dried material.
RIT Best Foods Division CPC International 1137 W. Morris Street Indianapolis, Indiana 46206	Household dyes.

St. Louis Crafts 44 Kirkham Industrial Court St. Louis, Missouri 63119	Copper, brass, aluminum tooling foil, tools.
Scorpio Imports 28 North Street Hingham, Massachusetts 02043	Finnish wood tapes, thirteen-page instruction book.
Seal, Incorporated Roosevelt Drive Derby, Connecticut 06418	Dry mounting tissue, silicone-impregnated release paper.
Spearhead Marketing, Inc. Minneapolis, Minnesota 55430	*Decoregger*, device for marking straight lines on an egg.
Paul Straight Craft Supplies Yarrow, Missouri 63501	Rye straw.
Surma 11 East 7th Street New York, New York 10003	Ukrainian-style egg-decorating supplies, dyes, regular and deluxe kistka.
Tandy Leather Company Tandy Corporation 1001 Foch Street Fort Worth, Texas 76107	Leather punches, pounding boards, mallets.
3 M Company Adhesives, Coatings and Sealers Division 3 M Center St. Paul, Minnesota 55101	Several varieties of spray adhesive.
A Touch O'Glass 2851C Kihei Place Honolulu, Hawaii 96822	Stained glass supplies.
Treasure House P.O. Box 22 Menlo Park, California 94025	*Scandia Straw* (flat straw plait—milliner's straw).
Triarco Arts and Crafts J. C. Larson Division 110 West Carpenter Avenue Wheeling, Illinois 60090	General art and hobby supplies, including glass stain, tooling foil, liver of sulfur.
Ukrainian Gift Shop 2422 Central Avenue, N.E. Minneapolis, Minnesota 55418	Ukrainian-style egg-decorating supplies, including dyes, *pysanky* pattern sheets, kistka (regular and electric).
Western Tree Cones 1925 S.W. Brooklane Drive Corvallis, Oregon 97330	Pinecones, dried materials.
Whitmore-Durkin Glass Company P.O. Box 2065 Hanover, Massachusetts 02339	Stained glass supplies.

Wilton Enterprises, Inc.
833 West 115 Street
Chicago, Illinois 60643

Cake-decorating supplies, including cookie cutters, sugar molds, meringue powder, run sugar mix, gum tragacanth.

J. Wiss and Sons Company
33-T Littleton Avenue
Newark, New Jersey 07107

Scalloping scissors.

United Kingdom Suppliers

Baker Smith (Cake Decorators) Limited
65 The Street
Tongham, Farnham, Surrey GU10 IDD

Cake-decorating supplies.

Cox and Barnard (Hove) Limited
56 Livingstone Road
Hove, Sussex BN3 3WL

Stained glass supplies.

Creeds (Southern) Limited
Pulteney Road
South Woodford, London E18 IPS

Cake-decorating supplies.

Dryad Limited
P.O. Box 38
Northgates, Leicester LE1 9BU

General craft supplies, including papers, dyes, batik supplies, wooden beads, felt, *Artstraws* (unsized white paper straws).

Dylon International Limited
Worsley Bridge Road
London SE26 5HD

Fabric dyes.

The Handicraft Centre
27 High Street
Princes Risborough
Aylesbury, Bucks.

Handicraft supplies, including straw and straw plait, wood shaving strips and curls, batik supplies.

Hobby Horse Limited
15-17 Langton Street
London SW10 OJL

General craft supplies, including wooden shapes, wood shaving strips, batik supplies, glass stain, leather tools.

Leisure Craft Centre
2/10 Jerdan Place
London SW6 5PT

General craft supplies, including straw, batik supplies, glass stain, tooling foil.

Paperchase Products Limited
216 Tottenham Court Road
London WIP 9AF

Assorted papers, foil, acetate, mirror-finish film, adhesives.

The Pot Shop
8 Shillingford Street
Islington, London NI

Craft supplies, including equipment for stained glass.

Reeves and Sons Limited
178 Kensington High Street
London W8

General art supplies.

George Rowney and Company
   Limited
12 Percy Street
London WIA 2BP

General art supplies.

Somerset House Wedmore Limited
Station Road
Cheddar B527 3AE

Straw for corn dollies.

Stockland
9 Little Clarendon Street
Oxford

Craft supplies, including straw and
   straw plait, wood shaving strips and
   curls, batik supplies.

World of Wood
Industrial Estate
Mildenhall, Suffolk IP28 7AY

Wood veneer, woodworking tools.

Index

INDEX